How to Write a Damn Good Thriller

■ ALSO BY JAMES N. FREY

NONFICTION

HOW TO WRITE A DAMN GOOD NOVEL

HOW TO WRITE A DAMN GOOD NOVEL II

HOW TO WRITE A DAMN GOOD MYSTERY

THE KEY

GIFT OF THE WHITE LIGHT

FICTION

A KILLING IN DREAM LAND

THE LONG WAY TO DIE

CAME A DEAD CAT

CIRCLE OF DEATH

THE ARMAGEDDON GAME

THE ELIXIR

THE LAST PATRIOT

U.S.S.A.

WINTER OF THE WOLVES

How to Write a Damn Good Thriller

A Step-by-Step Guide for Novelists and Screenwriters

James N. Frey

ST. MARTIN'S PRESS NEW YORK

www.stmartins.com

Book design by Level C

Library of Congress Cataloging-in-Publication Data

Frey, James N.
  How to write a damn good thriller : a step-by-step guide for novelists and screenwriters / James N. Frey. — 1st ed.
      p. cm.
  ISBN 978-0-312-57507-6
  1. Suspense fiction—Authorship.   2. Thrillers (Motion pictures)—Authorship.
I. Title.
  PN3377.5.S87F74 2010
  808.3'87—dc22

                                                        2009040245

First Edition: April 2010

10 9 8 7 6 5 4 3 2 1

To the memory of the Greek poet Homer,
the greatest thriller writer of all time

With thanks to my wife, Elizabeth, the brains of the operation

■ Contents

■ Introduction

The aim of this book is to help you design a damn good thriller. Thrillers are the most exciting of all the genres. Unlike writing, say, a literary tome full of angst and ennui that will sour your own stomach, let alone your reader's, writing a thriller is like riding a bobsled down Mount Everest. You can let your imagination run. You can make up wild and crazy characters and stuff them into woodchoppers. You can blow up cities. Lop heads off. Sink ships. Go to Mars.

In the world of thriller writing, anything goes—as long as you thrill your audience.

The first thing you need to know about writing thrillers is that it is not brain surgery. In fact, it's easy. That's right, easy as smacking a beached banana fish. You create the characters; the characters create a thrilling story. What could be easier?

I know—you're saying, Come on, even if it's fun, there still are sometimes big old speed bumps in the creative road. Didn't Hemingway say that to write fiction you had to go into your room every day and stare at a blank piece of paper until blood came out of your forehead?

Well, okay, there are those days. But most days, it's a hoot. No kidding.

■ What's a Thriller?

Before we begin, we'll need to settle on just what a thriller is.

There are all sorts of definitions for "thriller" floating around. *The American Heritage Dictionary of the English Language* defines a thriller as a work of fiction "that thrills, especially a sensational or suspenseful book, story, play, or movie."

That's okay, but to say a thriller *thrills* is not all that useful as definitions go. In fact, you might say it's circular, and as any good semanticist will tell you, a circular definition isn't worth spittle on your shoe.

Thrillers are most often described as "fast-paced" and thriller-type characters as "being in danger at every turn." Some say thrillers need to have "the thrill of the chase" or "gamesmanship." According to International Thriller Writers (their Web site: www.thrillerwriters.org), a thriller is characterized by "the sudden rush of emotions, the excitement, sense of suspense, apprehension, and exhilaration that drive the narrative, sometimes subtly with peaks and lulls, sometimes at a constant, breakneck pace. Thriller is a genre of fiction in which tough, resourceful, but essentially ordinary heroes are pitted against villains determined to destroy them, their country, or the stability of the free world. Part of the allure of thrillers comes from not only what their stories are about, but also how they are told. High stakes, nonstop action, plot twists that both surprise and excite, settings that are both vibrant and exotic, and an intense pace that never lets up until the adrenaline-packed climax."

This seems to be an excellent description of an international thriller, even though it is my firm belief that heroes should never be ordinary; they're far more clever than ordinary or they wouldn't be worth our interest. At first they may seem ordinary, but they'll be revealed as exceptional as the story unfolds.

Okay, the main ingredient of a thriller is pulse-pounding suspense. Nearly everyone, even a highbrow *New York Times* critic, would agree to that. Suspense is that quality of fiction that makes the reader want to turn the pages to see what's going to happen next.

A reader of any kind of fiction might want to turn the pages to see if, say, the hero is going to find love or happiness or come to terms with his feelings of guilt or remorse because he disappointed his parents by choosing to be an orthodontist. But this is clearly not the type of suspense we find in a thriller. In a thriller, the nature of the suspense is more intensely dramatic. A thriller is about characters who are, as Dean Koontz puts it in *How to Write Best-Selling Fiction* (1981), in "terrible trouble."

Terrible trouble may involve the fate of the world, or the fate of a city, or the fate of a dozen people stuck in a tram car suspended over the Grand Canyon whose cable is coming unraveled. Terrible trouble may even involve the fate of just one person. Jack London's wonderful short story "To Build a Fire" (1908) is a damn good thriller, and the stakes are but one man's life. The same is true for Alfred Hitchcock's gripping film *Strangers on a Train* (1951), from the novel by Patricia Highsmith (1950).

The type of terrible trouble will determine the subgenre of thriller: sci-fi, horror, political, techno, man-against-nature, fantasy, supernatural, western, medical, action/adventure, military, romantic, and so on. In Great Britain and elsewhere in the English-speaking world, by the way, the word *thriller* is sometimes used for any kind of suspense fiction, including mystery. In the United States, mysteries are not considered to be thrillers, though they share some common elements. So what's the difference? you ask. Putting it simply:

In a mystery, the hero has a mission to find a killer.

In a thriller, the hero has a mission to foil evil.

I discussed what's required of a mystery and how to create one at length in *How to Write a Damn Good Mystery* (2004).

Okay now, a thriller is a story of a hero who has a mission to foil evil. Not just a hero—a *clever* hero. Not just a mission—an "impossible" mission. An "impossible" mission that will put our hero into terrible trouble. Some examples:

- In Frederick Forsyth's *The Day of the Jackal* (1971, film 1973), the clever hero has an "impossible" mission to foil evil—the assassination of French president Charles de Gaulle.

- In *Gran Torino* (film 2008), the clever hero has an "impossible" mission to foil evil—a vicious street gang that is menacing the neighborhood.

- In Thomas Harris's *Black Sunday* (1975, film 1977), the clever hero has an "impossible" mission to foil evil—the killing of thousands of people at the Super Bowl.

- In *Miss Congeniality* (film 2000), the clever hero has an "impossible" mission (particularly after the boss leaves her to fend for herself) to foil evil—the bombing of a beauty contest.

- In *The Hand That Rocks the Cradle* (film 1992), the clever hero has an "impossible" mission to foil the evil that is mysteriously menacing her family.

- In William Peter Blatty's *The Exorcist* (1971, film 1973), the clever hero has an "impossible" mission to foil evil—Satan himself, who has possessed an innocent little girl.

- In *Fargo* (film 1996), the clever hero has an "impossible" mission to foil evil—the kidnappers of an innocent housewife. In this darkly comic story, the hero fails to rescue the victim, though she succeeds in bringing the villains to justice.

- In Nancy Price's *Sleeping with the Enemy* (1987, film 1991), the clever hero has an "impossible" mission to foil evil—her brutal and evil husband.

- In Ernest Hemingway's *For Whom the Bell Tolls* (1940, film 1943), the clever hero has an "impossible" mission to foil evil—the Spanish Fascists, who are in league with the Nazis.

- In Stephen King's *The Shawshank Redemption* (1982, film 1994), the clever hero has an "impossible" mission to foil evil—a sadistic and corrupt prison warden.

- In Ken Follett's *Eye of the Needle* (1977, film 1981), the clever hero has an "impossible" mission to foil evil—a ruthless Nazi spy.

By the way, at the end of this book you will find a list of films cited as examples in this book. The ones highly recommended are marked with an asterisk next to the title.

■

Okay, we now have a wide-angle-lens view of this thriller business.

By the way, I would love to take credit for inventing the principles of creative writing I teach and write about, but alas, in all good conscience, I cannot. The principles of dramatic writing I espouse have been passed down through countless generations. All creative writing teachers are lip-synching Aristotle, who admitted that the principles he was espousing were already countless generations old when he dictated *Poetics* to his students around 330 B.C. All I do in my classes and in my books on the subject is try to show how writers can apply these time-honored principles to their own work.

Now then, how do you go about applying them in a thriller? How do you create a story of a clever hero on an "impossible" mission to foil evil? As I wrote in *How to Write a Damn Good Novel* (1987), the place to start the creation of a fictional work is with the germinal idea, which, happily, is the subject of the first chapter.

1

■ Germinal Ideas: High Concepts and Bad Concepts

Types of Thrillers, Plus a Special Note About Psychological Thrillers

The germinal idea is simply the idea that you have that gives the spark to your creative fire. It's something you feel hot about, something you think you can turn into a damn good thriller and hope that the reader or audience will think so, too.

High concept is a Hollywood term. It refers to the germinal idea for a project that excites producers and makes their hearts go thumpety-thump when they hear it. It's usually something fresh, something that you think is original and will have broad appeal to a large audience. Because Hollywood producers can't pay attention to anything for more than 9.4 seconds, a high concept must be expressed in one sentence, and that sentence should never be more than thirteen words long.

I'll give you an example of a high concept from a few years ago, when Bill Clinton was president. You may recall Bill supposedly had a sexual tryst or two while in office. True or not, there were stories floating around that he was, well, a serial skirt chaser. David Baldacci, an unpublished thriller writer at the time, had a great high concept for a story. In his thriller, the president—not Bill Clinton, but a fictional president—has an affair with a woman, and during a night of passion there's a problem. The president and the woman get into a fight, things get physical, and she gets killed. Oops.

Ordinarily this would not be a huge problem for this sleazy fictional president. His flunkies could dump the body in the Potomac and no one would be any the wiser. But here is what makes Mr. Baldacci's idea a high concept: A burglar dangling from his climbing gear on the side of the building witnesses the murder. So what to do? The president has a dilemma: There's an eyewitness to the crime. No problem. The president and his cronies will blame the murder on the burglar and get the whole police apparatus of the country chasing the poor slob. This is a very high concept indeed. The novel that evolved from that high concept was called *Absolute Power*. It was first a damn good novel (1996), then a damn good film starring Clint Eastwood (1997).

You'll notice how "impossible" the burglar hero's mission is: Not only must he escape the thousands of law enforcement agents aligned against him, but he has to bring the murderer to justice. You'll also notice that even though there's a murder in it, this story is a thriller and not a murder mystery because there is *no* mystery. The hero knows and the reader knows who committed the murder right from the start.

The high concept for *Absolute Power* can be expressed in one sentence: A burglar witnesses the president committing a murder; the burglar gets blamed.

Even the busiest—or dimmest—of Hollywood producers can get it in less than nine seconds.

Another film that was made from somebody pitching a producer a high concept—at least that's the story I heard—was eventually made into the Mel Gibson film *Conspiracy Theory* (1997). It's the story of Jerry Fletcher, a nut who publishes a newsletter about conspiracies that are nothing but his paranoid fantasies. And then, by chance, one of his paranoid fantasies turns out to be true . . . and it gets him into terrible trouble when the conspirators come after him to shut him up.

Jaws, many in Hollywood say, was an extremely high concept. It was a sort of melding of two other plots that each had held audiences in thrall: Herman Melville's *Moby-Dick* (1851, film 1956), about a whaleboat chasing a huge white whale around the world; and Henrik Ibsen's classic *An Enemy of the People* (a play first produced 1882, film 1978), about a town that had a bad water supply and refused to clean it up because the bad publicity would hurt the tourist trade.

What is or what is not a high concept is, of course, somewhat subjective. The term is even sometimes used derogatorily to pan a film with a thin plot and thinner characters, one designed to appeal to a mass audience but with no depth or substance. For that reason, Roger Ebert, the renowned film critic, calls high concepts "low concepts."

Often high concepts have a lot of current cachet in the pop culture. A juicy scandal or lurid tragedy works well. The TV series *Law & Order* often fashions scripts that echo dramatic situations that have been in the news, and then they manipulate the true story, twisting it so they won't be sued. Look at the headlines of the tabloids at the checkout stand of any supermarket and you'll find out what's currently on the public's mind.

The trouble with high concept germinal ideas is that what is a high concept to you may not be a high concept to a producer. And since a high concept may be hot today and cold tomorrow—depending on the fickle winds of popular taste—your high concept may quickly seem old hat. Besides, there are always hordes of screenwriters with their fingers in the wind of pop culture who are pitching similar high concepts, so what's current may have legions of competition. There's a lot of bandwagon-jumping-on in Hollywood, my friend. Every hit film has a hundred clones before the first ticket is sold.

My savvy editor, Daniela Rapp at St. Martin's Press, tells me that the same sort of bandwagoning happens in New York publishing. With the success of Dan Brown's *The Da Vinci Code* (2003, film 2006), she says, "All of publishing was up to their eyeballs in religious conspiracy thrillers, all with the same concept: enigmatic, ancient scrolls and mind-boggling codes embedded in works of art, historical figures engaged in secret society conspiracies—but with slightly different angles than Dan Brown's tale. And after 9/11 came a flood of Middle Eastern bad guys thrillers that has yet to recede."

So there you are. Walk the tightrope, my friend. Write what's timely, but stay off the damn bandwagon. How to do that? you ask. Wish I knew.

■ The Great Hollywood Rip-Off

And then there's always the problem with high concept germinal ideas, that since they cannot be copyrighted, whoever you pitch it to may like it well enough to steal it. That's right, my friend, you could easily be the victim of out-and-out theft by somebody working for the Hollywood dream machine.

A friend of mine once had a great job working for a major studio. She had a nice office and a large desk and windows that got the morning sun, and she had her name on the door in gold lettering with a title something like "assistant acquisitions manager." Her job was gathering high concepts, great lines of dialogue, and fresh, dramatic situations from scripts and treatments that were submitted to the studio. A world-class speed-reader, she would scan the scripts and treatments quickly, then pass the gold she'd mine from these scripts to any producer working for the studio who could use them. She was a hired thief, which did not square well with her self-image. Her conscience bothered her so badly that she wrote a scathing magazine piece about the practice, quit, and moved to Vermont to become a creative writing coach.

One way to protect yourself from getting ripped off is to turn your high concept into a damn good thriller as a novel before you pitch it to Hollywood for a film. That way, you are somewhat protected. Of course, they can still steal your high concept, because high concepts are just ideas and you cannot copyright an idea.

There are some so-called screenwriters and pseudoproducers—you can find their Web sites by Googling "high concept"—who give seminars on how to pitch your high concept to harried producers. I don't know how successful the attendees of these seminars are with pitching their high concepts after they get trained, so I can't recommend any of them. My guess is, if you have a high concept that tickles producers' fancies, they will be busy two days later with their own screenwriters who they know can develop your high concept into a damn good thriller. What need do they have of you? Hollywood is a small town where it's who you know that counts.

Some of the best germinal ideas for a thriller might not sound good if presented in thirteen words or fewer anyway. One of the best damn thrillers ever penned, Frederick Forsyth's *The Day of the Jackal*, sounds idiotic as a concept. The concept is this: A master hit man is hired to kill Charles de Gaulle, who was then president of France. It is the story of how a clever policeman, with the help of every cop in France, stops him.

The reason this sounds idiotic—and many said so at the time—is that everyone in the audience knows that in fact Charles de Gaulle was not assassinated, and so, the reasoning goes, there would be no suspense.

Besides, the hired assassin—the villain and not the hero—is cleverly facing the most "impossible" odds. The hero is creating the "impossible" odds for the villain and not the other way around.

But to the skeptics' surprise, vast numbers of people read the sensational novel and even more vast numbers of people saw the Fred Zinnemann film starring Edward Fox as the devilishly clever Jackal and Michael Lonsdale as the hero cop. Apparently, in some perverse way, they identified with the lone assassin hunted by every cop in France—at least until about a third of the way into the story, when he started murdering sympathetic characters who got in his way. Apparently, people had no problem getting caught up in the story world where the threat to de Gaulle seemed very real, even though in the real world there was no threat. If you have not seen this film, I suggest you rent it today. It's one hell of a damn good thriller.

By the way, there have been a lot of damn poor thrillers made from high concept ideas. One of these was *The Jackal* (1997), the American version of *The Day of the Jackal*. It tried to overcome the problem of the audience knowing the target was not assassinated by not revealing the identity of the target, which was . . . well . . . really, truly, a first-class dumb idea. Fred Zinnemann and Frederick Forsyth both denounced it.

Most of the time, it's not the concept, but the execution of craft that counts, my friend.

■ Bad Concepts to Be Avoided at All Costs

What is a bad concept? you ask. In an effort to be fresh and original, some writers think they have locked on to a great high concept, which is to make the hero evil or the villain heroic in the beginning and reveal their true nature later. A truly terrible thriller, *Hide and Seek* (film 2005), with Robert De Niro, had such a concept: The crazed lunatic killer, we discover at the climax, is the guy we thought all along was the hero. The critics savaged the film. Kevin Crust in the *Los Angeles Times* called it "the year's first laugh-out-loud-funny thriller."

The Jack Nicholson character (Jack), who turns into a monster in *The Shining* (1977, film 1980), works because he's never a hero. He's a writer, a victim, who is driven mad by ghosts and becomes a homicidal maniac. The audience is never misled about Jack's nature.

The audience is misled about the nature of the hero in Roman Polanski's *The Ninth Gate* (1999). The protagonist is Dean Corso, a total sleazeball, who takes on the villain the way heroes do, even sleazeball heroes. So the audience identifies with him because his goal is to foil evil. But in the end, this protagonist embraces evil himself and walks through the ninth gate, the gate to hell, to join up with the Devil and share his power. I guess the writers thought this was—wow—really, really clever, making the hero turn villain in the end, but in my opinion it turns out to be one of the most unsatisfying movie endings ever made. Lisa Nesselson in *Variety* called the film "rather silly."

Perhaps there are cases where late in the story a villain could change sides, see the evil of his ways, and then act heroically, but I've not seen it done effectively. It was done rather clumsily and ineffectually in both film versions of *3:10 to Yuma* (1957, remake 2007) from a short story by Elmore Leonard (1952). That switch robbed the audience of the satisfaction of seeing the hero defeat the villain in the climax, one of the biggest thrills a thriller delivers.

Okay, let's say you have a sudden impulse to make the hero really the villain, or the villain really a hero. No matter how much the idea excites you, take a cold shower, drink a large bourbon smoothie, hit yourself in the head with a hammer, and forget it.

■ Turning Your Germinal Idea, High Concept or Low, into a Damn Good Thriller

Let's say you're the Greek poet Homer. It's 800 B.C. or so and you've just had a smashing international hit with your first epic, *The Iliad*, and you're casting around for an idea for your next project. *The Iliad* was a type of thriller, a war story; the most recent film version was *Troy* (2004). In it, Paris, prince of Troy, kidnaps Helen, the wife of Menelaus, king of Sparta, and takes her to Troy to be his mistress. The king of Sparta sends out a call to all the Greek city-states for help in getting his wife back. Warriors flock to join in the cause, and the largest fleet ever assembled (until the Normandy invasion, some historians say) heads for Troy. Hence, Helen of Sparta becomes known as "Helen of Troy." She's said to have had "the face that launched a thousand ships."

Anyway, *The Iliad* relates the battles that ensued between the Greeks and the Trojans: battles involving great warriors, great heroes, gods and goddesses, and a host of common soldiers led to the slaughter. It was a huge hit as an epic poem and had what in the entertainment biz is called "legs." That's lasting power—two and a half millennia and it's still enchanting readers and audiences.

It would be pretty hard for Homer to top that, eh? But he had to try. So he cast around for a germinal idea he thought might make a story to thrill audiences.

Luckily, the Muses bestowed their blessing again. In case you're not up on your paganism, the Muses were goddesses, who according to the ancient Greeks were the source of all creativity. This blessing was the germinal idea for his next work, and it was a truly damn good idea.

Homer had a wonderful minor character in *The Iliad*, a Greek warrior who was a good candidate for a thriller hero: Ulysses "the Cunning." He carried out various spy missions, fought in many battles, and showed his courage, resourcefulness, and cleverness over and over again. So why not make him the hero of the sequel? Homer must have thought.

Now as to the actions of the story, Homer had to brainstorm a bit.

Ah. The Trojan war is over, so what does the hero do? He does what soldiers do when peace comes: He retires to civilian life. Homer decided Ulysses would journey from Troy to his home in Ithaca.

But what kind of a thriller is that? Is a trip home a mission? A trip home might make a long, boring literary novel full of great poetic descriptions and nice little insights about life, but a *thriller*? Homer lived in the days when you had to have a gripping story—a thriller—or forget it, and there's nothing gripping about a long trip in a boat. I'm a sailor and I know. Unless, of course, there's a whole lot of danger and menace—terrible trouble—so that it's not just a trip, but a test of courage and ability, a mythic hero's journey. So if this germinal idea is going to be a high concept for a damn good thriller, it's obvious the mission has to be a difficult one. Not just difficult: "impossible."

Homer knew that to make things difficult you have to create obstacles for the hero to be tested against. Homer had Ulysses tested by storms; sirens trying to lure his ship onto the rocks; a cyclops that imprisons him in a cave and uses his men for food; a witch, Circe, who seduces him by looking exactly like his wife, Penelope; and so on. Along the way Ulysses loses his memory, his crew mutinies, he's shipwrecked . . . the guy has a hell of a lot of terrible trouble.

Homer knew, too, that the mission the hero is given should be not just for the hero's benefit, but for the benefit of others. That's right, the hero should be self-sacrificing. If he's only out for himself, he can't be a real hero. This tale of Ulysses, *The Odyssey*, is the kind of thriller called "the hero's journey," and this type of story is very old. I wrote about the hero's journey in *The Key: How to Write Damn Good Fiction Using the Power of Myth* (2002) to show modern writers how to use this ancient paradigm to make their stories more powerful.

So who is Ulysses going on the mission for? Homer had a problem here, but he solved it by having Penelope in terrible trouble back home.

Since Ulysses is thought to have died in the war, Penelope is being courted by a bunch of ill-mannered louts who are eating her out of house and home and bankrupting the little kingdom. The people are suffering. Ulysses must get home and save the day. But how does he even know about Penelope's terrible trouble? There are no cell phones or e-mail or text messaging, not even telegraph or snail mail. Sending a messenger might work, but between storms and pirates there was a pretty good chance the messenger would not make it.

Luckily, Homer had the gods at his beck and call. He simply has the gods tell Ulysses that he has to get home and foil evil. This adds *urgency* to his mission, another key ingredient of a damn good thriller.

The fundamental pattern, then, of a damn good thriller was started millennia ago. It was probably ages old when Homer used it. As models, he no doubt had other thrilling sagas now lost in the mists of time. To create a damn good thriller, you need to create a clever hero and send him or her on an urgent, "impossible" mission to foil evil for the benefit of others. Do that, my friend, and you will have an unbeatable high concept like *The Odyssey*, and it won't depend on the fickleness of popular taste.

Now then, is it possible to have a damn good thriller where the hero has a mission to save himself but is not acting for the benefit of others? Well, yes. Certainly Robert Ludlum's *The Bourne Identity* (1980, TV 1988, film 2002) was a damn good thriller. In it, the hero, Jason Bourne, is acting only to save himself from a vast evil conspiracy against him. He's not self-sacrificing for others.

But myth-based thrillers such as *The Odyssey* that have the added dimension of other people who will suffer should the mission fail makes a gripping story even more gripping. If the hero wins and others are saved from some terrible trouble, it is deeply satisfying to the audience.

In this book, when I say "audience" I mean it to include readers of the print version.

■ A Warning

The film *Ronin* (1998) with Robert De Niro and Jean Reno is a lesson in what happens when you leave out some important elements. In *Ronin*, the clever heroes are trying to get their hands on a fancy silver suitcase that contains something that a whole bunch of evil people want. In the hero's journey terminology, this suitcase is called "the prize." Alfred Hitchcock called it "the McGuffin"—the thing the heroes are after that is often a central element of a thriller. It's the microfilm in Hitchcock's *North by Northwest* (1959), the photos of the Allies' fake tanks in *Eye of the Needle*, the stolen money in *Charade* (1963).

The problem with *Ronin* is that the audience is never told what's in the suitcase. In fact, the heroes don't know, either. I suppose the author and director thought they were being creative and were opening a powerful story question, when in fact, I'm sure most people who saw this film found it maddening. If the audience knew what was in there, they might be far more interested in the film. Say it was a nuke, or a bioweapon, or a working model of a mind-reading machine, or a gas that would make armies go crazy. The list of fascinating prizes is endless. Any horrible thing to scare the audience would be infinitely better than nothing.

This is a good example of a widespread fallacy among people who teach the craft of writing: that you create suspense by what you withhold from telling the reader or showing the audience. This is complete and total bullplucky. You create suspense by what you tell the reader and what you show an audience. What you withhold are future events.

Another annoying thing about *Ronin* that's instructive for thriller writers: The heroes are supposedly on this mission for mercenary reasons. They are not self-sacrificing for others. In fact, we don't even know who they're working for; it could be Islamic terrorists for all we know. Not knowing removes the moral dimension; as a result, viewers are far less involved than they would be otherwise. It's a truly terrible film in my opinion. You might watch it to see what happens when you toss some of the principles out the window.

Right at the end, alas, we find out the De Niro character (Sam) is acting out of self-sacrificing motives after all and is on a mission to help end the strife in Ireland, a cause the audience would champion if the director had revealed it earlier. This film delivers its thrills via car chase scenes that are so incredible they're silly. You are asked to believe that it's possible to speed for miles going the wrong way on a freeway in moderate traffic and not hit anybody. You might feel at times you're being held prisoner in a video game. The point is, don't try to get creative and deconstruct the thriller paradigm and leave out essential elements. These elements are your bullets; fire them all as straight and true as you can. Be creative with the cleverness of the villain and the hero, not in remodeling the form.

The ancient pattern for the thriller that has not changed in thousands of years is this:

A clever hero has an "impossible" mission to foil evil. The hero is brave; he or she is in terrible trouble; the mission is urgent; the stakes are high; and it's best if the hero is self-sacrificing for others.

Over the years, this prescription for the thriller has held audiences captivated every time. Called "England's national epic," *Beowulf* (first in the oral tradition for centuries, then written down in the Middle Ages, say about 800 A.D., film 2007) involves a hero, Beowulf, who has a mission to kill first two monsters, then, later, a dragon. The legends of King Arthur and the Knights of the Round Table, with knights going off on all sorts of quests to rescue damsels in distress and kill bad knights and dragons, are thrillers about clever heroes on "impossible" missions to foil evil. These stories are from about the sixth century A.D. or even earlier.

Then there came one of the most enduring thriller heroes of all times: Robin Hood. He supposedly lived at the time of King Richard the Lionheart in the late twelfth century. His tale appeared in print as a ballad entitled "A Gest of Robyn Hode" (1492). *The Adventures of Robin Hood* (film 1938) is one of the truly great adventure thrillers ever made.

Here's a clever hero indeed, who has the "impossible" mission of foiling Prince John and the Sheriff of Nottingham, as evil a couple of dudes as ever lived. Thrillers have been around a long, long time, and the good news is, they're more popular than ever. And the pattern remains the same: A clever hero has an urgent, "impossible" mission to foil evil.

Okay then, we now know what our goal is. Before we begin crafting our thriller step by step, we'll have to decide what type of thriller we're going to write.

■ Types of Thrillers

Often you will see thrillers categorized by their formal genre, the way Hollywood sees the world. Examples: sci-fi, horror, political, techno, supernatural, Everyman, mystery-thriller, western, man-against-nature, and so on. The genres are based on the kind of menace the hero is facing. If the hero is up against the spirit world, it's a supernatural thriller; against a monster, it's a horror thriller; against terrorists, it's an espionage thriller; and so on. Sometimes the hero is a professional spy, say, like James Bond, or a cop, but other times he or she is just some ordinary sap who wanders into a bad situation. Alfred Hitchcock's film *The Man Who Knew Too Much* (1956) is an example of the ordinary sap type. Of course it turns out the sap is a clever sap. The basic design of the ordinary sap thriller is the same as any other thriller; a clever hero has an "impossible" mission to foil evil no matter which type it is. The exception, of course, is the comic thriller, where the hero is inept but lucky.

In addition to the formal genres (sci-fi, horror, political, Everyman, slasher, and so on), there are thrillers written in different, let us say, traditions or modes, from campy to cartoon, to serious, to literary. One popular tradition is the thrill-a-minute thriller. These are sort of like Road Runner cartoons, and sometimes they can be very entertaining. They include films such as the recent James Bond thrillers *Casino Royale* (2006) and *Quantum of Solace* (2008), which have little to do with the works by the creator of the series, Ian Fleming. Also the Indiana Jones series, *Raiders of the Lost Ark* (1981), *Indiana Jones and the Temple of Doom* (1984), *Indiana Jones and the Last Crusade* (1989), and *Indiana Jones and the Kingdom of the Crystal Skull* (2008). The *Lethal Weapon* series is of the same type: *Lethal Weapon* (1987), *Lethal Weapon 2* (1989), *Lethal Weapon 3* (1992), and *Lethal Weapon 4* (1998). These were followed by the *Bourne* series (based on the novels by Robert Ludlum): *The Bourne Identity* (2002), *The Bourne Supremacy* (2004), and *The Bourne Ultimatum* (2007). The *Die Hard* series (based on the characters from the novel *Nothing Lasts Forever* by Roderick Thorp) supposedly inspired them all, beginning with *Die Hard* (1988), followed by *Die Hard 2* (1990), *Die Hard: With a Vengeance* (1995), and *Live Free or Die Hard* (2007).

I think that the roots of these films go deeper than just the *Die Hard* series. They harken back to the serials shown at Saturday movie matinees in the 1930s, 1940s, and 1950s called "cliff-hangers," because every week they'd end with somebody dangling over a pit of tigers or trapped in a burning building or tied to the railroad tracks as the train was just around the bend and coming fast. . . .

Thrill-a-minute thrillers are cartoons you wouldn't want your six-year-old to watch; the characters are action figures rather than traditional fictional characters with any flesh on their bones. When you're watching them, your heart might beat fast, but the only thing you're likely to remember is the special effects.

There are no novel or short story versions of such films; they are an overpowering visual and auditory assault that can be made only on a screen. The heroes are supermen who can walk through a hailstorm of bullets, fall off buildings, get blown up, and come through with nary a scratch. These films often make enormous amounts of money, but they're usually written on assignment. It's extremely difficult to crack this market if you're not a Hollywood insider and on what they call "the white list."

I asked a Hollywood insider once if there really was a white list. When pressed, he reluctantly indicated the affirmative. So I asked how you get on the white list, and he said sagely, "Nobody knows."

There are other, more realistic, less cartoonish thrillers where the heroes are not indestructible. Of course, the heroes are larger than life, theatrical, extremely clever—still, they're believably human. The early James Bond stories, particularly *From Russia with Love* (1957, film 1963), and Len Deighton stories such as *The Ipcress File* (1963, film 1965) are realistic thrillers. So is *Single White Female* (1992). Frederick Forsyth's

The Day of the Jackal, as mentioned earlier, is a wonderful realistic thriller. By the way, *The Bourne Identity* TV film (1988) was not quite as cartoonish as the later *Bourne* films; in some ways, because the hero was not so superduper, it was a superior film. There are some great man-against-nature films in this genre. *The Snow Walker* (2003), a small-budget Canadian film based on Farley Mowat's short story "Walk Well, My Brother" (1975), is a great example of a realistic thriller. This is a must-see film for thriller writers who'd like to see how much can be done with few special effects.

Even more serious than the realistic thriller is the literary thriller. The literary thriller is not just realistic; it is frequently grim, and often the hero dies in the end. The "impossible" mission in the literary thriller is often not quite as "impossible" as in other thrillers. In *How to Write a Damn Good Novel*, I discussed a literary thriller at length, *The Spy Who Came in from the Cold* (1963, film 1965), by John le Carré. It is a terrific literary thriller that was later named "the best spy thriller of all time" by *Publishers Weekly*. It's about a spy sent behind the Iron Curtain during the cold war, pretending to be a turncoat in order to give false information to the enemy. The threat and menace and moral dilemmas are wonderful. The hero, Leamas, chooses to join his girlfriend in death in the end. Now how grim can you get?

Ernest Hemingway's *For Whom the Bell Tolls* is a wonderful literary thriller. Robert Jordan is behind the lines fighting for the Fascists during the Spanish Civil War. His mission is to blow up a bridge. Jordan dies in the end as well. Hemingway's novella *The Old Man and the Sea* (1951, film 1958) is also a literary thriller. Santiago, the clever hero, has an "impossible" mission to go into the deepest part of the Gulf Stream to catch a big fish. Of course, since this is a literary work, the fish gets eaten on the way home by sharks and Santiago is left with nothing but bones. Sad, but at least he gets to the end of the story alive.

Then there's the comic thriller. There are two types: the light comic thriller and the broad comic thriller. The film *Romancing the Stone* (1984) is one damn good example of a light comic thriller; its sequel, *Jewel of the Nile* (1985), is another. Joan Wilder, the hero in both of these comic thrillers, is clever but bungles from time to time and gets lucky from time to time. In other types of thrillers that aren't comic, letting the hero get lucky is regarded as bad storytelling. The villainous characters and other antagonists in light comic thrillers are often bunglers, too; this is unacceptable in more serious thrillers.

The film *Midnight Run* (1988) is another example of a damn good light comic thriller. It's a buddy film about a tough bounty hunter and a sensitive criminal up against bungling FBI agents and bungling competing bounty hunters.

In a broad comic thriller, everything is upside down. Rather than clever, the broadly comic thriller hero is totally inept. *La Chèvre* (1981), a hilarious French film, has such a hero: an accident-prone boob who is sent on a mission to recover a kidnapped girl in Mexico, who is also accident-prone. The American version titled *Pure Luck* (1991) is a bad imitation.

Besides the pure thriller, there's the cross-genre mystery/thriller, which is becoming ever more popular. The mystery/thriller starts off as a mystery—the hero has to find a murderer—but along the way, it's discovered that the murderer or some other character is up to something really evil and must be stopped. Robin Cook is famous for this kind of book: *Coma* (1977) is an example. It starts as a murder mystery, but the heroes soon find themselves up to their necks in a creepy medical research conspiracy. Cara Black has thriller elements in several of her Aimée Leduc mysteries; *Murder in the Rue de Paradis* (2008), with an underlying terrorist angle, is an example.

■ A Special Note About the Psychological Thriller

You may be wondering why I have not included the psychological thriller as a subgenre of thriller. As I see it, a psychological thriller is one that is written with a psychological focus and might be of any type—sci-fi, horror, Everyman, political, any kind—but in itself, it is not a subgenre. What is called the psychological thriller is more a matter of style and substance, and since all damn good thrillers spring from the character of the villain and his dark mission, all damn good thrillers are in some sense psychological thrillers.

The "cat and mouse" or "chess game" aspect of a thriller is often considered psychological. Perhaps the granddaddy of all cat-and-mouse thrillers is Baroness Emmuska Orczy's novel *The League of the Scarlet Pimpernel* (English-language version 1919, filmed as *The Scarlet Pimpernel* 1934). It was a primo example of the chess game, played with cunning, wit, charm, and daring and chock-full of delightful surprises. It was tried as a play in London in 1903 and flopped, but with a tune-up it was a smash hit two years later. It opened almost a hundred years later as a Broadway musical in New York in 1997 and had 772 performances. Amazing, isn't it, how thrillers capture the imagination generation after generation. They never grow old.

The Scarlet Pimpernel, the clever hero, is an effete English aristocrat who leads rescue missions to France to save "innocent" aristocrats from the guillotine during the Terror in the late 1790s. He's playing the chess game with wily Citizen Chauvelin, the head of the revolutionary government's intelligence corps. This wonderful and exciting story prefigures the other great stories of the seeming weakling who is actually a superhero—Zorro, Superman, Batman, Spider-Man, Plastic Man, Wonder Woman, and a host of others.

Sometimes the cat-and-mouse game is not quite as good swashbuckling fun as *The Scarlet Pimpernel*. The cat-and-mouse game can be horrific. One really great example is Shirley Jackson's brilliant *The Haunting of Hill House* (1959), made into the film *The Haunting* (1963, 1999). There is not a single drop of blood in the entire film, yet it is one of the most frightening films ever made because of the psychological mind game being played. It's about a group of folks invited to a spooky house to investigate a haunting. One of the folks is Eleanor, a lonely spinster who is being seduced step by step by the ghosts in the house, who want her to join them in death. It's not clear whether she's bonkers or she's become possessed. Before the others can get her out of there, she dies. The ghosts may have gotten her or she may have committed suicide; we never know. The ambiguity makes the death even more horrific. Stephen

King in his study of the horror genre, *Danse Macabre* (1981), cited it as one of the greatest horror stories of the twentieth century, and indeed it is.

Often in thrillers the critics call *psychological,* suspense is built slowly, by indirection. There's a lot of ambiguity, fogginess, eeriness. The reader or audience doesn't quite know what's going on, but whatever it is, it's not good. Things are going bump in the night, doors open and close by themselves, chains are rattling in the basement, mysterious moaning is heard. The Gothic thriller genre relies heavily on these kinds of creepy techniques that drive the characters—and the audience— insane. Maybe that's why they're thought of as psychological.

Recently, because of the ability of moviemakers to create absolutely dazzling special effects, a type of psychological thriller is emerging that blurs the edges of what is real and what is delusion—films like *Jacob's Ladder* (1990) and more recently *The Matrix* (1999), which question the nature of reality. In *Jacob's Ladder,* the mission of the hero is to find his sanity. In *The Matrix,* it is to save humanity from computers who have created the delusional reality in which we've been living for some time now.

Sometimes when the head game between the villain and the other characters is exploited, the critics will call that psychological. John D. MacDonald's *The Executioners* (1958), later titled *Cape Fear* (film 1962, remake 1991), is considered to be a psychological thriller by many critics. It's a domestic, Everyman thriller, the story of a family menaced by a maniac. Each of the films handled the situation differently (in the early version the family is happy, well-adjusted; in the second, dysfunctional), but both versions are damn gripping.

John Katzenbach's novel *The Wrong Man* (2006) is also damn gripping. Katzenbach is often called a modern master of the psychological thriller. In this one, a woman has a one-night stand with a charming psychopath who stalks her afterward. As in *Cape Fear,* the woman's whole family gets involved in the cat-and-mouse game with the psychopath.

Alfred Hitchcock's film *Psycho* (1960), from the novel by Robert Bloch (1959), is often called a psychological thriller. It's the shocker with the knifing in the shower scene, about a killer who appears to be a friendly and helpful motel proprietor. But evil villains pretending to be someone else is pretty much the stock-in-trade of the thriller writer. One brilliant example is *Bunny Lake Is Missing*, a novel by Merriam Modell writing as Evelyn Piper (1957, film 1965), where it turns out Bunny's uncle has snatched Bunny and is fixing to kill the tyke.

Another of this type of thriller is Alfred Hitchcock's *Suspicion* (1941). This film was based on the novel *Before the Fact* (1932) by Francis Illes (a pseudonym for British author Anthony Berkeley Cox, often cited as "the father of the psychological suspense novel"). It's the story of a rich but somewhat frumpy heiress, Lina McLaidlaw, who is courted by Johnnie Aysgarth, a petty thief and fortune hunter. They marry. Gradually it's revealed what a lowlife Aysgarth is: a crook, adulterer, and so on. Ah, but she loves the mutt and can't bear to leave him. In the book, her suspicions prove true and he kills her in a wonderfully horrific and terrifying ending. Unfortunately, the film studio did not want to show Cary Grant as a murderer, so in the film it turns out he's really in love with her, has no intention of doing her in, and all ends happily. So Hollywood once again destroys a great story with a heavy sugarcoating.

Many damn good thrillers center on the hero's efforts to figure out the mind of the villain in order to catch him, and that makes it, I suppose, psychological. Thomas Harris's damn good *The Silence of the Lambs* (1988, film 1991) has the puzzle as to how the killer's mind functions at the core of the story, as an example.

One type of psychological thriller is about psychology itself—say, a shrink's efforts to jump-start the memories of an amnesiac, as in Alfred Hitchcock's *Spellbound* (1945), based on Francis Beeding's novel *The House of Dr. Edwardes* (1927). Another great film about treating a mental abnormality is the brilliant and gripping *The Sixth Sense* (1999), guaranteed to give you a bad case of the creeps. I loved it so much that when it was over, I bought a ticket and went back into the theater to watch it again.

Psychology gone amuck is the subject of *Das Experiment* (2001), the German film made from the novel *Das Experiment: Black Box* by Mario Giordano (2001), a fictionalized account of an actual psychology experiment done at Stanford University, where volunteer students were randomly assigned the role of guard or prisoner. The guards quickly became masochistic (gee, what a surprise), and their oppression became so severe that the experiment was halted. This is certainly a psychological thriller. The fictional version has been denounced by the folks who did the experiment, saying most of the violence, torture, and other good stuff in the film never happened. Oh well.

The king of all psychological thrillers is, of course, *Gaslight* (1944). The impact of this film is so great that the title has entered the language as a verb ("gaslighting") meaning to drive someone nuts by making him think he's losing his mind. It was adapted from the play *Angel Street* (1938) by Patrick Hamilton.

A recent, really wonderful comic thriller, Carl Hiaasen's *Skinny Dip* (2004), reverses the usual situation where the villain is driving someone nuts: Here the heroes are driving the villain nuts. The villain, Chaz Perrone, is polluting the Everglades for profit, and when his wife finds out, he tosses her off his yacht; but, alas, she survives and teams up with ex-cop Mick Stranahan to get even by driving him insane. It works well. It's a great read if you like your characters a bit on the wacky side, and I do.

Critics will often label a film such as Hitchcock's *Rear Window* (1954) a psychological thriller, but to me, it's a mystery/thriller. There's a lot of gray area surrounding the borders of the psychological thriller. If you write a thriller and people call it a psychological thriller, well, that's not a bad thing. Psychological thrillers are considered by critics to be a cut above the standard thriller. Psychological thrillers are considered more literary and so have a snob appeal. People who read *The New York Times Book Review* are more likely to read them. So when you pitch your story to an agent, call it a psychological thriller even if it ain't.

2
■ What You Should Know Before You Start Pounding Keys

Some Sample Germinal Ideas and Other Good Stuff

So far, we've covered germinal ideas and high concept and outlined the basic pattern of a damn good thriller—a clever hero on an "impossible" mission to foil evil. And we touched on different types of thrillers and discussed the psychological thriller.

Now then, since this is a step-by-step guide, what is the first step in creating our damn good thriller? That's right. You'll need to come up with a great germinal idea, one that gets your blood racing, one that will have you calling in sick during the busy season at your day job, one that will keep you up until four in morning, that might land you in divorce court, that will make your children sue you for being a delinquent parent.

A great germinal idea will hit you *pow!* right between the eyes. It may make you dizzy or giddy, and if you're dead drunk, it might sober you right up. A great germinal idea is something that appeals to you so powerfully that as soon as you get the idea, you want to write it. It takes possession of your soul and demands to be written or you'll burn in hell.

Where do these germinal ideas come from? A thriller writer sees something in the news or hears something on the radio, or something in an old movie or book strikes him or her as an idea that would make a damn good thriller. If somebody plants a bomb in a railway station or a poison gas canister explodes at a post office, thriller writers everywhere click on computers and crank up the story machinery.

Some great germinal ideas just seem to pop up out of nowhere. They sneak up on you when you're in the shower or driving on the freeway or getting a root canal. When your spouse wants to talk about the damn bills, your mind will float away on the pleasant cloud of creativity as a great germinal idea starts working on you.

Once a damn good germinal idea has stuck, your subconscious mind blows it up like pretty pink balloons. Who knows why one will take hold of you and another—equally good—will not. The imagination is such a mysterious organ. More is known about subatomic particles than about the imagination. The imagination lobe in your brain makes stuff up out of the soup of the unconscious, and nobody knows exactly how that works; critics and college professors often proclaim this or that literary influence caused the idea to germinate, but they're just spewing stuff that sounds erudite. Nobody knows where Tolstoy got the germinal idea for *War and Peace* (1869, English version 1886, film 1956 in English, and 1968 in Russian), the greatest damn good war thriller since *The Iliad*.

Since I can't know what your idea is, I intend to show you how I take my ideas and develop them, step by step, into a damn good thriller and how you can do the same.

■ Germinal Ideas, Fresh from the Oven

DXP

You'll sometimes find a germinal idea strikes you because it's a clone of another story. Most stories have common elements with other stories—it can't be helped. All romances are like all other romances. There are common elements in procedural detective stories: finding the body, the autopsy, lying suspects. Nearly all possible dramatic situations have been explored by other writers; you're probably not going to find one that is totally fresh. If you do, throw a party.

The idea of twins or look-alikes being switched has been a well-used motif. One example is *The Man in the Iron Mask* (1848) by the great French thriller writer Alexandre Dumas, père, whose works are now part of the French canon of classical literature. He was famous for saying he wrote about the only things that made life worth living: love and violence.

The Man in the Iron Mask was made into the wildly popular film *The Iron Mask* (1929) starring Douglas Fairbanks, and again with the title *The Man in the Iron Mask* (TV film 1977) starring Richard Chamberlain, and then again with Leonardo DiCaprio (1998). The stars all played a dual role: the vile king and his wronged twin, who replaces him on the throne. In this twin-switching story, a bad man is replaced by a good one. Audiences loved it.

The Prisoner of Zenda by Anthony Hope (1894, film 1937) also has a bad man replaced by a good one. Famed Japanese director Akira Kurosawa used the core plot in *Kagemusha* (1980). A general is fatally wounded and is replaced by a look-alike thief who is about to be executed for his crimes.

Mark Twain used the twin-switching device in his exciting historical thriller *The Prince and the Pauper* (1881 in Canada, 1882 in the United States), which has had several successful film versions (1920, 1937, 1962, 1977).

The romantic comedy *Dave* (film 1993) starring Kevin Kline was another incarnation of the twin-switching plot. This time, the president of the United States is switched with his look-alike so he can have a dalliance with one of his female aides, and while in flagrante he has a stroke, leaving his look-alike as president while he recovers. It turns out the look-alike is a better president than the real one. In the sci-fi *Futureworld* (film 1976), doubtless the king of twin-switching stories, the villain, Dr. Duffy, is trying to take over the world by replacing *all* of the world's leaders with exact twin clones that are programmed, of course, to mindlessly obey Duffy.

When one is using a well-worn plot device such as this, the key to success is to make it fresh. I have a germinal idea for a twin-switching story that I think is fresh. Here it is:

Let's say the first American pope is campaigning against the new globalism and against one American company in particular, DXP International. In certain African and Asian countries, this company uses labor so cheap that it is virtually slave labor. The corporation gets rich while the people are working eighty-hour weeks for five bucks, living in squalor, half-starved and beaten into submission by an oppressive regime that DXP keeps in power. The pope is on the way to the UN to make a speech calling for the international body to end this form of slavery. He wants everyone to join him in a consumer boycott of DXP, which will cost DXP billions in profits. A plot is hatched to switch the pope with a look-alike who is, say, a crooked cop in New Orleans.

I like this story. You'll see when discussing the possibilities of this idea that this story can be made both plausible and gripping.

Code Red

I love politics. Politics is drama. Senators playing footsie in airport bathrooms. Bribes and scandals are everywhere. Congressional aides are murdered and their bodies dumped in the woods. What a source for inspiration—gads. Germinal ideas are lying everywhere in the streets of Washington. What fun!

Code Red is a political thriller. Of course, politics is often the stuff that makes great thrillers. Fletcher Knebel and Charles W. Bailey II's *Seven Days in May* (1962, film 1964), as an example, one of the best, was about a right-wing political zealot, a general, carrying out a coup d'état against the president of the United States. The satiric *Dr. Strangelove* (1964), inspired by *Red Alert*, a 1958 novel by Peter George, was a great political thriller that could scare the pants off a British marine.

Okay, what's the idea for *Code Red*?

I was doing some research on nuclear war sometime back and was horrified to discover that it just might be possible for a president of the United States to launch a first strike all on his own. That's right, he could just press the button and *boom!* millions of people would be incinerated. This shook me to my socks. I thought, Gee—all this trust is put into the hands of the president, but what if he has a secret agenda? What if he's evil? What if he's under someone's evil spell, drugged or psycho-whacked like in Richard Condon's *The Manchurian Candidate* (1959, film 1962)?

Nuclear war at stake—the stuff of a great thriller. Very tense. The future of civilization at risk, even the earth itself.

The hero might be some young gal working in the code room who, say, gets a male Secret Service agent to help her. We could have a romantic interest. The ticking time bomb of Armageddon.

Wow. I like it.

Day Three

This is a Hitchcock-type thriller. An innocent person is dragged into murder and mayhem and international skullduggery.

Let's say an American secret germ warfare researcher got a conscience a few years ago and managed to change his identity and disappear. He knows some secrets a bunch of evil guys headed up by a really dastardly villain want to know; they want to use the secrets to make some stuff to kill a lot of people. The researcher's wife does not know of his past. As far as she knows, he's a high school chemistry teacher in the small town in Ohio where they live in *Leave It to Beaver*–style bliss.

There have been several films that start like this. Harrison Ford starred in one, *Frantic* (1988). But many stories have the same germinal idea and may have a similar beginning but turn out to be totally different, so that's okay. As I said, many thrillers share similar elements with other thrillers.

In my story, the couple go on vacation in Florida, say, and the husband just vanishes. The villain has him and plans to wring his secrets out of him. The hero might be the guy's wife, who has a mission to find her husband and save the world. Or could be a cop. Or a private cop the wife hires.

I like it.

The Legend of Hungry Wolf

I've had this idea for a while and am particularly fond of it. I think it could be made into a great film. Any producer out there who likes this idea, let me know.

The idea is framed in yet another well-used motif that works every time. A bunch of innocent people are held hostage by a gang of crooks.

Humphrey Bogart starred in two hostage films: *The Petrified Forest* (1936), from the play (1935) by Robert E. Sherwood, and *The Desperate Hours* (1955), from the novel (1954) and play (1955) by Joseph Hayes. *The Desperate Hours* suffered a badly done remake (1990) starring Mickey Rourke. Dustin Hoffman starred as the villain protagonist in the hostage film *Dog Day Afternoon* (1975). The hostage motif has been used in westerns a few times. A good one with a lousy title, *Rawhide* (1951), starred Rita Hayworth and Tyrone Power. My idea is for a western thriller as well.

Here it is:

It's the Old West—let's say 1888. A gang of outlaws captures a remote railroad station and takes a bunch of people hostage. A train will be stopping there in a few hours. The outlaws want something on that train. The Templeton gang has been the terror of the West for a dozen years. Let's say, months before, a posse hired by the railroad president, Jacob Fisk, caught up with the gang and killed twenty-two of them. The remaining six are here awaiting the train. Jacob Fisk is on board. They plan to kill him in some hideous way to avenge the death of their fellow gang members.

There are various characters in the station to be held hostage. I could have a ball making up colorful characters for hostages and outlaws. Let's say there's a prim Chicago schoolteacher who's been west for the summer working as a dance hall girl. Maybe there's a famous former gunfighter who took a shotgun blast in the face and is now blind and a self-pitying drunk. There's a rich rancher dying of tuberculosis with his spoiled, whiny son. And then there's Hungry Wolf, the hero.

I think of him as a Geronimo kind of guy. Let's say in his youth he was at war with the United States and was chased by the cavalry all over the Southwest and half of Mexico. He killed ten cavalrymen for every brave he lost, but the whites had an unlimited supply of men. With his resources dwindling, Hungry Wolf finally cut a deal with the government and retired to a reservation, where he's been living for twenty years. Now in his mid-seventies, he's gotten permission to leave the reservation to accompany his granddaughter to Seattle, where she has been accepted at a nursing school. He's now considered a tame reservation Indian, a beaten man. This assessment, we'll soon see, is not quite accurate.

The best dramatic stories are those that show the transformation of character through the dramatic conflicts of the story. That's what I have in mind here. A defeated man regains his warrior's soul. How, exactly, I don't know yet.

■ *Hunting Season*

This is a sci-fi thriller germinal idea.

For me personally, sci-fi is the most difficult of the thriller genres because it's so hard to be fresh and original. I think a lot of sci-fi writers and movie producers also find it difficult. Perhaps that's why there have been so many film versions of Jack Finney's novel *The Body Snatchers* (1955), a wonderfully gripping and creepy thriller. First there was *Invasion of the Body Snatchers* (1956) with Kevin McCarthy and Dana Wynter. Then in 1978 it was remade starring Donald Sutherland, Jeff Goldblum, and Brooke Adams. It was made again as *Body Snatchers* (1993) with Gabrielle Anwar, Terry Kinney, and Meg Tilly. Its most recent remake, which drifts far off course, is *The Invasion* (2007) starring Nicole Kidman and David Craig, a made-for-TV movie that most of the critics said was pretty lame.

Story elements and motifs in other thriller genres often appear in sci-fi thrillers. *Outland* (1981), as an example, was said to be "*High Noon* in outer space." *Forbidden Planet* (1956), often cited as the grandfather of space operas, was said to be inspired by Shakespeare's *The Tempest* (1610). The plots are indeed similar.

My story idea is this: An Idaho deer hunter is taken prisoner and then is hunted for sport—by space aliens. It shares some elements with one of the most gripping thrillers ever penned, Richard Connell's *The Most Dangerous Game* (1925, film 1932), about a loony Russian aristocrat, General Zaroff, who owns his own private Caribbean island game preserve. Having tired of hunting wild animals that no longer pose a challenge to his skills, he now hunts men and mounts their heads on the walls of his library. In the film version, he causes the shipwrecks that net him his victims. The idea of a man being hunted for sport is also found in Ian Fleming's *The Man with the Golden Gun* (1965, film 1974) and also in *The Naked Prey* (film 1966). In this truly scary adventure/thriller, the hunters are Africans and the prey is a Great White Hunter. The times have changed: It seems now more racist than was intended when it was made.

Here's my idea for *Hunting Season* fleshed out a little:

Five buddies known to be a little on the wild side are out hunting in a remote part of Idaho when they spot a spaceship and a couple of space creatures resembling men in weird suits. They seem to be stalking a bear with just a spear. The five move in to get a closer look and are spotted by the aliens, who fire some kind of advanced, high-tech, wave weapons at them that ignite the forest. One of the five—the one with the camera—is missing when the rangers finally get the fire out. The remains of his body are found in a remote canyon some distance away: He's been roasted and eaten. Nobody believes the survivors' story, so the hero—one of the survivors—and his sidekick go back to find the camera. On the trail, the sidekick vanishes mysteriously.

My hero finds the camera and sees digital photos of the inside of the ship and the aliens. He searches frantically for his sidekick. He runs into a mysterious, beautiful woman all alone in the wilderness, who claims at first to be a UFO hunter. He thinks she might be a government agent or just crazy. She's funny and seductive, and he finds himself attracted to her, even though he doesn't trust her. . . .

Later on, our hero discovers she's a scientist from another planet who's been observing on Earth disguised as an earthling and suddenly got orders to find the spaceship, which has been stolen by a bunch of hooligans (yes, her culture has them, too) who are joyriding in the ship and hunting humans for sport. She wants to use our hero to attract the hooligans so she can repossess the spacecraft. It's a very expensive space-craft, and getting it back without further expense will be good for her career. Wanting to bring these outer space killers to justice, our hero agrees to help and soon finds himself prey in a bizarre game of hunter and hunted.

The more I work on this idea, the more I like it.

Stay tuned.

■ Shadow Self

This one's in the horror genre, a doppelgänger story.

A doppelgänger in German folklore is a ghost of a living person. If you see yours, look out: Its appearance usually means something bad is about to happen, often a death. Probably yours. Percy Shelley, the British poet, told his wife he saw one at the time she almost died having a miscarriage. Another British poet, John Donne, said he saw his wife's doppelgänger the night she delivered a stillborn daughter. Abraham Lincoln saw one—and reported it to several witnesses—a week before he was shot dead. Emilie Sagée, an obscure French teacher in Latvia in 1845, was said to frequently have a doppelgänger appear when she was teaching, often witnessed by other staff members as well as her forty-two students. In 2006, in a science experiment in Geneva, Switzerland, a doppelgänger appeared in the room while a patient's brain was being stimulated electrically. It was witnessed by a dozen people and photographed.

Supposedly, you have no control over your doppelgänger. They sometimes do things to help you out, like play tricks on your competitors or enemies. Doppelgängers are sometimes reported to be impersonating their living doubles and wreaking havoc with the living person's life. Dostoevsky's *The Double* (1846) is about a doppelgänger that keeps showing up in the hero's life and eventually drives him insane. Depending on how you read it, it's either a damn good thriller or a literary novel of a man having a schizophrenic break.

Here's the germinal idea for my doppelgänger story:

The hero, a woman, is married to a man who is always busy with his business, sports, his buddies. The protagonist has a woman friend who dabbles in esoteric religion, psychics, and so on. The two women witness a session of astral projection (spirit travel). On a lark, our hero takes a shot at astral projection. She floats her soul to a motel where her husband is having sex with his mistress. When she returns from her journey into the netherworld, she comes back with her trickster, evil doppelgänger right behind.

Weird stuff begins to happen. Maybe her husband's mistress turns up dead and our hero is blamed. Hell, a dozen people saw her pull the trigger.

We'll see.

The Hunt for Jethro Potts

This is a lightly comic thriller like *Midnight Run*, *Romancing the Stone*, and *The Man with One Red Shoe* (1985), from a French film (1972). Let's say a mad bomber (Jethro Potts) has blown up sixteen TV stations because he hates television. It broke up his marriage, made him impotent, made the boys at the Silver City social club hate him, and gave him pounding headaches. He is hiding out in the rugged mountains of the Appalachians, a folk hero to the locals and an endless source of stories on TV reality shows. He's a survivalist and a former U.S. Navy SEAL, a sharpshooter who loves being hunted: To him, it's a sport. So far, he's shot six men who went after him—all with rock salt in the buttocks— and left two more hung up in the trees by their ankles.

This would be not-quite-so-super-Rambo with a comic touch.

How Joe Smigelski Saves the World

This is a germinal idea for a broadly comic thriller. Broadly comic thrillers are often satires, such as *Dr. Strangelove* or *Austin Powers: International Man of Mystery* (1997), both of which satirize international thrillers. Or they can be slapstick farces, such as *Airplane!* (1980) or *It's a Mad Mad Mad Mad World* (1963), which satirize domestic thrillers. The broadly comic type of thriller usually takes a common thriller motif and twists it and pushes it to the limits of reason to make it absurd. Two broadly comic thrillers, parodies of *The Da Vinci Code*, are good examples of perhaps going even beyond the limits. One is *The Da Vinci Cod: A Fishy Parody* (2005), by Don Brine (Adam Roberts), and the other is *The Da Vinci Mole: A Philosophical Parody* (2006) by Dr. Ian Browne.

Okay, as to our broadly comic thriller: Let's say somebody in the military—a not-too-bright tech sergeant—has lost an atom bomb. It's disappeared from the inventory the sergeant was responsible for. He's got to have it back or he'll be doing twenty years in Leavenworth breaking rocks. He sells his car, his girlfriend's engagement ring, and his beloved stereo system to raise money to hire some good detectives, but it's not enough. The money he raises ($848) will get him only one broken-down old dick named Joe Smigelski. He's a colorful bungler who discovers that this missile has been stolen by a motorcycle gang, which peddled it to some high school kids who want to launch it at a graduation party, but then it's stolen by a maniac who escaped from a government brain-altering experiment . . .

This one could be truly wacky and great fun to write.

Peace Day

This idea struck me one evening while watching a special on TV about the Middle East. They showed angry Jews and angry Muslims shrieking at one another like kids in a schoolyard, and I thought, Now who could put an end to this madness? Then it hit me. Young people! That is the only thing both sides care about. So here's what I came up with as the germinal idea for a story:

A bunch of young adults in their teens and twenties from the turbulent Middle East and elsewhere, calling themselves the International Association of the Sane, have met on the Internet. They're going to attempt something their elders have failed to do: make peace between the Jews and the Palestinians. This group is made up mostly of Muslims and Jews, and they are going to have a conference in the birthplace of the UN—San Francisco—to hammer out an agreement to settle the Middle East crisis using peace, love, and world opinion as their weapons. I like this because I think it's an important topic, and I would love to write this thriller. I've decided to create the story for this one in detail, as you will see. In my previous damn good fiction writing guides, I've created outlines for rather simple plots. This one will be complex, as many thrillers are, so you can see how it's done.

Now here's the thriller element: A villain wants to sabotage the conference and menace a bunch of sympathetic characters. I don't know who he is at the moment, but I'll make him up.

The killing of innocents is an old story, one that never fails to get readers and audiences on the edge of their seats.

■

Enough ideas from me. I hope you agree that any one of them has potential, and I hope yours does, too. Of course, it's all in the execution.

Once you have the idea, what do you do next? Read on, my friend.

■ Fiction Writers' Terminology

In fiction writing, the meaning of the terms that creative writing coaches use often gets blurred. And sometimes, being human, we just misspeak. We sometimes say *hero* when we mean *protagonist*. And to further compound this babble, different experts often define the terms differently because there is no widespread agreement on what structural literary terms mean. One book you read may define *viewpoint*, say, as "where the camera is" and another as "the attitude of the character" (it's both, actually). What I call a *premise*, others call *theme* or *central idea* or *controlling emotion*. What I call *germinal idea*, others call *premise*. It's no wonder students of the craft get confused.

So before we begin plotting, it's best that we get the terms straight so that you and I are in synch.

Let's start with the terms *hero* and *protagonist* and *villain* and *antagonist*.

A *hero* is a character, any character, who self-sacrifices for others. It is a moral term. But not every character who acts heroically is the hero. The hero of a story is a hero *and* the central character. In *The Adventures of Robin Hood*, the characters of Little John, Friar Tuck, Will Scarlett, Maid Marian, and a host of Merry Men all act heroically from time to time, but Robin Hood is the central character, so we call him the hero.

Villain is also a moral term. It refers to a character who takes villainous actions; that is, he has a baseness of mind or character: He's vicious, treacherous, evil. Any character who takes villainous actions is a villain, but not *the villain*. *The villain* is the chief villain.

The term *protagonist* is not a moral term; it's a literary structural term and refers to a character who "takes the lead in a cause or action." Usually, the hero is the protagonist of your story. But you could have, as an example, a villain as the protagonist in a story. Macbeth, in Shakespeare's *Macbeth* (play 1606, film 1948), is a villain *and* the protagonist.

In the film *Bonnie and Clyde* (1967), the central characters—the protagonists—are villains. Hey, they're bank robbers. Still, it's a wonderful film. Another truly wonderful film with great characters and gripping action, *Charley Varrick* (1973) from the novel *The Looters* (1973) by John Reese, is about a bank robber who has inadvertently ripped off the Mob and is pursued by an evil Mob enforcer. In this case, the protagonist is a bank robber and, therefore, at least in the eyes of society, a villain. But this gets blurred because the guy who's after him is a total scumbag and far more villainous than is the protagonist villain.

Many early films had thieves and robbers and even killers as protagonists, such as *The Public Enemy* (1931), *Scarface* (1932), and a host of other gangster epics.

Antagonist is another literary structural term; it refers to any character who opposes the protagonist. So in those rare cases where you might have a villain as a protagonist, the hero would then be the antagonist. In *Bonnie and Clyde*, Frank Hamer, who tracks down Bonnie and Clyde and brings them to justice, has a minor role. He appears in only about three or four scenes in the whole film, but he is, in fact, the hero.

Can you have two protagonists? Sure. Bonnie and Clyde are co-protagonists. Buddy stories, such as *Butch Cassidy and the Sundance Kid* (1969), have co-protagonists. TV's *Law & Order* episodes feature teams of two detectives, each being a hero and co-protagonist.

Okay? Here's a short recap:

A *hero* is any character who is self-sacrificing for others. *The hero* is the chief hero, usually the central character in the book or film.

A *villain* is any character who acts villainously. *The villain* is the chief villain, who opposes the hero.

A *protagonist* is any character who takes the lead in a cause or action. *The protagonist* is the central character of a story, be he a hero or a villain.

An *antagonist* is any character who opposes a protagonist.

In almost all damn good thrillers, the hero will be the protagonist and the villain, the hero's chief antagonist. Beware trying to be too clever. He who is evil should remain evil—unless he learns his lesson at the very end.

There is one more structural term you might find useful. Lajos Egri, in his seminal work, *The Art of Dramatic Writing* (1946), discusses what he calls *pivotal characters*. A pivotal character is one who at any given time in the story is "pushing the action." Various characters may be pivotal in a story at different times. In *The Day of the Jackal*, the Jackal is pushing the action at times, and at other times the hero, Claude Lebel—the best detective in France—is pushing the action. It's best if some character is pushing the action at all times; otherwise the story loses its narrative drive.

This does not mean, of course, that you can't have a scene, say, where the hero and his sidekick discuss strategy. Planning an action or adding up clues is part of pushing the action and is dramatic. Other kinds of talky scenes, even though they may "inform the audience about the characters," often need to be cut. You should at all times be showing a *well-motivated character overcoming obstacles in pursuit of a goal.* That is dramatic conflict. Dramatic conflict is the essence of good storytelling.

■ Thrillers and Morality

There may be no right and wrong, only endless, dreary gray, in a literary novel (or even some bad thrillers), but in the popular genres of thrillers— in the damn good ones, at any rate—there is right and wrong, and the audience is cheering for the heroes and hating and fearing the villains. Snooty literary types, in between nibbles of their Brie cheese, will look down their aquiline noses and deride the thriller as being a "morality tale." And you know what? They're right for once. It's true, my friend, a thriller is a morality tale. A modern thriller is an echo of morality tales told millennia ago by storytellers sitting around campfires, keeping their listeners enthralled, and, yes, teaching them by example what it means to have courage, to confront evil for the sake of others, and to act heroically in the face of mortal danger.

The evil, of course, is sometimes a mindless evil, such as a plague or virus or mindless life form, as in Michael Crichton's *The Andromeda Strain* (1969, film 1971, TV miniseries 2008), *Alien* (film 1979), and *Aliens* (film 1986), but it is a manifest evil nonetheless. The heroes are self-sacrificing, acting heroically, showing us how to live by their example.

John Gardner in *On Moral Fiction* (1978) attacked modern literary fiction for its lack of concern for morality. His attack is even more relevant today than it was when he made it. He calls morality "the highest purpose of art." According to Gardner, morality is not an arbitrary construct of society, but an eternal truth, "taking on different forms but not essentially changing through the ages." He says that moral fiction "attempts to test human values, not for the purpose of preaching or peddling a particular ideology, but in a truly honest and open-minded effort to find out which best promotes human fulfillment."

This is exactly the job of the thriller hero.

It's my firm belief that in the years to come, novels that are today considered popular fiction will become the classics. Likely candidates are *The Godfather* (1969, film 1972) and *Gone With the Wind* (1936, film 1939) and many written by one of the greatest fiction writers of all time, Stephen King, including such masterpieces as *Misery* (1971, film 1990), *Dolores Claiborne* (1993, film 1995), and *The Green Mile* (1997, film 1999). It's difficult to choose a particular book of his because he is so talented and extraordinarily prolific. But in general, the brilliance of his work is the equal of that of Edgar Allan Poe, author of a dozen or more horror masterpieces, including the short stories "The Pit and the Pendulum" (1842, film 1961) and "The Premature Burial" (1844, film 1962). Poe is today considered one of the greatest writers America ever produced, and that is certainly going to be what future generations will say of Stephen King.

How do I know these popular writers of today will be the literary lions of the future? Because most of the novels considered classics today are what we'd call genre fiction. Poe was a popular fiction writer of Gothics and penned the first detective novel, *The Murders in the Rue Morgue* (1841, film 1932). *Moby-Dick* by Herman Melville, often thought of now as the Great American Novel (1851, film 1956), is a sea adventure story. Jane Austen's *Pride and Prejudice* (1813, film 1940, 2005, TV miniseries 2005) is a comic romance. *Moll Flanders* by Daniel Defoe (1722, film 1996) is a "rogue biography," a picaresque romp that lampoons the morals of bourgeois society. *The Last of the Mohicans* by James Fenimore Cooper (1826, film 1992) is an adventure story; *Ivanhoe* by Sir Walter Scott (1819, film 1952), a medieval romance; *The Count of Monte Cristo* by Alexandre Dumas, père (1844, film 2002), a swashbuckling adventure story; *The Hunchback of Notre Dame* by Victor Hugo (1831, film 1939), a Gothic thriller; *Treasure Island*, a sea adventure by Robert Louis Stevenson (1883, film 1934, 1950, 1972); and countless others—all works of popular fiction in their day that are today considered to be great classics.

Write your thriller well, my friend; it may make you immortal. You will improve your chances of immortality if you keep in mind that all damn good thrillers are built on seven pillars, a discussion of which comes next.

■ The Seven Pillars of a Damn Good Thriller

To create a damn good thriller, construct it on the following seven pillars. Leave any one out and you may fail. So beware.

1. **HIGH STAKES.** In your thriller, there should be lives at stake, sometimes even all of humanity. Occasionally, the stakes may be other than life or death: Sanity or the fate of an immortal soul are high stakes indeed, as an example.

2. **UNITY OF OPPOSITES.** When you have a unity of opposites, the hero cannot run away from the challenge. The hero is "in the cauldron," as dramatists call it; this is the term I used for this dramatic principle in *How to Write a Damn Good Novel*. Egri, in *The Art of Dramatic Writing*, called it *the unity of opposites*. Without it, the audience thinks, Why doesn't the hero just get the hell out of there? When you have it, the audience understands that the heroes are bound to keep up the fight by some strong motive—say, loyalty, patriotism, love, duty—or, as in the case of Robin Hood and other cultural heroes, they yield to the heroic impulse for self-sacrifice. Think of the unity of opposites as the glue that keeps the hero stuck in the plot.

3. **SEEMINGLY IMPOSSIBLE ODDS.** The situation of the story should be such that it will seem impossible for the heroes to defeat the villains, even though they almost always do.

4. **MORAL STRUGGLE.** Your thriller should embody the moral nature of the struggle the audience will witness. In other words, there's right and wrong in the thriller world, and your hero is on the side of right. The heroes will be locked in a desperate life-and-death struggle with

manifest evil. This evil includes natural evils, such as virus, fires, volcanoes, earthquakes, floods, and so on.

5. **TICKING CLOCK.** You should create some kind of deadline that the heroes must beat to defeat the villains. This gives your thriller urgency, and a sense of urgency is a very good thing: It keeps the reader turning pages or the audience cemented to their seats. Get the ticking clock started as soon as you can.

6. **MENACE.** Not only should you have high stakes, but the heroes and other sympathetic characters should be in danger throughout much of the story.

7. **THRILLER-TYPE CHARACTERS.** Apart from being determined and larger-than-life theatrical characters that you'd find in any damn good dramatic work, thriller characters, both heroes and villains, must be clever and resourceful. Pitting a clever and resourceful villain against a clever and resourceful hero is at the heart of a damn good thriller.

■ Examples of the Seven Pillars in Damn Good Thrillers

If you examine damn good thrillers, you will see that they all stand on these seven pillars. What? you say. There are no exceptions? Nope, there are no exceptions.

In *The Exorcist*, as an example, the situation had *high stakes* indeed: An innocent little girl is possessed by Satan! How creepy . . . how horrible . . . how delicious. The heroes cannot abandon this possessed little girl, so they're locked into a *unity of opposites*. Satan is a powerful antagonist, so the heroes face *seemingly impossible odds*. And, of course, doing battle with Satan is a *moral struggle*. If the heroes fail, the little girl will be condemned to hell, so there's a *ticking clock*. Gads. There's no telling what Satan might do at any moment, so everyone faces *menace*. Both the priest hero and Satan are clever and resourceful *thriller-type characters*. Though literary elitist Vincent Canby in *The New York Times* called the film "elegant occultist claptrap," the more astute

Roger Ebert in the *Chicago Sun-Times* saw it as a work of "great crafts-manship." Indeed it was. And it was one of the biggest-grossing movies of the decade, taking in $402.5 million, at that time a staggering amount.

The Day of the Jackal is another good example of a thriller standing on the seven pillars.

This was supposedly based on the true story of a clever and resource-ful professional hit man code-named "the Jackal," hired to assassinate the president of France, Charles de Gaulle. *High stakes?* You bet. The hero sent to stop him is a clever and resourceful professional detective, Claude Lebel. These are *thriller-type characters*. Lebel is put in charge of all the police apparatus in France with a mission to find the Jackal. Could the hero quit? No way. He's locked into a *unity of opposites* by duty. Since the cops have no clue as to the identity of the Jackal or what he looks like, the hero is facing *seemingly impossible odds*. Because the Jackal kills to protect his identity, nearly everyone he encounters faces *menace*. Killing a head of state is definitely evil, so this is a *moral struggle*. And since the assassination is to take place at a certain date and time, there is a *ticking clock*.

How about *From Russia with Love*?

This is the best of Ian Fleming's Bondiad. In many ways it's a typical spy story, but the novel is deftly crafted and the film is an exciting ride. A professional British spy, James Bond (007), is sent to Constantinople to snatch a decoding device from the Soviet embassy that could help win the cold war, so we have *high stakes* and a *moral struggle*. As a pro, Bond must carry out his assignment, so he's locked in a *unity of oppo-sites*. What makes this rather standard spy plot both fresh and good fun are the colorful helpers and antagonists and all the derring-do and sur-prising plot twists. Bond is up against the clever and resourceful villain, Ernst Stavro Blofeld, and two extremely clever and resourceful and nasty minions, Rosa Klebb and Red Grant, great *thriller-type characters*. Bond is outnumbered and faces *seemingly impossible odds* and great *men-ace*, not only from Blofeld and his clever and resourceful minions, but from the Soviets who are after him, too. Bond must get to safety in Italy before the villains get him, so there's a *ticking clock*.

Academy Award winner *High Noon* certainly had a *ticking clock*. The camera kept showing it to the audience. The marshal can't run from his desperate situation—his sense of honor won't let him—so he's locked in a *unity of opposites*. The villain is arriving on the noon train for a showdown with the marshal: That's plenty *high stakes*. Because the town is threatened by evil, we're in a *moral struggle* with plenty of *menace*. Marshal Kane can't get anyone in the town to help him, so he's left facing the villain and his three bloodthirsty minions alone, and that's *seemingly impossible odds*. The marshal and Frank Miller and Miller's gang are determined, *thriller-type characters*.

In *Romancing the Stone*, Joan Wilder, a romance novelist with no romance or adventure in her life, is contacted by her sister's kidnappers, who demand a treasure map for ransom. So there are *high stakes*. Joan can't just run away; she's locked in a *unity of opposites*. She must get the ransom by a certain time or her sister will be killed, so there's a *ticking clock*. Because she's trying to save her sister from evil guys, there's a *moral struggle*. Joan is pursued by clever and nasty villains creating lots of nice *menace* and *impossible odds*. There's a cast of wonderful *thriller-type characters*, including Jack, the adventurer she falls in love with.

You get the idea. You will need to build your thriller on the same seven pillars.

3

■ All About Your New Best Friend, Your Villain

The villain in a thriller is not just evil: The villain is evil right down to the soles of his or her feet. Villains think and act for selfish and self-centered motives and have no regard whatever for the welfare of others—except possibly for family. Otherwise, they are self-centered creeps.

The villain is ruthless, relentless, and clever and resourceful, as well as being a moral and ethical wack job. Determined to get what he or she wants, the villain is willing to crush anyone who gets in the way.

The villain is your best friend, because the villain creates the plot behind the plot—the plot that has to be foiled by the hero—and that, my friend, is what thriller writing is all about. There are some damn good thrillers where the villain does not have a plot behind the plot but is simply an evil force permanently in power and needs to be dislodged: an evil king, perhaps, who does all kinds of evil stuff but does not have any narrow, dark mission. And, of course, there are other damn good thrillers where nature has turned evil and is menacing a whole bunch of people. This nature-gone-bad scenario serves as the villain: the shark in *Jaws*, the volcano in *Dante's Peak* (film 1997), and the earthquake in *San Francisco* (film 1936).

There are also survival thrillers, where it's not nature that's turned evil, but where the disasters are simply accidents, such as *Titanic* (1997) and *The Towering Inferno* (1974).

The villain is often something of an enigma in thrillers. The audience may not know anything about the villain or why or how he or she became evil. The Jackal is such a character. The hero, Claude Lebel, tries to find out who he is, but even after the Jackal is killed in the end, the police still don't know even what country he was from, where he got his training, or how he became an assassin.

Often the villain has become evil as a result of a wound, such as the title character in Ian Fleming's *Dr. No* (1958, film 1962). Dr. No, who lost his hands doing radiation research and was an unloved, out-of-wedlock, mixed-race child, is such a case. And so is Carson Dyle in *Charade*, who was a casualty of war and left behind to die by his buddies. Wounded villains often wear their wounds like a badge and use them to justify their villainy.

Sometimes the villain is evil because he was raised to be evil, such as Faber in Ken Follett's *Eye of the Needle*, who was brought up to be a Nazi. A villain might be born evil, such as the creatures in *Alien* and *Aliens*, and the pods in *Invasion of the Body Snatchers* and its many clones, and in William March's supercreepy *The Bad Seed* (1954, film 1956, TV film 1985), which features a sweet little girl as a serial killer, just born that way.

The chief villain may be off somewhere giving the orders, and the villain's sidekick or underling, who is acting out of loyalty or patriotism or is simply a mindless follower of the villain, serves as the chief antagonist of the hero. The villain's sidekick may be deluded by the villain to act on his behalf but not be evil himself, merely misled. That can work.

Readers and audiences want the background of the main characters revealed, because identifying and empathizing with the characters is one of the delights of the fictive experience. As readers and audiences, we are getting vicarious experience of others' lives when we enter the fictive dream; getting to know the hero's background helps us to have a deeper fictive experience. But not knowing the details of the villain's background does not trouble us much, because hopefully we feel fear and loathing of the villain anyway.

This is why, in even some of the best thrillers, the villain may not be a fully fleshed-out, well-rounded character; instead, the villain is a force of evil with a unidimensional personality. The villain's personality is a black hole: All we see of the villain is greed or overweening ambition, voracious hunger for power, perhaps, the narcissistic part that is evil, and that's it. And it's not a problem.

More serious thrillers such as *For Whom the Bell Tolls* have a tendency to use more well-rounded and fleshed-out villains, but many other damn good ones don't.

It doesn't even seem to matter much that villains act contrary to the portrait of them that the author has painted. Goldfinger in Ian Fleming's *Goldfinger* (1959, film 1964) is an example. Goldfinger loves gold; it seems to define him as a character. It's his ruling passion. How he got that way, nobody knows. If Ian Fleming knew, he never said. Goldfinger lusts after gold, the yellow metal itself; he can never have enough of it, he says. Yet he is going to blow up the Fort Knox gold depository with an atom bomb that will destroy the very thing he lusts after. He's doing this so that the gold he has stockpiled will have more value. He will be richer but will have not a single ounce more gold. This seems to be a pretty stupid plan if what he wants is more gold; he's going to have to pay much more for the gold he'll be getting in the future. But if any readers or anyone in the audience noticed, they didn't seem to give a fig.

What accounts for the easy acceptance of this obvious contradiction? I think it has something to do with the powerful, deeply psychological nature of the thriller. Each of us has within us the evil that is being acted out by the villain and his minions. Though we may be rooting for the hero, we have a secret fascination with the villain, who has a twin deep within our psyche. That a villain is mysterious allows us to watch him or her in a removed sort of way without admitting that we, too, have these feelings, which we, as mature and civilized human beings, find unacceptable. Whatever the reason, it is something that is useful for thriller writers to understand, because in some cases it is neither necessary nor perhaps even desirable to create the villain as a fully fleshed-out, well-rounded multidimensional character.

Let's take a look at a few villains found in damn good thrillers. First comes the granddad of English-language thrillers: the Robin Hood story. The villain is Prince John, who is trying to steal the crown from his brother, Richard the Lionheart, who is being held for ransom by the Austrians. While pretending to collect taxes for the ransom of his brother, Prince John is actually filling his treasury to buy an army that will be used to put himself on the throne. Now how dastardly is that? Prince John's character sketch might look like this:

- He is powerful.

- He is vain, smug, and a braggart.

- He is prissy and narcissistic.

- He is maniacally ambitious.

- He is insanely jealous of his brother, the king, and his brother's power.

- He is ruthless and murderous and powerful.

- He is coldhearted and has no pity for the poor people he is overtaxing.

- He is determined, clever and resourceful, and seemingly unstoppable.

If he were a well-rounded, multidimensional character, he would have inner conflict about carrying out his dark mission. A less evil character might have remorse and regret, but Prince John has no remorse or regret and no inner conflicts whatever. He is evil down to the bone. And the audience loves him for it.

His second in command is the Sheriff of Nottingham. He is not totally evil: After all, he is loyal to Prince John, and loyalty is a positive quality, even if misplaced. But he loves his work: beating, hanging, branding, whipping, eye gouging. No cruelty is too great to get those taxes collected. He's pretty much like his boss.

How about *Eye of the Needle*? The villain is Hitler himself, who is offstage for the entire story. The villain's follower, who is really the acting villain of the story, is Faber. Although he may see himself as a patriot, we see him as

- powerful

- ruthless

- murderous

- merciless

- determined

- cunning

- clever and resourceful

- seemingly unstoppable

- coldhearted

I see a pattern emerging. In the Bible, there is the story of Samson and Delilah. I discussed this story at some length in *The Key: Using the Power of Myth to Write Damn Good Fiction*. Samson and Delilah is really a wonderful story. The villain in the film version (1949) is the Saran of Gaza. What is he like?

- He is powerful, a despot with the power of life and death over everyone.

- He is merciless.

- He is full of hatred and jealousy for Samson.

- He wants revenge for the destruction Samson inflicted on his army.

- He is ruthless and murderous.

- He is coldhearted.

- He is vain, self-centered, and narcissistic.

- He is cunning, determined, and seemingly unstoppable.

Yes, there definitely seems to be a pattern. Goldfinger—what's he like?

- He is powerful.

- He is greedy.

- He is psychopathic.

- He has maniacal ambition.

- He is self-centered.

- He is ruthless and murderous.

- He is coldhearted.

- He is merciless.

- He is selfish.

- He is narcissistic.

Ah, you say, seems like these villains are a lot alike once you strip away the outer trappings of their lives.

At times, a villain is mindless, such as the pods in *Invasion of the Body Snatchers*, the creatures in *Alien* and *Aliens*, the great white shark in *Jaws*, and the virus in *The Andromeda Strain*. How does the audience think of these antagonists?

- They are powerful.

- They are ruthless.

- They are merciless.

- They are cunning.

- They are clever and resourceful.

- They are determined.

- They are murderous.

- They are seemingly unstoppable.

As you can see, even though these forces, these creatures, are not really characters in the usual sense, they have many of the same qualities as any other villainous character.

Okay, your villain will be creating the plot behind the plot that is the engine behind your plot. Your villain, of course, embodies the evil that has to be foiled. Your villain should not be creating the plot behind the plot for altruistic reasons. He or she should be evil, ruled by unbridled ambition or lust or greed or revenge or any other base motive, but never to do good for others. It is just not in his or her nature.

Oh, sure, a villain may claim to be acting for others—family, country, comrades, an ideal—but it's always a lie. In other words, you don't want your audience to come to the end of your story and find that, gee, the dark side of the Force does have its good points. No. Evil is evil, and in the end the audience should cheer when the villain gets what's coming to him or to her. In those rare cases when evil is victorious, as in *The Spy Who Came in from the Cold*, the audience should feel shocked and deeply saddened.

It does not matter to the audience that evil villains may not see themselves as evil. The pod people in *Invasion of the Body Snatchers* see themselves as good—free of all those pesky, enslaving emotions like friendship, desire, and love that flesh-and-blood people are infected with.

But the audience is scared to death of them. And the more scared they are, the bigger the thrill in your thriller.

■ Big Menace Thrillers and Small Menace Thrillers

So how do you go about creating this villain, who will be the author of the plot behind the plot?

You're going to create this character to fill the role of villain in a thriller once you have a germinal idea for it, and, of course, I have no way to know what that germinal idea might be. The way I can help you is to show you how to go from the germinal idea to creating the character of the villain, no matter what germinal idea you might be working with.

There are two broad categories of thrillers. There is the big menace thriller and the small menace thriller. In small menace thrillers, there are high stakes, but only a small number of people are at risk. In *Charade*, as an example, the menace is to just a few: mainly Mrs. Lampert—she's the one we're worried about. The same with *The Day of the Jackal, The Desperate Hours, Misery, The Hand That Rocks the Cradle* (film 1992), *Sleeping with the Enemy* (1987, film 1991), *SWF Seeks Same* (1990)—made into the film *Single White Female* (1992)—and a host of others. Slasher films are all small menace films, they tell me. I have never actually seen one and don't plan to.

In a big menace thriller, the menace is to a great number of people. In *Black Sunday*, fifty thousand people attending the Super Bowl are menaced. In *The Andromeda Strain*, the whole world and everyone in it is threatened by death. In *Invasion of the Body Snatchers*, all humanity is in danger of being turned into vegetables. In *Blindness* (1995; film 2008), the world is threatened with an epidemic that causes people to lose their eyesight. These are all big menace thrillers.

Often in my plotting classes new writers think they have to menace the whole world in order for the audience to be riveted. Not so. A small menace thriller may be just as riveting as a big menace thriller.

In *The Key: Using the Power of Myth to Create Damn Good Fiction*, I discussed a damn good small menace thriller, *Inferno* (film 1953), which was gripping as hell, about a man left to die in the desert by his unfaithful wife and her lover, his business associate. The hero's wife and her boyfriend try to kill him by pushing him off a cliff. Alas, he is not killed but breaks a leg in the fall. It's miles to civilization, and there's nobody around, so the would-be killers leave him there to bake in the sun and die of thirst. This is a thriller with small stakes indeed—one man's life. And it is truly a gripping film, often rated as one of the greatest survival films ever made. It's right up there with *The Snow Walker.*

So when you're creating your villain, the nature of the villain in a small menace thriller may be slightly different from that of the villain in a big menace thriller. Villains in both types may be psychotic, of course, and, at least in the views of sane people, motiveless. The difference is, in the big menace thriller the villain has more grandiose plans and is not just evil but often an around-the-bend megalomaniac, such as the cat-loving Blofeld in many of the Bond films.

Okay, you have a damn good germinal idea. Now for the next step. You will need to create your villain with a dark mission, and that dark mission is the engine for the plot behind the plot. All of that comes next.

■ Creating the Villain to Fit Your Idea

I've discussed the principles of character building for any novel in *How to Write a Damn Good Novel II: Advanced Techniques for Dramatic Storytelling* and *How to Write a Damn Good Mystery.* I showed how all damn good dramatic characters are larger than life, theatrical, determined to overcome the obstacles that are put in their path. They are an *extreme of type*, larger than life, and they have a *ruling passion* that defines who they are.

I followed the method Lajos Egri outlined in *The Art of Dramatic Writing*, urging writers to first create the character's physiology (how he or she looks, size, weight, age, defects, deformities, sexual appeal, scars, tattoos, IQ [native intelligence])—everything you can think of about the character's physical attributes, right down to acid reflux and the scent of his or her breath.

Then I suggested you create the character's sociology, do a sort of fictional biography for the character, what some writers call the character's *backstory*. Create the neighborhood the character grew up in, the school, friends. What kind of a subculture was he in, choirs and clubs, gangs, what were the sports she played, who were the bullies he (or she) fought with? Were his or her parents free spirits? Drug addicts? Button-down Presbyterians? What were the parents' politics? What schools did the character go to, what troubles did he or she get into? How about his or her love life?

This combination of physiology and sociology produces the character's psychology. They may be real neat freaks, perhaps, or slobs, or pious religionists or militant atheists. Whatever they are, the writer needs to know what made them what they are.

Now then, how does the physiological and sociological combine to create the psychological? Say a pretty girl is doted on by everyone while her plain sister is ignored or, worse, made fun of. The pretty girl might grow up to be self-centered, vain, narcissistic. She's a product of her physiology and her sociology. Meanwhile, her plain sister has low self-esteem and is perpetually angry. She's unhappy, perhaps drinks too much. Flies into rages. Her physiology and sociology have combined to create a volatile psychology.

A boy is born strong and quick. He's good at sports. His sports-minded father pushes him . . . but, alas, no matter how hard he tries, he can't make it to the top. He feels his father's disappointment: He didn't measure up. He starts running with a rough crowd, doing petty crimes, then burglaries. He becomes a great second-story man. If he can't make his father proud, at least he can make him look at him. . . .

Your physiology and your sociology forge your fate.

I also suggested that writers, when creating their major characters, identify their *ruling passion*. The ruling passion may or may not be revealed to the audience. It is a device for giving you, the writer, a way of conceptualizing characters and thinking of them as dynamic rather than as flat and flabby. A ruling passion might be, say, to be the world's greatest cellist or to break the world record in the forty-meter sprint. It might be more abstract, such as "a desire to control everyone" or "an excessive need to be loved."

The dark mission for the villain may be the villain's ruling passion or may be motivating it. "To kill all the McCoys" might be hillbilly Jeb Hatfield's ruling passion *and* his dark mission. "To serve God" might be a ruling passion of a religious fanatic: "to blow up the stock exchange" might be the fanatic's dark mission.

Creating a character with this kind of detail may seem like a pain, but it will help you to better create living, breathing, dynamic characters.

I also recommend writing journal entries in the character's voice. This, I've found, is an important step: You will come to understand the character at a much deeper level. And often, when you write a journal and the character speaks to you, the character will say things that may surprise and delight you, things you had not imagined when you designed him and made up his sociology, physiology, and psychology.

I once was doing a character's journal and my character said, "Of course, you know, I did murder my mother. . . ."

I hadn't known that. But as soon as she said it, I had a much more profound grasp of her character and the depth of her depravity.

■ The Villain Profile

I discussed several villain characters from various thrillers to demonstrate the common characteristics they shared at their core. Characters with these characteristics fit, let us say, the *villain profile*. As an aid to creating your damn good thriller, when you create your villain it might be helpful to make sure that he or she fits the villain profile. Here it is:

- Villains are powerful.

- Villains will act out of base motives, such as jealousy, greed, desire for revenge, hatred, lust, maniacal ambition.

- Villains may be psychopathic or psychotic and are often paranoid.

- Villains are self-centered, selfish, narcissistic, and often vain.

- Villains are coldhearted and merciless, ruthless, determined, cunning, clever and resourceful, seemingly unstoppable, relentless.

The villains that I'm about to create, and the villains that you create, should fit this profile.

Does this mean that all villains are stereotypes? Absolutely not. It means that they share some common characteristics at their core, but they can be different in thousands of ways. One might be young and sexy and seductive; another, old, cranky, and nasty. One might be intellectual and cool; another, prone to rants and rages. They can be young, old, gay, straight, rich, poor, educated, uneducated . . . anything, just as long as they otherwise fit the profile.

■ Fitting the Character to the Profile

I have written in my other books on craft, and have repeated it earlier in this chapter, that the way to create characters is to create a fictive biography—the character's backstory—that starts with the physiology and the sociology and together produces the psychology. Now, in addition, we'll create a character that will fit the villain profile, a character who will have a dark mission and will be driven to create the plot behind the plot. So as we proceed, we'll keep in mind that we're planting the seeds of evil.

It's best to create that character with a backstory that you feel down to your bones. The character's biography must account for the evilness, after all, and even if you don't let the audience in on much of the villain's backstory, it is critical that you do know and understand your villain as you know and understand any other character.

When creating villains for your damn good thriller, you should create them as believable characters. The villain's evil should grow believably out of the background you invent and not be just a sniveling evil cartoon monster. You should invent far more background for your villain than ever bubbles up through the actions of the story. The audience will sense it if you have not done a thorough job.

And like all good dramatic characters, villains should be theatrical— bigger than life. Your villain should be an *extreme of type*. In other words, if your character is a neat freak, he or she should be an extreme neat freak, such as Felix Ungar in Neil Simon's *The Odd Couple* (play 1965, film 1968). If a miser, he should be an extreme miser, such as Scrooge in Charles Dickens's *A Christmas Carol* (1842, film 1910 and at least two dozen remakes, the best being the 1951 version starring Alistair Sims). Goldfinger didn't just like gold; he was murderously psychotic about it. He lusted for gold the way some men lust after a beautiful woman. The most memorable characters in literature are villains who are an extreme of type. Ahab in *Moby-Dick,* as an example. He's willing to sacrifice everything, including his own life and everyone on his ship, to kill that damned white whale. Now there's a damn good character. I really love that guy, and in the 1956 film Gregory Peck played him big, as he should be played.

Your hero should have been been wounded, physically, socially, or psychologically. The wound makes the character human. As we shall see, the hero should also have been wounded. The difference is, the hero will heal the wound by sacrificing for others; the villain will attempt to salve the wound by doing evil. Wounds may be physical, as in the case of Ahab, but more often the wound is psychological. Red Grant in *From Russia with Love* has a bad case of class envy, as an example.

In the best thrillers, the villains, remember, are powerful. There's no sense putting your hero up against a weakling. The villain may also have powerful henchmen and allies. Often the villain's sidekick is extremely deadly in mortal combat. In *From Russia with Love*, the villain is Blofeld, who pets cats and schemes against James Bond. His henchmen, Rosa Klebb and Red Grant, are far more deadly, personally, to the hero.

So, starting with your damn good germinal idea, you will need to create a villain with a dark mission to put your germinal idea into action. Earlier, I dreamed up a few germinal ideas for thrillers. In the next chapter, I'll sketch out some villains to give you an idea of how to make the leap from germinal idea to villain with a dark mission, one who will create the plot behind the plot for you. Then we'll move on to creating the hero and finally the plot itself.

I find this part of the process to be a real kick. It's fun to play God.

4
■ Creating Villains and Exploiting Their Dark Missions

L et's begin with the villain for *DXP*.

DXP is my retelling of the well-used twin-switching plot that is endlessly fascinating to thriller lovers.

You may recall that DXP is a ruthless international conglomerate enslaving thousands of poor Africans. DXP is opposed by the pope, so the villain, DXP's CEO, has a plan to switch the pope—the first American pope, Pope John Peter I—with his look-alike twin brother, who is a crooked cop in New Orleans. I like this one because it lays bare the dark side of the new globalism, which I believe is the greatest threat to human dignity and democratic ideals since Genghis Khan.

I'm a libertarian, and like most libertarians, I'm all for free trade, as long as it's really free and the workers are adequately compensated for their labors. But hey, anybody with a brain and a heart is against low-wage slavery, even if it is disguised as job creation and nation building.

Unlike the literary writers of today who believe that beautiful use of language is what fiction writing is all about but don't give a damn about telling a great story with a sociological angle, thriller writers do give a damn, and they often care deeply about injustice. *Dr. Strangelove* attacked the stupidity of the MAD (mutual assured destruction) nuclear deterrence policies of the cold war. Peter Maas's *Serpico* (1973, film 1973) attacked police corruption in the New York City Police Department. John le Carré's *The Constant Gardener* (2001, film 2005) is an exposé of the skulduggery of pharmaceutical companies in Africa. *Blood Diamond* (film 2006) attacked the illegal international diamond trade, which finances terrorism.

There's a long history of thriller writers attacking injustice, warning against abuses of science, as in Robert Louis Stevenson's *Strange Case of Dr. Jekyll and Mr. Hyde* (1886, film 1931) and Mary Shelley's *Frankenstein* (1818, film 1994); or political oppression, as in George Orwell's *Nineteen Eighty-Four* (1949, film 1984) and Ray Bradbury's *Fahrenheit 451* (1953, film 1966). One of the most influential works of fiction of all time was Harriet Beecher Stowe's *Uncle Tom's Cabin* (1852). It's an adventure/melodrama with a lot of thriller elements, particularly in the opening chapters, which dramatize Eliza's escape from slavery. It was the best-selling novel of the nineteenth century. It had a profound impact on the country and helped to turn public opinion against slavery. So writing thrillers is not just fun: You can feel that not only are you making a buck and getting your mug on TV, but you're warning folks about various evils and giving a voice to the voiceless. That's what I'd hope to do in *DXP*.

So who is the villain? After a little pacing around, drinking strong Colombian coffee, and brainstorming, here's what I've come up with:

Henry Zink, DXP's CEO. He's fifty-two, trim, fit, athletic, brilliant, and as evil as Satan. He makes all kinds of deals with corrupt third world dictators to keep the workers in his sweatshop factories under control. His company has a private security force that uses intimidation against its enemies and will not stop at murder.

In person, Henry Zink's a charmer. A backslapping, smiling good ol' boy from Atlanta, friend of presidents and a huge supporter of breast cancer research at the Henry Zink Cancer Research Center in Atlanta. He has a heart-shaped birthmark on his forehead. He's handsome, tall, silver-haired.

His backstory: Henry grew up poor in Atlanta, the son of Polish immigrants. His father took off when he was seven, and his mother had to scrub floors to make a living. Henry wanted to help out, but he hated hard work. He soon discovered he could use his charm on people and started selling soap door-to-door, claiming to be working to raise money for the Boy Scouts. He later became a used-car salesman, specializing in stolen sports cars. He had one arrest, beat the rap, and went on to manufacture after-market parts and car burglar alarms. By then he was able to buy his own bank and got into home electronics at the start of the boom, and he made a fortune smuggling chips and then another fortune smuggling Freon.

He married a doctor, who heads up his breast cancer research center. They have no kids. Henry hates kids.

Okay—so far, so good.

I love this guy. He hides his evilness behind the cloak of respectability, yet inside he's self-centered, ruthless, cunning, greedy, power-hungry, egomaniacal: He has the villainous qualities found in the villain profile.

He's not just a greedy businessman, he's the greediest of the greedy businessmen, and that makes him, as he ought to be, an extreme of type, out on the bell curve. Good dramatic characters are way out on the bell curve, and that's where we'll find Henry.

Now, it's important that you think of the villain as having a dark mission. Henry Zink, through acquisitions and mergers, plans to create the largest corporation on earth, one that controls trade and credit and that no nation can stand up to.

The pope is opposing him, and this is why he has his dark mission to switch the pope with his man.

Once he has his man installed as pope, he figures, nothing will stop him not only from creating the largest corporation on earth, but from becoming the most powerful man who has ever lived.

■ Getting to Know Your Villain Intimately

I have found that the participants in my workshops who write journals in the voices of their characters really get into the characters and find out things about them they didn't know, even if they have written lengthy biographies of their characters and really know their physiology, sociology, psychology, and ruling passion.

The idea is to get into the heads of the characters as much as possible to try to speak as they would speak. Find the rhythm of their speech and the depth of their feelings. I asked my workshop participants to include the characters' feelings about their parents and their background. The following examples are brief, intended to give you an idea of how these journals would read. When you write them for your characters, I suggest that you make them much longer. Five or ten pages would be good; twenty pages, even better.

Let's hear from Henry Zink in his own voice. His dark mission to switch the pope with his evil twin is to sway a billion Catholics worldwide to support his corporate enterprises in the name of modernization and economic development. Here is his view of things:

> Hi, Jimbo,
> I can't tell you how happy I am that you are writing about me and my gosh-darn troubles with the papacy, God damn it to hell, and I mean it. If anybody ever was the Antichrist, it's this John Peter I. Hey, Jimbo, I believe in doing good. My company and its subsidiaries around the world employ 2 million people. And those 2 million jobs have lifted 25 million people out of the depths of poverty in countries like Nigeria, Honduras, the Philippines, Brazil, Pakistan, and dozens more. Our corporate infrastructure is on every continent and many South Pacific and Caribbean islands. Time magazine said my corporation was a nation to itself. And that's what it is, and a damn good citizen of this world it is.
> I've done very, very well since growing up in Atlanta the son

of a shoemaker. In every interview I've ever done I always said my mama and daddy were just great people—Southern Baptists, working-class Democrats, so warm and loving and kindly— who taught me that looking out for his fellow man was the most important job in any man's life. I know these are lovely sentiments and I wish it were true, but you know different. In fact, Daddy was a drunk and Mama was a whore.

I got into some bad things as a boy, but six months in the Fulton County jail set me straight and got me into learnin'. In jail they got me into a high school equivalency test class and for the first time I figured out just how dang smart I really was.

I was nineteen years and four months old when I walked out the doors of that place, and I was a new man. I met a black used-car dealer in there, a successful man who was railroaded by a no-good wife. He told me that the most important thing in the world was to have a corporation that can move money around and take a rake-off, like he did in his business. I never forgot that. It's like you put yourself with your hand out into the money stream and grab all that you can get. That has been the key to my success. . . .

You'll find that writing these journals will pay tremendous benefits. Your villains—and all your major characters—will take on a life of their own.

■ The Villain for *Code Red*

This is a nuclear war thriller. The germinal idea: Someone is manipulating the president, and he wants a first-strike nuclear attack on another country, which will then nuke us back. This could be a nightmare scenario if ever there was one. A nuclear Armageddon is upon us.

So who could be trying to make this nightmare a reality? Could be the president. Could be a general. Could be the secretary of defense.

Could be the First Lady. Could be a high-ranking adviser to the president. There's a lot of terrific possibilities here.

Often in thrillers there's some kind of secret, evil cabal. Let's have one here—we'll call it the Brotherhood of the Shield—that is manipulating things behind the scenes so that the heroes don't know who's good and who's evil. What a great idea—makes my blood run cold.

Say this villain is the vice president and he is a psychotic paranoid, but he's able to act sane. It's always best to start with a name. Charlie Thompson, how's that? A plain name to mask an evil genius. He's from upstate New York. His father was a lieutenant general in the army during Vietnam and came home a nutcase: brutal, bad-tempered, mean. Charlie grew up facing terror every day, and it twisted him. He learned to seem cool, while underneath he felt rage and despair and dreamed of murdering his father, but he never got up the nerve.

He's fifty-four, a onetime college football starter for Notre Dame, where he was a hard-hitting linebacker. He's gone to fat, pudgy now, and in demeanor he is a careful, serious man who many think is the brains behind the administration. He's a genius at getting people elected, and many are grateful to him. He's a Washington power broker with friends in business and in the military.

He has paranoid fantasies about, say, Russia. He was once a CIA operative and had disappeared for two and a half years while on assignment in Beirut. After an exchange of spies, he was freed. While in custody, he was tortured by the Russians—and he ratted out other agents, but only he knows this. After the collapse of the Soviet Union, he watched the rise of the new Russia with more than just alarm: He's terrified. He imagines they're getting ready to strike America at any hour, and the only defense is to strike first. To that end, he manages to get Russia haters in dozens of key positions, and they've formed the secret cabal dedicated to destroying Russian power. They manage the intelligence reports and create false assessments that point to a Russian plan to strike first.

Let's hear what Charlie has to say for himself. Remember now, the character is not supposed to keep things hidden; this is strictly between villain and author as an aid to getting into the character's head.

> *Greetings.*
>
> *The Russian economy is in free fall. Their president is a maniac. Look at history. The only way for him to pull out of the nosedive his country is in is to pull his people together and give them a common cause, and that cause, sir, will be the destruction of the United States.*
>
> *I was in their care for thirty-one months. They tried their damnedest to break me—they beat me, they used electricity, they kept me from sleeping—but I defeated them. They bared their dark souls to me, and that gives me a third eye that can see inside them. I know what they're thinking; I know they're in league with Satan. They must be obliterated from the face of the earth.*
>
> *Of course I don't expect others to see what I can see, those who do not have prophetic vision like I have.*
>
> *I knew with mathematical certainty that the path to power was to raise political money, and I raised billions. I have managed, over the last eleven years and four months, to maneuver the right people into the right positions, and now I am ready. . . .*

Charlie sounds like just the guy we need. He fits the profile of the thriller villain: He's cunning and clever and a self-centered, paranoid psychopath, determined and seemingly unstoppable. And he's got minions in his cabal, ready to carry out his evil plan. He's going to create a great plot behind the plot, one that will sizzle.

■ The Villain for *Day Three*

This is the Hitchcock-type thriller involving the disappearance of a seemingly innocent guy while on vacation. He's actually a former germ

warfare researcher who found religion and got a conscience and assumed a new identity. He is menaced by the villain, who wants to know
his secrets so he can kill a whole bunch of people. So who is this villain,
and whom does he want to kill? Let's brainstorm a little.

How about he's going to get hold of some of the bioweapons
and blackmail the government into releasing his brother from
the death house?

How about he belongs to that Japanese terrorist cult Aum
Shinrikyo, the one that set off a sarin poison gas canister in a
Toyko subway in 1995? How about he intends to do it again,
only this time with a far more lethal substance, a bioweapon
that will kill millions?

How about he's a scientist whose bioweapons project was
canceled by the new administration, and he wants to scare the
hell out of everyone so the country will go back to researching
these weapons so it can defend itself against them? Okay, let's
go with this guy. In fact, since we've had a couple of male
villains, let's make this one a woman.

Now then, who is this character?

The place to start, as usual, is with a name. Let's say her name is
Amy Love. No good. Too comic. How about Aimée DeLuv? She's from
a long line of military people and considers herself a patriot, taking a
great risk. She is willing to sacrifice many people because it is the only
way to get the country to wake up to the threat of bioweapons. I know
she seems a little nutty, but most thriller villains are nutty.

What does Aimée look like? How about she's a little overweight but
attractive, with a nice smile? She intends, of course, to die with the people she is sacrificing. Being suicidal makes her even more dangerous.
She is a megalomaniac, self-centered, determined, ruthless, murderous,
clever and resourceful, if not brilliant, a really great villain who fits the
villain profile nearly perfectly, except she's not as powerful as some who

have minions and millions to spend on equipment. The villain does not have to fit the profile 100 percent. Aimée is close enough.

Working with such evil characters is really great fun, but I wouldn't want her dating my nephew.

Aimée's journal:

Dear Mr. Frey,

I have given my life to protecting my country from what is potentially the worst threat imaginable. I have been a voice in the wilderness and have been ignored. I have written over two thousand letters to legislators and get nothing but form letter responses and polite phone calls promising hearings on the matter when the proper appropriation bills come up. But the hearings never happen.

I have never, when presented with an obstacle of any kind, been one to play the poor-me-they-won't-listen-to-a-woman card. I have a Ph.D. from MIT and got it without any extra credit for using my vagina. I got it with hard work and brains. In my career, I've created some of the most virulent strains of bio-toxins the world has ever known. Some of them could kill every man, woman, and child on the planet.

I have decided my conscience can no longer be placated: The world has got to know what I know. The world has got to know the threat that it is facing from rogue nations that are preparing for biowar, and the only way to do that is to give the world a small taste of what's in store for them. And for that, I'll need to create a small demonstration which will require me to obtain the services of the man who headed up Project Candyslam. I have tracked him down and I'm now ready to snatch him up and force him to help me show the world, by killing off eight or ten million people, the terrible destructive power of these weapons. . . .

She's scary. I'm in love.

■ The Villain for *The Legend of Hungry Wolf*

In this one, the germinal idea determines the character of the hero. He will be put to the test, and he will pass. We already know the hero's name is Hungry Wolf. He's a sort of fictional Geronimo, the brilliant Apache war chief who fought the Mexicans and Americans from 1858 to 1886. His American enemies called him "Geronimo the Terrible."

Okay, our fictional Hungry Wolf was defeated in war some years back by the cavalry and is now an old man who has been studying to become a medicine man and is fighting to keep hold of his tribe's customs and religion. Fine, but who is the villain? And why has he taken over the railroad station?

How about this: On the train there is going to be the judge who once sentenced the villain to hang. The villain's sentence was commuted to life, and now he has escaped and is seeking revenge on this hanging judge. That's his dark mission. Let's go with that. We need to give the villain a name. How about "Deuce"? Deuce Slade. A great name for a villain in a western.

Oops, wait. The name is okay, but our villain's mission is too much like that of Frank Miller in *High Noon*: getting revenge on the guys who sent him up. How about, instead, Deuce is waiting for his brother, who's on the train because he's being taken to the insane asylum. Deuce needs his brother, who's nuts, but, gee, he's a great outlaw and Deuce can control him. The villain's dark mission, then, is to free his psycho brother from the clutches of the authorities. I like it. His brother is mean as a snake and a murderous lunatic, scary as Manson.

But Deuce is the villain. Let's say Deuce has a pockmarked face from a bout with smallpox when he was a little guy growing up in the hardscrabble town of Rattlesnake Creek in West Texas. His father was a brute, his mother a mean, sullen woman who had nineteen kids. Deuce grew up bad, stealing cattle, robbing stagecoaches, going into Mexico and raising hell. In the Civil War, he fought for the South as an irregular in Quantrill's Raiders, raping, burning, and pillaging, mostly in the border states of Kentucky and Tennessee, but also into Kansas. After the war, he robbed trains with Cole Younger's gang. The only person in the world he loves is his psychotic brother, Zeke.

Deuce is afflicted with arthritis and seeks to steal a lot of money and head down to Mexico to retire where it's warm.

So is Deuce Slade a great villain: determined to get what he wants and ruthless, cunning, and so on? Seems he fits the profile perfectly, like a chambered .44 slug.

This from Deuce:

> *I don't go much for palaberin'. Look, growin' up as I did with a whole lot of misery and a belly full of nothin' gives me a special way of lookin' on things. I figured out real young the devil was ownin' this world and I best be his friend. There plain ain't no mercy for the weak. I got the devil's own pain growin' in my joints and I got to go to Mexico and lay in the sun. Sleepin' on the hard ground is no longer something I be toleratin'. One more job for me and Zeke—that fat cattleman's bank in Toscosa—and we can live out our lives where it's warm and the tequila is smooth and the señoritas are friendly. The only thing is, first I got to get Zeke away from those dogs who think he's loco. Well, maybe he is a little, but he does what I tell him. Me and the boys are gonna take this here train stop for just a day or so, collect Zeke, and then head for the Silver City Bank to do a little business. Plannin' is uppermost, like in the war, being foxy, that's what Quantrill learnt me when I rode with him. Quantrill was a cunning jackal, he learnt me everything. . . .*

He'll do. I have to work on the accent, obviously. And he needs to come across as smarter. Oh well, let's say he's a work in progress. But you can see, I hope, how working with his voice and his background, I'd be able to have him fleshed out as a dramatic character before drafting this story.

■ The Villain for *Hunting Season*

Okay, this is the one about the hunter who's hunted by a renegade space alien and his gang out for sport. He's a hooligan, a criminal, who is joy-riding in the spacecraft. I think of him as a sort of plot device. The interesting character, the real villain of the story, is the alien woman who supposedly is helping the hero get justice for his friend's murder. Once she gets the spacecraft back, she plans to do away with our hero so he's just one more guy who reported a UFO and never came back.

One of the problems with writing sci-fi is that you don't just create characters, you often have to create whole worlds with strange cultures. Fantasy and sword-and-sorcery writers have to do this well. This is called *world building* and is an important first step before you can create the characters.

The world in this story is our world, the world you and I live in. The only difference is that living among us are aliens. Okay, these aliens look just like us. They have been genetically modified and surgically changed, and they have been trained to blend in. They are not preparing for an invasion. They are studying us; we are a kind of laboratory. You and I and everyone else in this world are lab rats.

They are the Krell. Individuals are called Krellians. Those of you who've seen *Forbidden Planet* know that the Krell were ancient, technologically advanced people. I might mention in my story that a Krellian posing as a human worked on the script.

The technology that the Krell possess is thousands of years ahead of ours. They can send spaceships through time warps. They have eliminated disease and aging. Their society has advanced beyond the need for money. Their home planet operates as smoothly as a beehive.

They have a passion for gaining knowledge. They want to understand the past and all biological systems. Okay, let's brainstorm this one a bit.

Maybe they can read minds. Human minds, no.

Maybe they no longer use their bodies to reproduce but do it in a lab.

Maybe they like sex and have developed it into an art form, highly stylized like tango dancing. The important thing is doing the positions and the progressions correctly.

Maybe they have some kind of gadget that gives them a feeling of well-being when they feel low, like a drug but without side effects.

Maybe they have love relationships, but they always take a backseat to careers. Class III and Class IV Krell do sometimes mate for life, which can be thousands of years.

Maybe the alien woman has contempt for humans, who are dirty and messy. Maybe she's a neat freak, highly organized; everything she does, she does systematically.

Maybe the UFO crazies in this world really have it right, and what they're seeing is Krell scientists coming and going. Their main station is underseas in the Bermuda Triangle.

Maybe the Krell pose a threat, because just as our scientists kill all the lab rats when the experiment is over, they will end this planet when they are through with it, and it looks as though that might be soon. It's becoming so polluted that it's no longer a good platform. This will raise the stakes nicely.

So this Krell woman, my villain—what's her name? How about Kitty Apple? Let's see . . . she's over five hundred years old and has been passing for human for over three hundred years. She's had nearly thirty different identities on Earth. Currently, she looks about twenty-five. She's a serious scientist and career woman working her way up in the Krell scientific hierarchy. She's hoping that rescuing the purloined craft will give her a boost. Her current assignment is as a barmaid at Duffy's in Santa Monica. Her unit is studying human mating behavior.

When you're creating superbeings like this with a background in another world, it's a challenge not to make them cartoonish. My villain is beginning to come alive to me. She's bright and controlling, and her ruling passion is to get to the top of the scientific establishment. She's a workaholic and does not have much fun. She does not allow herself to be distracted from her ambitions with trivial things like relationships with other Krell.

Here's Kitty Apple's journal:

I've been pretending to be human for so long, I can barely remember what the home planet is like. For one thing, it's a very cloudy place. We all live underground most of the time, so the natural environment will not suffer from our presence. I was born in subclass IIA. We're scientists and glomers—those who direct development of the culture and compose music. Musicians on our home planet have great prestige and power. They are in subclass IA. From the time we breathe air until adulthood is only 94.112 Earth days. So there is really no childhood as such. Our brains are programmed and supplemented with memory chips, so there really is no need to go to school. Humans waste so much time on schooling. But we do develop and practice creativity, and meditate on the nature of Krell. Our natures are our politics and our philosophy. Our religion has to do with being absorbed by Krellness, a process that humans cannot understand. It would be sort of like teaching your dog to play chess. The Krell call it "remembering." It's a way of soldering our pieces together and becoming more truly Krell. We spend a lot of time in a remembering chamber. I can only describe it by saying that when you're in a remembering chamber, things are more real than real. It is a kind of paradise.

I was young, only the equivalent of about a 90-year-old human, when I won the competition to enter the Earth culture studies program. We ended the aging process long ago, and disease is unknown. We can be killed, of course, but we rarely get sick; if we do, we can cure it no matter what it is. Death does come eventually, in about a thousand Earth years, but our DNA labs are working on this.

We are animals—highly evolved though we may be. But the pesky problems of humans like lust, loneliness, and despair have long given way to technological solutions. We still have ambition and envy, though, because culture cannot progress without them. Competition is part of our nature. We want to get ahead. We're programmed to focus on cultural and personal development. I speak 11 human languages and am working on some hypermath problems.

By the end of my next tour of duty, I hope to be in charge of de-commissioning Project Earth, returning it to an elemental state, and moving on. We've found 2,318 planets with highly organized civilizations to study just this Earth-year alone in this quadrant. Some of them have never had any experimental treatments—a very exciting prospect.

Writing science fiction is fun. You can really let your imagination run amuck. Getting into the minds of aliens is not easy, however, since their worldview is so different. I'm hoping as I work with Kitty that I'll get to understand her better and new aspects of her background and personality will emerge.

One thing you've probably noticed: She does not totally fit the villain profile. She is powerful and self-centered, coldhearted, determined, cunning, clever, seemingly unstoppable, and so on, but she is not operating out of base motives found in the villain profile, such as jealousy, greed, desire for revenge, hatred, lust, or maniacal ambition. Hers is the evil that comes from the indifference of a scientist, and maybe that is even more chilling.

It's going to take a great hero to defeat her. We'll see who will fill that role later.

■ A Villain for *Shadow Self*

This is the horror story about the doppelgänger. Again, it's going to take some brainstorming. The doppelgänger is the ghost of a living person, but it is not a ghost in the usual sense. It does not have the soul of the living person (let's call her "the victim"). It is a spirit that has only the appearance of a living person and has the ability to become solid and to mascarade as the living person. The doppelgänger has its own agenda.

> Maybe this doppelgänger enjoys playing games with the living person at first. Maybe it will drive the victim's husband's mistress away.
>
> Later, the doppelgänger enjoys being solid and wants to replace the victim.
>
> Maybe the victim and the doppelgänger have a life-and-death struggle in the slam-bang climax and they're both killed, but there's only one body.
>
> Maybe the doppelgänger will at some point try to make a deal with the victim to share her life.
>
> Maybe the victim will find someone who's an expert on spirits to help her. She may even try to send the doppelgänger back to where she came from through a kind of exorcism.

The doppelgänger does not have a name. On the other side, she was simply a spirit, like an energy, waiting to come into existence. Okay, let's see what she has to say for herself.

The doppelgänger's journal:

I'm supposed to tell you my true feelings. Okay, I guess I have no choice. Since I've come over the barrier, I've grown to dislike this worm you call "the victim." Hell, she's no victim—I'm the damn victim. Everyone would think that just because we look alike, we are like. But we're nothing alike. For one thing, I like a good time and she's a stuffed shirt that likes to suck on pickles. She has no sense of humor. She completely flew off the handle when I borrowed a dress that belongs to her and wore it to see her shrink. That guy couldn't analyze a carrot. And when I tried to put the make on him, just for fun, he freaked. You'd think he'd never seen a woman's breasts before.

You know, having a body is sooooo much better than not having a body.

I got a kick out of it when her shrink called up "the victim" to tell her she was even nuttier than he suspected and he never wanted to see her again.

You'd think when I showed up while her husband was having sex with his business associate, Miss Tweeg, that your "victim" would have been pleased. But no, she tried to explain to her husband that it wasn't her. You know, she really doesn't get it. I mean, she doesn't understand who I am and where I'm from and how powerful I am.

You, my author, do not know what it's like on the other side of the barrier. You don't understand what it means to live in a place where there is no time. Time, on the other side, is stalled. Having never experienced it, you just don't know. I was stalled there myself. You don't live in the spirit the same way you live in the flesh. I was not able to be myself there, but here in this universe, gloriously living in sequential time, I am able to be myself. And I decided there's nothing I want more than to live the life of a human.

You want to know about my physiology: I have none. My sociology: I was a mist, lost, with no identity. My psychology: I saw this bonehead coming over the barrier playing astral projection and I grabbed my chance.

I know you find it shocking that I would get rid of the woman that I look like, but remembering that cloying feeling *of timelessness, I see that this is my one chance to break free. . . .*

I like her a lot. She'll light up the story all right and be a great villain.

■ The Villain for *The Hunt for Jethro Potts*

This one will be lightly comic. Jethro Potts is a bit off-kilter and thinks that TV destroyed his marriage and his life. Well, maybe he's not so off-kilter. The villain here is not Jethro: The villain is a TV producer who is gaining fame by pursuing Jethro and making him into the villain of a reality TV show.

The villain, then, is Morton Gluck. He's rich, selfish, self-centered, vain, a megalomaniac, seemingly unstoppable, clever, and cunning. Gee, sounds like he fits the profile, except he's not murderous. After all, it is a comedy.

Of course, he appears to be a crusader, after a man who has violated the law by blowing up his TV stations. Let's make Morton short and round, with cherubic looks. He's a self-made man who started out selling recycled golf balls he pulled out of a lake next to the golf course. His parents were middle-class folks who loved square dancing. His mother was a sort of naïve innocent all her life; his father, a manager of a bowling alley, was a self-absorbed pencil pusher with a pimply girlfriend.

Morton now owns a cable network and has made a fortune with sleazy reality TV shows.

This could be a great comic thriller as the two men try to destroy each other.

Here's Morton's take on things:

My mom and dad were great people, the salt of the earth, but, you know, I never did really connect with them. It was like, well, like I was born into the wrong family. My reality was TV. I love TV. Really love it. I never loved anyone as much as I loved Cindy on The Brady Bunch. *I wanted to be in that family so, so bad. I used to dream that I was Cindy's older brother sometimes. No, it wasn't sexual. I was her brother. I loved her like a brother.*

That's why I got into TV. I just had a knack for knowing what the audience likes. I connect to the audience; it's like they're an extension of my soul. I am fused with the audience. It's a spiritual thing.

Producing for TV is like playing God. I decide not just what people watch—I decide what they think. Not even God decides what people think—but I do. Yeah, I feel my power.

Then here comes Jethro Potts and he's challenging this power, and I know he's got to be dealt with. He's a crazy man, but it doesn't matter. People are defying their God and siding with Potts, listening to his insane ravings. He says I'm evil, that TV is evil, that it's ruining America. This is blasphemy!

He must be stopped at all costs.

This could be funny and still make some good points about the evils of TV, which around Berkeley, where I live, is called "the one-eyed monster." Lots of bumper stickers here saying, "Kill your TV."

■ The Villain for *How Joe Smigelski Saves the World*

This is a comic farce, you'll recall. Joe is the hero. He's a bumbling private eye hired to recover an atom bomb.

I wrote a couple of short stories with Joe as the hero, so I know this character well. I thought of him as the son of a Sam Spade kind of guy—a tough-guy P.I. Joe's mother, who now works for him, is even tougher, even though she's in her eighties. Joe's dad was killed on the job, and Joe's mother brought up her son to fill his shoes. Only trouble is, Joe is a pretty dim bulb. But he does have some clever moments. He wears a piece of iron plate inside his overcoat so that when somebody shoots him they're usually wounded by the ricochet. He's also been training for some years in Igotsunami, an obscure Japanese martial art where you defend yourself with just your middle finger. The rest of him is pretty vulnerable, but that finger—it's deadly.

Most detectives are able to catch killers through the use of logic, reason, science, and inspiration, but Joe—he wins by following wrong clues and cockamamie theories that lead him to bungle into terrible trouble.

You might say, Hey, Jim, isn't Joe a detective? Doesn't this make his story a mystery?

Nope. You've got a hero with a mission to foil evil; that's a thriller, even though the hero is a detective. Well, sort of a detective. He thinks he's a detective.

Okay, Joe's our hero, but the plot starts with the plot behind the plot, and that's cooked up by the villain with his dark mission.

So who is he? Let's start with his name. How about Kirk? Kirk Yonkers, how's that?

Let's say Kirk escaped from a government brain-altering experiment that was designed to cure him but only made him worse. He grew up on a Northern California marijuana farm. His parents loved dope, and he grew up smoking it, shooting it, sprinkling it on his cornflakes. He's evil right down to his socks, a man who enjoys torturing kittens, determined to blow up, say, Happytown, a suburb of Cleveland, where the girl who jilted him is living happily with her dentist husband.

We can fit him into the villain profile box, no problemo.

His journal:

You have said it wrong, asswipe. "Jilted" is not the word to describe what that bitch did to me. I found her having sexual congress with the man slated to be my best man. I can't tell you what that did to me. My brain froze! And when I took her to court, the judge in Ohio said I had no case. I could not even get the money back for the ring.

Don't you see? It's not only Cindy that's at fault, it's the judge and the community that has made these laws that lets a man be mortified without judicial redress. So you see, this community has condemned itself to vaporization, and I, like Pontius Pilate, wash my hands of the matter.

I know I will suffer condemnation by the media for my justifiable actions, so I have decided, since life without Cindy is not worth living, that I will set the bomb off myself and will go into eternity with the community. They will see then that I am no coward. They will know I was a worthy man of principle. . . .

A pretty scary guy. Maybe Joe can save the day by getting him and Cindy back together. But for Joe to pull that off . . . well, it might be a little much even for a superhero like Joe. But it would be funny if he tried.

Anyway, I think of this as the same type of comedy as the Austin Powers films. Really goofy and great fun to write.

■ The Villain for *Peace Day*

The previous character sketches are slimmed-down versions of what you should be doing; they are meant to give you an idea of how to create a villain, assuming you have your germinal idea. I will now show you how to develop the villain in detail by creating one example more fully. I've decided to use the germinal idea for *Peace Day*. I will be showing you a complete plot-behind-the-plot outline and a complete plot outline that I call a *step sheet*.

The germinal idea for *Peace Day* is, I think, timely and potentially gripping: A group of kids, Arabs and Jews, meet in San Francisco to hammer out a peace treaty to settle their differences for all time, and the villain is going to try to sabotage this meeting in some horrible way, a way that will scare the hell out of the audience.

I flipped this idea around in my head for a while, trying to figure out who the villain might be. I thought first of terrorists, of course, and then that seemed too obvious or exploitative, so I canned that idea. Besides, ever since 9/11, thrillers have been doing the Islamic terrorist scenario to death. Maybe my villain will make it *look* as if terrorists are doing it.

Then I thought maybe some escaped lunatic or some nutcase living in a cave somewhere with his computer like the Unibomber pulls this off, some monster you wouldn't want to spend the night in your guest room. But then I hit on an idea that really appeals to me: I'll make the villain a writer.

Hmm, wonder where this idea came from? Oh yeah, I'm a writer. Write what you know, as they say.

Isn't it wonderful the way the imagination works? Suddenly I have a picture of a guy in my mind and have no idea where he came from. It's like there's a pool of people in Central Casting deep in my subconscious.

I know writers who clip pictures out of magazines for their characters. That seems to work for them. I know others who imagine a certain actor playing the part. That works, too.

Now then, when you go to make up your villain, remember: This is not supposed to be hard work, this is fun. Let your imagination run.

Let's begin by giving the bastard a name. Here's one that popped into my *cabeza*: Josh Pape. Okay, his name is Josh Pape and he's a writer.

What do we know about him? Nothing so far. Just his name.

Let's say he has a personal vendetta against the leader of the peace group and really has no connection at all to Arabs, Jews, or the International Association of the Sane. I like that; it'll make him hard to find.

Let's also say he had a wildly successful book about recovery from drugs and alcoholism, but he fell out of grace with the public and sales went into the tank when it was exposed that he had plagiarized much of it.

Mary Cathcart, the woman who exposed him—on a nationally televised TV show—worked as a freelance book reviewer. She heard it from her boyfriend, who had met Josh Pape in drug rehab and knew that he had copied someone else's memoir. Mary did some digging, got the full story, then contacted the TV show he was scheduled to appear on. She was added to the show and showed her proof. In ten minutes, he was ruined and she was famous.

Sounds great. A disgraced, best-selling writer out for revenge. I love him already. Revenge is always such a nice, clean, well-understood motive. Audiences have wanted to take revenge a time or two themselves, so they can identify with the villain's motive and loathe him at the same time.

Now we've got what happened to him. Let's press on.

■ All About Josh Pape

As with any other major character, his physiology and sociology will combine to make his psychology.

Physiology:

Let's say Joshua Randal Pape is tall and the nervous sort. Age, thirty-seven. He's not muscular, but he was always good at games where quickness counted, like tennis. He was always quick-tempered as well. He's fairly handsome, except he has a bent nose that got broken twice in fights in the tough Boston neighborhood where he grew up. But when he was young he had wonderful, wavy blond hair. Later it would thin somewhat, and that bothered him. He had always been proud of his hair.

His tendency to be outspoken got him into lots of scrapes. His lips are thin, and his teeth are large and slightly crooked. Josh has a high IQ and a lot of musical ability, but he was always something of a dreamer and could not force himself to sit down and practice the violin, even though he loved it. He has buttermilk skin that burns easily in the sun, and his eyes are narrow, but clear and blue. He looks serious to others, but not unfriendly.

Sociology:

Josh's mother is Irish and his father Italian. They were dirt poor. The family name was Papatonni; Josh changed it when he was twenty-one. He didn't like being Italian. He was blond and preferred to tell people he was Swedish.

He has four sisters and two brothers. Josh was next to the youngest. His father worked two menial jobs and was rarely home; his mother was overwhelmed by their poverty, and the house was in chaos. One of his brothers—Anthony, the youngest—was a good-natured boy, with a bright smile and a sunny disposition. He was everyone's favorite, especially his mother's. Josh hated him and picked on him, which caused a lot of enmity between him and everyone else in the family.

In school, Josh tried to fit in, but he was smarter than the other kids and they resented him, even though he got poor grades. He had an "above it all" attitude.

Psychology:

As a child, Josh felt neglected and unloved, that he did not belong, so he developed a feeling that he was ever the outsider. He desperately wanted to be liked and loved, but except for his maternal grandmother, who died when he was eight, no one ever gave him either attention or love. In high school, he never had a girlfriend. He once tried to kiss a girl in a kidding way—she was a friend of his sister Maria—and she hit him with a book bag and gave him a black eye.

In his isolation and loneliness, Josh turned to books; he read science fiction and dreamed of becoming a great writer. One of the nuns in grammar school told him she thought he had a lot of talent because of a story he wrote about a rat whose head was too big to get into the cupboard with the other rats. In high school, he won an essay contest, "Why I love Boston," which was the greatest day of his life, he often said. It was as if, he said, the hand of God had reached down from heaven and touched him and made him a writer.

Much of the essay was lifted from a 1956 *Life* magazine article, but no one ever noticed.

Josh was an angry kid. Despite his brains, he dropped out of high school and ran with a bad crowd that drank, smoked dope, and stole cars for parts. It was the only time in his life he felt as though he belonged. He landed in juvenile hall for six months. It was this experience that he would write about. He started publishing from his cell, small pieces. When he got out, he became involved with drugs again, but the writing was going well, and to meet a deadline for a book, he plagiarized some of it from the diary of a former cell mate who had hung himself.

Josh later ended up in drug rehab, where he met the love of his life, Ellen Tashkent. He moved in with her. She was unhappy and miserable, and trying to stay off heroin was a daily battle that left her exhausted. But she relied on him, and he felt wanted, needed, and loved.

On the sale of his book, Josh soon became rich and famous and happy, and life was wonderful. He and Ellen moved to a luxury flat on Nob Hill. He got Ellen into the best clinic with the best doctors and into a good drug therapy that seemed to bring her to life. She looked radiant. They hobnobbed with the rich, spent weekends with film stars, traveled, took cruises to exotic places.

Then, alas, Mary Cathcart discovered he'd plagiarized parts of his book and, on prime time, she destroyed him. Ellen killed herself with an overdose on the day he was sentenced to prison for fraud.

Josh was devastated. He tried to kill himself twice in his cell. He entered into a despair so deep, he called it a black hole. It felt, he said, as if hell were crushing his head. But then he started to imagine what he might do to Mary Cathcart when he got out.

He had an inferno of hatred in him, and all of it was focused on her. He swore oaths that he would have his revenge and have it in such a way that even she would see he was a creative genius.

So Josh's ruling passion was to be a great writer; that's what he had been all about all his life. But now that the love of his life has killed herself, his ruling passion is his dark mission to get revenge on Mary Cathcart.

He's my kind of guy. A street-smart punk with a high IQ and the morals of the gutter, full of murderous impulses.

Josh's journal:

I know you want to get to know me better by having me speak in my own voice and to get yourself in touch with how I think and feel.

You described me as being quick, the nervous sort, which is not quite true, and I take offense at you saying that. I'm not a Don Knotts kind of guy. I'm edgy, that's the way I think of myself. I'm always in self-protective mode. I have fast reflexes. A couple of times I've avoided car accidents because I am quick. And I have a quick mind. Being edgy is a by-product of having a quick mind, and, yes, I have a hot temper. Passionate people always do.

You said I was outspoken. I believe I'm forthright and my opinions count because I'm smarter than just about anyone you're likely to meet. I have an IQ of 154. That's genius, in case you didn't know it. I could have been anything, but I think God chose me to be a writer. As I see it, writing is not a vocation, it's a life. Writing is not what you do, it's who you are.

One thing, Frey, you got dead wrong. My eyes are not "narrow." They may appear to be so because of the glasses. You never mentioned it, but I have 20-2400 vision in my left eye and 20-1800 in my right eye.

You made me sound like a vain asshole because I'm a little pissed that my hair is thinning. Well, hell, I'm a human being and I like to look good. All that wavy hair made me look great. It is not vanity to mourn its loss.

You said I didn't like being an Italian. You said very little about my father. Something you missed. He had taken a fall when he was young, cracked his skull, and was in a coma for 188 days. It affected his brain. He was brain-injured and mean as a junkyard dog, but I loved him. My anti-Italian attitude had nothing to do with my father. It had to do with the way society saw Italians as being a bunch of spaghetti benders with greasy hair. So I used to tell people I was Swedish, big deal. You had it right about me feeling as if I were an outsider. At home, my brother Anthony got all the attention, all the love, and I was like a lightning rod for everyone's antipathy. Anthony could do nothing wrong and I could do nothing right and so I hated my mother, and that's all you're going to get out of me on the subject.

When you have a great mind, you have to continually stimulate it with great thoughts. That's what drew me to science fiction, where in my time all the great writers roosted from

Heinlein to Frederik Pohl, to Arthur C. Clarke to Doc Smith, to Ray Bradbury to Isaac Asimov, to Philip K. Dick, and, of course, the guy who could make me laugh myself sick, Douglas Adams. I lived in places imagined by the greatest minds on earth, and I lived in a world of my own where I was not called a Wop and the girls did not think I was strange and the boys did not think I was a geek.

That crowd you said I ran with, the bad boys that got me into trouble, were called "the Outlaws." We all read sci-fi, and, yeah, we thought we were different, and we were different. I was trying to write and to expand my consciousness—we all were. We experimented with peyote and pot and we learned we could steal car parts and make a lot of money easy as pie. And we experimented with the hard stuff, too—coke and hash and ludes, and finally heroin—that had a strange and powerful effect on me, and that's how I got to the rehab where I met sweet and wonderful Ellen Tashkent and fell deeply, madly, drunkenly in love.

Everything was perfect. That TV show Sally Queen Presents made me a best seller and every dream I ever had was coming true. . . .

Then Mary Cathcart came along and accused me of plagiarism. That is sort of like being accused of witchcraft in the nineteenth century. Once the accusation is made, you are convicted. Hell, all writers do it. She never gave me a chance—she completely blindsided me on television in front of a national audience. For once my quick mind failed me. I was in shock. And had she but given me a chance to respond or to prepare an answer, or to interview me in private and find out what actually happened, none of the tragedy that followed would ever have been. Ellen and I would still be happy, I would still have my reputation, and all would be well. Instead, I descended into the hell of prison. And disgrace.

I believe that there is very little free will involved in human *activity. We do what we must, what we are driven to by the meanness of God. But there does come a time when a man must make a decision and must act in order to preserve his own human dignity, and that he will do by choice. Mary Cathcart destroyed me. I must destroy her. It is an equation as simple as two plus two equals four. If I do not rectify the injustice done to me, I will not be able to hold on to my sanity. Therefore, as a matter of existential choice, I have decided to eliminate Mary Cathcart and, with her demise, I will also destroy her vision of peace. This gives me a reason to live. This has become the focus of my life and my passion. . . .*

■

You may notice that I sometimes deviate from what I wrote in the biography. That's all right. The purpose of this is for me, the writer, to get into the thought patterns and the feelings of the character, much as a Method actor gets into the character of the part he or she is playing.

You may think that this might be a huge waste of time because Josh may not be onstage in front of the audience all that much in the course of the story. And that may be true. He may appear only in a scene or two, but he is a pivotal character driving actions. And it's very important, critically important, that I as the author understand why he is doing what he's doing, and to feel it, not just know it. To make this technique work even better, I should spend more hours writing in his voice until his way of thinking, feeling, acting, and reacting is a part of me.

■ Josh's Dark Mission

Okay, the International Association of the Sane is getting a lot of media attention. Mary Cathcart is making a video documentary about their impending conference and is writing a series of articles for the *New York Journal*. She has managed to get the conference worldwide attention. All the major networks have done pieces on the conference, including interviews with her.

I realize that as you read this, you may get the impression that scenarios and character sketches are pumped out of my imagination like water from a fireboat hose. I'm accused of being off in the la-la land of my imagination so often that I ought to be given Prozac with every meal. But, in fact, ideas don't come that easy all the time. I often spend hours pacing the floor, coming up with ideas and rejecting them, which sometimes can be like shooting off your toes one by one.

When I created the character of Josh, I thought I'd have no problem figuring out what he'd do to get his revenge. I thought I could always come up with something brilliant, but then I discovered that the firehose imagination had shut off. Every idea I cooked up for Josh was a fizzle and for lots of different reasons.

IDEA #1. I thought, How about Josh gets the Jews and Arabs feuding with one another so that the conference disintegrates? I rejected this because it would not be very dramatic. While in a social sense the stakes would be high, they would not be high in the audience's mind. The feud between the Jews and the Arabs would continue, but it's been going on for five or six thousand years, so what's the big deal?

IDEA #2. How about Josh plans to poison-gas everyone at the conference and blame it on radical Palestinians? This could be an exciting climax. So the story would be about trying to stop him. I got really excited about this idea until I figured out it was a bust. The problem here is the FBI would be involved in this, and they would take my story away from my hero and, hell, they'd just cancel the whole thing and send everyone home. Not much drama there.

IDEA #3. This one I also got really excited about before I decided that it wouldn't work. I mean, my heart was beating fast, I was so sure this was a winner. Here's the idea: I'd have Josh invent a group of terrorists who would not want the peace plan to succeed. The group would be made up of Jews, Arabs and other Muslims, and anarchists, and they'd sabotage the conference. But then I realized that I would not be able to make it believable. What's not believable? That you could get these people to work together for any cause. Hell, you'd never be able to get them to sit down in the same room, let alone work together. I went to Israel and talked to Jews and Arabs. You've never met people with minds shut so tightly on both sides. It's like talking to bricks.

So I fell into a funk. I just couldn't figure it out. I did my usual tricks: I interviewed the character, I brainstormed, I went out on my sailboat, *Spirit of Arnaldo*, and let the wind and the waves massage my imagination. All to no avail.

I was beginning to think I'd have to go with one of my other ideas, even though it did not really excite me, when I finally hit on it:

IDEA #4. Josh, pretending to be a radical group, could kidnap Mary and announce to the media that he is going to behead her at the moment of the signing of the peace treaty.

I love this. It gets the clock ticking. We could be in Mary's viewpoint part of the time while she awaits the ax. Wow. Chilling.

How about the FBI? Well, of course they're on the case, and they keep getting in my hero's way. Hey, it's my job to make obstacles for the hero: The FBI could be a huge one. But not as huge as if the problem were stopping a gas attack. If there's a kidnapping, they might put a few men on the case because of the media attention, but for a mass gas attack they'd take over San Francisco, and my story. And I don't want to write about the FBI.

I decided I'd go with the beheading idea.

A note about finding the right idea: Once you find it, it seems so right and so ridiculous that it didn't occur to you before that you can't believe you ever had a problem dreaming it up.

Now Josh has to get to work for me cooking up a plot behind the plot. That's next.

5
■ The Secrets of Clever Plotting Revealed

Examples to Show How Easy It Is

So far, we've discussed how you start with a germinal idea and what makes a good one; then we discussed the villain profile and how to create a villain with a dark mission, who will take actions to get what he wants. These actions are the plot behind the plot. The hero's job in a thriller, remember, is to foil evil. The villain's plot behind the plot is the evil the hero must foil. These actions the hero and others take to counter the plot behind the plot make up the plot of your thriller. Simple, no?

The first thing you will need to do is make a plot-behind-the-plot step sheet. The early steps may include important things that have happened in the villain's backstory that you might want to keep in mind. Next come the steps he takes in carrying out his dark mission. Some of these steps might be shown to the audience and become steps in the plot itself or are actions taken by the villain offstage, behind the scenes, that the audience does not see.

Here's an example of what a single step looks like, written in a short-hand manner.

13. *Josh buys a gun.*

Don't like shorthand? You may write a longer description, like this:

13. *Josh goes to an ex-con he knows, Freddy Smith, who sells weapons out of the trunk of his car at the Oakland flea market. He buys an old Colt .45 automatic and a box of shells and a sawed-off Savage double-barreled shotgun. Josh feels great: Things are going exactly as planned.*

There's no right or wrong way to do it. It's for you, after all, to help you construct your plot. Write as little or as much as you want.

Even if you do a diligent job of creating the plot behind the plot, you may discover when you start making up the plot itself that the villain could have been more clever. That's okay. You can always go back and change the plot behind the plot and fix it. The plot behind the plot—and the plot itself, for that matter—is as flexible as warm taffy. If you get a brilliant idea, you should be open to changing anything and everything, including the dark mission, the character of the villain, the germinal idea itself—anything at all, if it will make a better story.

Of course, once you get past the first-draft stage, the changes you can make are limited to the amount of rewrite you're willing to do. Sometimes the best ideas come too late to use. Oh well. Writing is a bitch.

■ Plots Behind the Plot, Complex and Simple

There are some damn good thrillers that have a complex plot behind the plot. *Charade,* for example. The villain is Carson Dyle. During World War II, Carson Dyle and four of his buddies got hold of a bunch of enemy loot and hid it, planning to come back after the war at an arranged time and split it up. Unfortunately for Dyle, he was soon after wounded in an engagement with the enemy. His buddies left him to die.

The Germans took Dyle prisoner, and he survived. Years later, one of the four who left him to die, Charles Lampert, went back ahead of the others to where they'd hidden the loot and grabbed it up for himself. The remaining three—Tex, Herman, and Leopold—discovered Lampert's treachery and killed him before he told them where he'd stashed the loot. Or maybe Dyle killed him; it's never really clear in the story.

The three remaining culprits figure Lampert must have given the loot to his wife, and so does Dyle. This, then, is Carson Dyle's dark mission: to get the loot from Mrs. Lampert (played by Audrey Hepburn in the film) before the other three can get their hands on it. Dyle impersonates a security man at the U.S. embassy and appeals to Mrs. Lampert's sense of patriotism to elicit her help in getting the loot.

Please note that Carson Dyle is ruthless and bent on revenge, cunning and determined, merciless, seemingly unstoppable, murderous, powerful, and so on, fitting the villain profile pretty much perfectly. I know this is repetitive, but it's important. So many thrillers fail because the villain is not villainous enough. A wussy villain will sink your thriller quicker than a nuke torpedo.

If you were to write a step sheet for Carson Dyle, it might look like this:

1. After the war, Carson Dyle looks up his old buddies and discovers they're going to Germany on, say, May 10 of a certain year.

2. He discovers that Lampert, who has been living in Paris, is going to betray the others and get there on, say, May 7.

3. Lampert gets the loot, and Dyle tries to get it back from him but accidentally kills him and throws him from a train.

4. Dyle goes after the loot, but so do the other three.

5. Impersonating a U.S. embassy employee, Carson Dyle enlists the aid of Lampert's widow. (This is a step that's in the plot and is shown to the audience, who are taken in by the ruse.)

6. Dyle kills off the three others one at a time, offstage, as the plot unfolds.

To make it even more complex, Mrs. Lampert's suitor, Brian Cruikshank, played by Cary Grant in the film, has an agenda of his own. He's the real embassy security man, who is after the loot as well. This is a wonderful, complex plot that works amazingly well. In case you haven't seen it, love does conquer all, you'll be happy to know.

■

The plot behind the plot of Ira Levin's *The Boys from Brazil* (1976, film 1978) seems complex because it involves so many characters, but when you boil it down to its elemental state, the plot behind the plot is elegant and simple. This is a truly great science-fiction/political thriller that was so far ahead of its time when it came out that it seems contemporary even today. It is a big menace thriller of the first rank.

During the war, evil villain Dr. Josef Mengele ran experiments on human beings at one of Hitler's death camps. Mengele was a historical figure, a real-life human monster who fit the villain profile, one of the rare, real human beings who would. He was a fanatical follower of Hitler and a hater of Jews. Ira Levin made a fictionalized version of him that's even more horrible, because he's not only evil, but a genius at cloning thirty years ahead of all the rest of the bioscientists in the world.

While Hitler is still alive in his underground bunker in Berlin as the Russians close in, Dr. Mengele collects a little of his blood so he'll have cells to make clones of him. Mengele escapes from the Allies at the end of the war and makes his way to South America. There, he sets up a clinic in the jungle where he can perform cloning experiments. Not willing to take the chance that a single clone of Hitler will turn out right and produce a perfect Hitler, he makes ninety-five of them. He impregnates surrogate mothers with embryos that carry Hitler's genes. To make sure that these clones are raised properly, Mengele sees to it that the boys are adopted into households with overly strict fathers and loving mothers— Adolf Hilter's family dynamic.

Since Hitler's father died when he was young, Mengele arranges for all of these fathers—from various countries all over the world—to be murdered when they're about the same age Hitler's father was when he died. As the story opens, Mengele has contacted former Nazi thugs still loyal to the Nazi cause who are in hiding all over the world and summoned them to South America to carry out these murders, and that's where the plot begins.

Mengele is a towering villain and fits the villain profile just great. He acts out of base motives all right—hatred of Jews, revenge, and maniacal ambition. He's coldhearted, ruthless, and not only clever and resourceful, but an evil genius and powerful. He must be vain and narcissistic: He always wears a white suit and is constantly preening himself. He is, of course, a seemingly unstoppable megalomaniac, not just a follower of Hitler, but the creator of nearly a hundred new Hitlers to be unleashed upon the world. This is a monster any thriller writer could love.

So even though it's complex, as the plot unfolds, the audience does not get lost in the complications.

Another complex, damn good thriller that does not lose the audience is *Eye of the Needle*.

Faber, a German agent, as I've already pointed out, fits the villain profile quite well. He has photographic proof that what appears to be a whole army and all its equipment apparently ready to assault northern France at Calais is really just made of cardboard and that the real forces are preparing for a landing at Normandy farther to the south. He must get those photos back to Germany. The fate of the Third Reich is at stake! The photos are what Alfred Hitchcock called "the McGuffin," the thing that spies in spy thrillers are killing one another over. Anyway, this spy—code-named "the Needle"—is going to meet a sub off an island where the hero, Lucy Rose, is living with her nasty, invalid husband. So this big menace thriller boils down to a chess game on this tiny island between the hero, Lucy Rose, and Faber, the villain. A good read as a novel, it was made into a great film.

The Day of the Jackal has a simple plot behind the plot. The 1954 war in Algeria and de Gaulle's decision to let Algeria break off from France sends a bunch of guys in the army really, really mad, so they decide to kill de Gaulle. That's the first thing we see when we watch the film: the 1962 assassination attempt. When it fails, they hire the damnably clever Jackal, a paid assassin.

High Noon also has a pretty simple plot behind the plot. While I have no way of knowing how the author put this western thriller to-gether, I've made up a plot behind the plot to show you what it might look like:

Will Kane was appointed marshal of a wild town, Hadleyville, New Mexico, a dozen years ago or so and, with the help of a large number of deputies, tamed it. His chief antagonist was a violent psychopath, Frank Miller, an outlaw gang leader. Marshal Kane and his deputies killed a bunch of Frank Miller's thugs and managed to get Frank convicted and sentenced to hang. They sent him to the state capital to be executed.

By some kind of crooked manipulation that is never explained to the audience, Frank Miller gets his sentence commuted to life in prison. In prison, he seethes and plans his revenge. His dark mission: to get out of prison and kill Marshal Kane and install a new reign of lawlessness in Hadleyville. You will notice—need I say it?—that Frank Miller fits the villain profile.

Frank Miller contacts confederates, who pay bribes with loot from Frank's crimes. These confederates get him a pardon from a corrupt governor, and now he's free to go ahead with his dark mission. He sends for three vicious killers, members of his old gang, to meet him in Hadleyville on a certain date. He plans to arrive on the noon train—by chance on the day that the marshal is getting married to the lovely Amy.

■ The Psychotic Villain

Many damn good thrillers succeed because the plot behind the plot involves a psychotic villain who is not only menacing, but unpredictable as well. An unpredictable psychotic is very scary, and audiences can't get enough of them.

Take Stephen King's *Misery* as an example. Annie Wilkes is a nurse who, we later discover, killed her father and a college roommate in the past, as well as a host of patients at the hospitals where she's worked. At the opening of the story, she lives as a recluse with her pet pig. She spends much of her time reading romance novels. Her favorite romance novels are in the Misery Chastain series, written by Paul Sheldon.

When she hears by chance that Paul is missing somewhere near where she lives, Annie knows just where he might have left the road. Her dark mission is to take Paul Sheldon prisoner and make him write a novel she'd like to read. A simple plot behind the plot indeed, but the story it produced was as gripping as lobster claws.

Of course, she fits the villain profile as a dagger fits its sheath. She's coldhearted, merciless, ruthless, cunning, clever and resourceful, seemingly unstoppable, and psychotic.

Charles Williams's *Dead Calm* (1963, film 1989) has a psychotic as the villain, and like nearly all psychotic villains, he exactly fits the villain profile. John Ingram and his wife, Rae, are out on the ocean in their sailboat when they spot another sailboat that's sinking. They rescue the lone survivor, Hughie Warriner, who turns out to be a homicidal maniac. Hughie has killed everyone on board his boat. We never learn quite why, other than he's a paranoid psychotic.

While Hughie is napping, John takes a dinghy to the sinking boat and discovers that all the crew members are dead. Meanwhile, Hughie wakes up and sails off on John and Rae's boat with Rae as his captive. This made a damn gripping film; the producers improved the story it was based upon.

In *Play Misty for Me* (film 1971), the psychotic homicidal maniac is a female fan of a disk jockey, who stalks him relentlessly with great rising tension. A very simple plot behind the plot that was made into another damn gripping film.

Three homicidal maniacs menace a blind woman played by Audrey Hepburn in Frederick Knott's *Wait Until Dark* (play 1966, film 1967). They are after a doll filled with heroin they think she has in her apartment. This one has its flat spots, but it delivers some pretty damn good thrills.

Most homicidal maniacs are out for revenge, such as the nanny from hell in *The Hand That Rocks the Cradle* and the ex-con tormenting the lawyer who failed to get him off in *Cape Fear*. The psychotic villain out for revenge seems to have a lot of tension inherent in the concept. I'm hoping it will work just as well in *Peace Day*.

■ The Plot Behind the Plot for *Peace Day*

Let's take a look at how we might go about creating a plot behind the plot for *Peace Day*—that is, how the villain creates the plot behind the plot for us. All you have to do is let your imagination run.

Remember, it's the villain's plot, not ours. You've got to let him do his own thing.

You'll recall that Josh was a brilliant but angry young man who got mixed up with some bad companions and landed in juvenile detention. He wrote a book about his time in the can and became a media sensation: a movie deal in the works, number one on the best-seller lists. Life was great. That is, until Mary Cathcart, freelance book reviewer, exposed him as a fraud: A lot of his memoir was plagiarized. He was disgraced, and the love of his life, Ellen, a fragile, recovering drug addict, killed herself. Josh's dark mission is to get revenge on Mary Cathcart.

First, you need to ask yourself if your villain fits the villain profile. Let's see—Josh is certainly acting out of base motives, primarily his desire for revenge. He is self-centered and narcissistic, cunning, a genius, clever and resourceful, and seemingly unstoppable. Ah. Sounds good.

We know all about Josh and how he came to be what he is and how he hates Mary Cathcart and plans to kidnap and decapitate her. He intends not only to end her life, but to destroy the cause of peace in the Middle East that she was promoting. He revels in the idea that she's going to know her dream has been wrecked before she dies. How evil is that, eh? What a great villain.

And being an egomaniac who has been to prison, he's going to really enjoy the game of chess to be played with the FBI. What he doesn't know is he will also be playing chess with our hero—whom we have yet to invent.

Okay, how's Josh going to carry out his dark mission? Let's brainstorm a little:

He might leave clues that will lead the cops to innocent people.

He might make it look as if some terrorists have done it. Arabs, probably.

He might leave clues that Mary Cathcart is staging a publicity stunt if the cops get hot on his tail.

He might leave fake DNA and fiber evidence around to throw the cops off the track.

He might fake his own death so that no one looks for him.

He will need some well-hidden place to keep Mary Cathcart a prisoner.

He might keep her on a boat that is anchored out someplace.

He might keep her in some kind of container or vehicle that has been buried in a pit and covered over with dirt.

He might try to collect a ransom for her, and he might even succeed.

He might work with disguises.

He might have some money stashed someplace.

Some of these things we might use, some not—that's the beauty of brainstorming. At the moment we're just letting the imagination run a little bit. I've found, by the way, that when you're cooking up a plot behind the plot and the plot itself, it's helpful to bounce these brainstormed ideas off your writer friends. They will often point out the difficulties of using various elements and will point out the clichés. They will also, sometimes, light up when you hit them with a great idea. And they may have some of their own that you could use.

Now let's put these ideas into some steps. The point at which you start is really arbitrary, since none of it will be shown to the audience.

1. Josh is in Sing Sing prison, seething with hatred for Mary Cathcart. He works making furniture for the state and is a model prisoner, hoping for an early release. He volunteers to work for a charity, and that's how he gets access to a computer and does a lot of research on Mary Cathcart and the International Association of the Sane and their peace for the Middle East project.

2. He plans to fake his suicide, so he goes to a shrink and talks about how he caused his girlfriend's death and how all he thinks about is killing himself. He pretends to get better as the sessions go on.

3. He arranges to have a guard beaten so he can rescue the guard and make points with the parole board.

4. He joins a born-again Christian group and persuades the pastor that he's been born again and is now a different man, willing to dedicate his life to Christ.

5. He has money hidden on the outside. He has a friend pay the family of a prisoner a few thousand so the prisoner (doing six life terms) will do him a favor: make an escape attempt that he can foil.

6. He is beaten by other prisoners for ratting on the guy trying to escape. Josh has arranged for this beating. He has a lot of black and blue marks—nothing serious. But it will gain him sympathy with the parole board.

7. He gives a great performance for the parole board and is given parole under terms of "supervised release." He is forbidden to drink alcohol or take nonprescription drugs or associate with known felons, and he must work at a regular job and be in by eight p.m. at the halfway house where he will be living. So he's free, and no one has a clue what he has in mind.

8. He gets a job at Mighty Burger on West Sixty-seventh Street in Manhattan as an apprentice fry cook, from eleven to three and five to seven, Monday through Friday. It's perfect. In the morning before work and during his off-hours, he goes to the library, where he reads everything

he can about the International Association of the Sane and Mary Cathcart. The conference where the young people will work out a peace treaty is about to start. He also reads about terrorists so that he can get the FBI chasing after them.

9. *He does volunteer work for the Fifth Avenue Theater Company, sweeping the stage after performances, being an usher during performances. He helps the actors with their makeup and leans the tricks of the trade. Disguises are part of his plan.*

10. *He works on a memoir called* Fallen. *In it he writes of his guilt and feelings of remorse over his disgrace and the death of his beloved Ellen. He writes that he does not blame Mary Cathcart but sees himself as fully responsible. He knows they will find this memoir when he fakes his suicide.*

11. *When he was charged with grand theft and fraud, he had $2 million. The law swept in and grabbed most of it, but he did manage to hide $360,000. He gets a false ID under the name of Michael Rudko and opens a bank account.*

12. *He sees a psychologist as part of his parole and talks of depression and his thoughts of suicide.*

13. *He fakes a suicide and uses his fake ID to fly to San Francisco, where the Sane peace conference is to be held.*

14. *In San Francisco, he moves into a Tenderloin apartment under a phony name and rents space in a closed factory, where he plans to keep Mary Cathcart captive.*

15. *He buys a few guns from an illegal dealer.*

16. *Disguised as an Orthodox Jewish reporter, he manages to forge a press pass to the peace event.*

As I write this, I find that the character is coming alive for me and the plot is beginning to take shape in my mind. Josh is clever and resourceful, as well as having the other wonderful qualities found in the villain profile embedded deep within him.

So what comes next? We'll need a hero to go after Josh and foil his evil plot.

■ **The Great Principle of Character Orchestration**
and
The Making of a Hero
and
Other Stuff Worth Reading About

Good orchestration is a vitally important ingredient of damn good fiction of any kind. When creating characters for your damn good thriller, you'll need to keep in mind the principle of character orchestration. This means, simply, that your characters are *different* from one another.

Look at *Samson and Delilah*, a favorite story of mine. Samson is as strong as a hundred men, a pious Jew blessed by God, a hero to his people, an innocent in the ways of the world. Delilah is a Philistine harlot, a pagan, beautiful, worldly, cunning, ruthless. This is an example of terrific orchestration.

In *Midnight Run*, you have Jonathan, an accountant/criminal health food nut, who has ripped off the Mob to use the money to do good. He's a softhearted innocent in a cruel world he little understands. He's up against Jack, a hard-nosed, ex-cop bounty hunter bringing Jonathan back for the reward money. Jack chain-smokes, swills coffee, eats anything as long as it's loaded with fat. He's cynical and tough, hard-bitten, worldly.

In the film *The Snow Walker*, the orchestration of the two main characters is wonderful. Charlie, the pilot, is a little crooked, a two-fisted, beer-guzzling bush pilot in northern Canada who detests the native Inuit Indians. His passenger in his small plane is Kanaalaq, an Inuit. She's a primitive—innocent, childlike, yet skilled at survival, having grown up in a hunting-and-gathering Stone Age culture. And she's ill and probably dying.

Good orchestration is the foundation for good drama. And it's not just the hero and villain who should be well orchestrated; all the major characters should be well orchestrated with one another.

Let's take a look at *The Godfather*, a damn good story if ever there was one. Though not a thriller, it has a lot of thriller elements. The character orchestration is truly wonderful.

Vito Corleone. He's a crime lord, the Godfather himself. He's old and full of deep, peasant wisdom. He's meditative, building his empire by cultivating friendships and trading favors. He's loyal to his friends and devoted to his family, yet he's ruthless and cunning and murderous when he has to be.

Frederico Corleone. He's the Godfather's eldest son. He's weak, has bad judgment, and is cowardly. And he's stupid. He is well orchestrated with his father. In other words, he's just about as different from his father as you could make him.

Sonny Corleone. He's the Godfather's next oldest son. He's a hothead, oversexed, quick to fight. He takes things personally. He is well orchestrated with his father, who is patient and wise, and well orchestrated with his brother Frederico, who is weak and cowardly.

Michael Corleone. He's the Godfather's youngest son, destined to become the next Godfather. Michael is a war hero, smart, clever, and bold. Though he loves the family, he sees the family business as immoral. He seems the least Sicilian. He's idealistic, a patriotic American, moral—well orchestrated with his father and brothers.

Tom Hagen. He's the Godfather's German/Irish adopted son. He's a brilliant and well-educated lawyer—shifty, devious, completely immoral, but loyal to the Corleone family. He's more intellectual and better educated than any of them, colder and cooler.

These well-orchestrated characters are also, you will notice, *extremes of type*. Vito, the Godfather, is the extremely thoughtful, peasant philosopher. Sonny is not just a hothead, he's a superhothead. Fredo is not just stupid, he's superstupid. Michael is not just Americanized, he's a war hero. Tom Hagen is not just a lawyer, he's the slimiest.

How about the Robin Hood legend? Were the storytellers of old following the rules of good orchestration? Let's take a look at the cast of characters.

Robin Hood. He's a war hero, back from the Crusades. He's self-sacrificing for others and the best archer in England. He's handsome, bold, brave, daring, clever. A Saxon baron and an outlaw, but loyal to the people and the legitimate king, Richard the Lionheart. Robin's a patriot.

Prince John. The villain. He's King Richard's younger brother. Prince John is trying to take over the kingdom in his brother's absence and get himself crowned king. He's a weasel, completely immoral, disloyal, a thief, the total opposite of Robin Hood. Great orchestration indeed.

The Sheriff of Nottingham. Prince John's sidekick, a lackey, totally ruthless, cruel, and inhumane. An opportunist. Now there's a great sidekick for the villain. And he's well orchestrated with Robin and his bunch.

Maid Marian. She's beautiful and brave and, in the beginning, a loyal follower of Prince John. She's a Norman. Get it? She's loyal to Prince John; Robin is against him. Robin is a baron turned outlaw; Marian is a ward of the prince. Robin's an experienced man of the world, having just come back from the Crusades. Marian is young and naïve, an innocent. Of course, she's going to change a great deal, but in the beginning they are very well orchestrated.

Little John. Robin's sidekick. He's huge and strong, a peasant, a follower who does as he's told. Still, he's brave and heroic and eager to be self-sacrificing. The best man in England with a staff—well orchestrated with Robin, the archer nobleman.

Friar Tuck. He's a great swordsman, fat as a sow, a pious churchman, and an unrepentant glutton, yet heroic and self-sacrificing.

Will Scarlett. He's a troubadour, a poet, smart and cunning, and he'll avoid a fight if he can. He's a peace-loving rebel.

So even the ancient storytellers knew the principle of orchestration.

When you make up your characters, be sure to orchestrate them well. It will pay huge dividends.

One thing we know for sure, then, after we create the villain and his dark mission: We know we have to create a hero to stop him. And that hero will be well orchestrated with the villain—even though they might have only a single face-to-face confrontation in the whole story.

Okay, as far as the plot behind the plot is concerned, the most important character in your thriller is your villain, but as far as the audience is concerned, the most important character is usually the hero. So let's take a look at what qualities make for a great hero before we go about creating one.

6

■ All About the Thriller Hero, the Flawed Thriller Hero, and a Not-So-Flawed Hero for *Peace Day*

Heroes, like villains or any other important character in a dramatic story, should be fully three-dimensional, well-rounded, dramatic characters. What goes into the making of a dramatic character I discussed at length in *How to Write a Damn Good Novel* and *How to Write a Damn Good Novel II: Advanced Techniques for Dramatic Storytelling*. Dramatic characters are larger than life, theatrical, and determined to overcome the obstacles that are put in their path. They are an extreme of type and have a ruling passion that defines who they are. And when you create your heroes, as when you create your villains or any other major characters, you should make them three-dimensional and know their physiology, their sociology, and their psychology.

In *The Key: A Fiction Writer's Guide to Writing Damn Good Fiction Using the Power of Myth*, I documented how the character of the hero in heroic stories has not changed much throughout the centuries—in fact, not at all. Despite their differences on the surface—James Bond and

Robin Hood wear different suits—the two are the same cocky, clever, determined, gifted hero. Because heroes through the centuries are virtually the same character, Joseph Campbell called his groundbreaking work about the hero's journey *The Hero with a Thousand Faces* (1949).

So, what do we know about heroes, in addition to their being dramatic characters?

The hero profile:

Heroes are courageous. In comic thrillers sometimes they aren't, but in almost all other types of thrillers they are as courageous as a cannonball. Other than in comic thrillers, heroes who are cowardly or tentative in the beginning soon find their courage. Their unbounded courage is one powerful reason readers and audiences love thriller heroes and want to identify with them and be like them.

Heroes are good at what they do for a living. At the gut level, the audience distrusts characters who are not good at what they do for a living and finds it hard to bond with them psychologically. Again, there is the comedy exception.

Heroes have a special talent. The hero's special talent draws readers and audiences to him or her. Robin Hood can hit a bull's-eye from halfway to China. Samson has the strength of ten Humvees. James Bond has a sack full of special talents: He can shoot skeet from the hip, he is irresistible to the most gorgeous women on earth of any ethnicity, and he can take a sip of brandy and tell you where the grapes that made it came from. By the way, the special talent of a hero may or may not be an aid to the hero in accomplishing his or her mission. The brandy talent has never helped Bond an iota.

Heroes are clever and resourceful. All thriller heroes except those in comedies are clever and resourceful. This is right at the heart of what makes a thriller a thriller. A thriller plot is a chess game, remember, between a clever and resourceful villain and a clever and resourceful hero. When thrillers fall flat, a lack of cleverness and resourcefulness on the part of either the hero or the villain is often the reason.

Heroes have been wounded. The hero's wound may be physical, psychological, or sociological. The hero may be a shunned outcast, a wronged lover, or the victim of a grave injustice. The wound touches the audience's heart. The villain may also be wounded, of course. The difference is, the hero is trying to heal his or her wound by being heroic; the villain is trying to heal his or her wound—or plaster it over—by doing evil.

Heroes are outlaws. Heroes are outlaws because they make their own rules. James Bond has a license to kill. Well, even if they don't have a license, heroes often do kill or commit other felonies. They may be outlaws in any number of ways: their fashion, their manners and mores, their way of life. A man cut off from his community, such as Ernest Hemingway's Santiago in *The Old Man and the Sea* (1951, film 1958), is an outcast and something of an outlaw. Robin Hood is a rebel posing as an outlaw. Luther Witney, the hero of *Absolute Power,* is a professional burglar, and you can't be more of an outlaw than that.

Heroes are self-sacrificing. This is what separates and distinguishes the hero from the villain. The villain will self-sacrifice only for himself and for his ego and his own self-interests. The hero willingly self-sacrifices for others—at least at some point in the story. Rick, in *Casablanca* (play *Everybody Comes to Rick's,* 1942, film 1942), does not get around to taking self-sacrificing, heroic action until the very end of the film, and it is at that point he becomes a hero. A protagonist who should take heroic action but does not is an antihero, not a villain.

Rick, then, almost makes it to the end of the film as an antihero, but, alas, he redeems himself at the last moment when, in a dramatic, self-sacrificing action, he breaks it off with Ilsa, his true love, so she can support her husband, who is fighting Nazis.

■ **Examples of Heroes and Their Qualities, the Good**
and
the Bad
and
A Note About the Flawed Hero

In *Eye of the Needle,* you'll recall, the villain, Faber, is trying to get photos of the Allies' fake army to his bosses in Germany. He is a hunted man. He lands on a windswept island in the north of England, where he encounters the hero, Lucy Rose.

Lucy's husband, once the love of her life, has turned into a mean drunk since being crippled in an auto accident on their wedding night, so she's *wounded,* too. She has a loving heart—that's her *talent*—and she turns out to be *clever and resourceful* in the duel with the villain, showing extraordinary *courage.* Because she's a lighthouse keeper, she's outside of society, and this makes her something of an *outlaw,* and, well, she has an extramarital love affair with Faber. But then she *self-sacrifices* for her country and kills the man she's fallen deeply in love with. Very dramatic. A truly thrilling thriller.

The Snow Walker, a great survival story, also has a woman as the hero. The pilot, Charlie Halliday, is not the hero of the story. He's the pivotal character (the one pushing the action) at the beginning of the story, but he is not the hero. The hero is Kanaalaq, a young Inuit Indian woman. After the two crash-land in the arctic wilderness, Kanaalaq is *self-sacrificing*: She risks her fragile health to save Charlie. She's *courageous* and has a *special talent* for hunting and fishing—which is what she *does for a living*—and is very damn good at it. She shows herself to be *clever and resourceful* at every turn. She has TB, a *physical wound.* When it comes to Charlie's society, she's an *outlaw* of sorts, a member of an out-cast tribe. This is a small menace thriller with heart and charm, and I highly recommend it.

In *Midnight Run,* another small menace thriller, Jack, the hero, has a mission to bring back a bail jumper. He's menaced by the Mob and vicious competitors and shows great *courage* and is always *clever and re-sourceful,* being very *good at what he does for a living.* He's an ex-cop, unjustly kicked off the force, so he's nicely *wounded* psychologically and socially. At the end, he's *self-sacrificing* for a friend; he brings the Mob guy to justice and lets the man he's captured go. He has a *special talent* for finding people and will break the law when he needs to. Why? Be-cause he's an *outlaw,* of course.

The same is true for all heroes. Except for comic heroes, of course, who are neither clever nor resourceful. You may find other rare excep-tions someplace, but they're as hard to find as a four-fingered slime sloth. I don't advise you to try to be original by plowing new ground and leav-ing out these qualities in your hero—you'll probably lose your audience. Readers and moviegoers like their heroes to have the same inner core. If you believe psychologist Carl Jung, the qualities of the hero are an inte-gral part of the architecture of the human mind. He called them *arche-types.* Make this a rule to live by: Don't mess with the archetypes.

■ A Few Words About Sympathy, Likability, and Goodness

You might be wondering why I didn't mention three qualities of the hero often claimed to be essential by creative writing coaches and books on the craft: that the hero must be *sympathetic, likable,* and *good.*

While the hero may be sympathetic, likable, and good, and often you will find that they *are* sympathetic, likable, and good, these qualities are *not* essential.

In one of the really great westerns of all time, *Hombre* (1961, film 1967), the hero, John Russell, is hardly sympathetic or likable or good. He's cold and indifferent to the sufferings of others and wants only to be left alone; he's an antihero for nearly the entire story.

But does he have a *special talent*? More than one. He can survive in a desert, he's quick with a gun, he's a great shot, he's brave, and he's good at breaking horses (what he *does for a living*). He was orphaned (*the wound*). He has rejected his own people and lives apart, making him, that's right, a sort of *outlaw*.

Millions of fans think Harry Callahan in the film *Dirty Harry* (1971) is a great hero. He's brash, full of himself, self-righteous, seething with anger, violent, abusive, cold, rude. Likable? Hardly. Sympathetic? Not very. Good? Well, maybe if you stretch the meaning of the word from here to the Fourth of July.

But he is *courageous*, damn *clever and resourceful*, and he's got a *special talent*: shooting his .44 magnum. As a cop, he's the best at what he *does for a living*, but he makes his own rules, forever a thorn in the side of his bosses, and that makes him a sort of *outlaw*. But he's *self-sacrificing* in risking his career for others, and he's *wounded* in the course of the story by the death of his partner.

So don't worry about making your guy or gal likable, sympathetic, and good. It's okay, either way.

We now know what we'll find at the core of the character of our hero that we're about to create. I've long believed that good fiction of any kind comes from having dynamic, vivid, interesting, multidimensional characters. In *How to Write a Damn Good Novel II: Advanced Techniques for Dramatic Storytelling*, I discussed creating characters that, in addition to being multifaceted, are interesting in the way real people are interesting. They've done things, they've been places, and they have unusual views. In other words, they've "lived."

Such characters have an individuality that stamps them as fresh. They have their own way of going through life, a style of living all their own. I suggested some of them might even be "wacky" like TV's Monk or dual characters like Hawkeye in Richard Hooker's *M*A*S*H* (1968, film 1970), a supercompetent surgeon and an oversexed clown. After all, we already know heroes are an extreme of type, outlaws who make their own rules.

Okay, next we'll create a hero for *Peace Day*. I urge you to try creating a few heroes of your own. I know, you need only one, but it's good practice to make them up, so do a few. You might just fall in love with one of them.

■ Building a Damn Good Hero from the Ground Up

In plotting workshops that I conduct here in Berkeley and elsewhere around the country and in Europe, I ask everyone to help me out in creating a plot out of thin air. That's right, we begin without any pre-conceived idea whatever and we make a plot outline, a step sheet, from beginning to end.

I start with a blackboard and a hunk of chalk. I have no idea what we're going to create: the characters, the time, the place, or even the genre of story. We always begin by simply making up two characters that are well orchestrated with each other. Once we have these two characters, we can figure out what kind of a story we're writing and who will be the villain—the author of the plot behind the plot.

I recently did a plotting workshop with a wonderful bunch of creative and enthusiastic writers in Reno, Nevada. The villain we created was fifty-one, white, fat, rich, and married to a native American. He was do-ing business with her tribe, bilking them out of hundreds of thousands of dollars every year. We named him Arnold Drake. We created him so he'd fit the villain profile: vain, self-centered, selfish, narcissistic, greedy, ambitious, and all the other useful traits that darken his soul and make a villain the audience will love to hate.

We then needed a hero. We kicked around some ideas and finally settled on David McDonald, whom we created very much opposite of the fifty-one-year-old, fat Arnold Drake. We made David thirty-four years old, tall, handsome, fit, an ex–U.S. Marine. He has a couple of tat-toos and some battle scars. That's his *physiology*. He was a stealth fighter in the Marine Corps and can kill you with his bare hands a dozen ways, and that's his *special talent*. He served two tours in combat in Afghani-stan and received a Silver Star, so we know right off he's *courageous*. He was a kind of a hotdog marine, a risk taker, brave but foolish—sort of an *outlaw*. He got a couple of his buddies killed, an action he regrets every day, all day. That's his *wound*.

We gave David a pretty sorry childhood, and that would be his *sociology*. His parents were hippies living in Northern California. His mother floated off the floor by about a foot and a half and saw the world through a Valium haze. She thought of herself as a poet, but she never wrote any poetry, and she thought of herself as a mystic but, alas, without a mystical practice. His father, though proclaiming a philosophy of love, was a brute who smacked his son around whenever David got within arm's length. David hated his father and joined the U.S. Marines at seventeen. Before that, he was the class clown in high school, rarely studied, and got into lots of fights. In the marines, he was quick to learn and found he loved the excitement of combat—until he made that one horrible mistake.

Now out of the marines, he's depressed most of the time, drinks too much, and smokes dope. He's the night manager of a seedy pizza joint called Pizza Nut and lives in a broken-down trailer. The Pizza Nut has a rowdy crowd that he manages well, so he's good at what he *does for a living*. Obviously, he's an *extreme of type*, a burned-out ex-marine burned to a crisp.

His *psychology*: Occasionally David does bodyguard work for an old friend who owns a security service. He has a high IQ. He's moody and sarcastic, gloomy, pessimistic. Life is going nowhere, and he will tell you he doesn't give a damn. Like all good dramatic characters, he has a ruling passion: His is to blot out the past.

Is he *likable*? That's a matter of taste. I like him, but, hey, I'm one of his creators. Many readers and moviegoers won't. Is he *sympathetic*? Hardly. He's too moody and sarcastic. *Good*? I wouldn't want my sister to marry him, but the real question is—is he worth writing about? I think so. I think he's a damn good thriller hero.

By what magic did we create this damn good thriller hero? We started by just trying to think of a guy who was different from the villain, so he would be well orchestrated. We knew that he was going to have to contend with the villain, so he would have to be smart and tough, and that's the way we made him. And whatever trait we gave him, we thought of pushing it to the extreme if it made any sense.

You may notice David is flawed. He's depressive, melancholy, pessimistic, a dope smoker. He's full of angst, seething with anger and remorse. Right, he's got flaws aplenty. There are some among my venerable colleagues in the how-to-write biz who say that the hero *must* be flawed.

Not true. Wounded, yes. Flawed, no. It's fine if he is, but it's not required.

I think whether you give a hero a flaw depends on the type of book you are writing. The tragic hero, such as Leamas in *The Spy Who Came in from the Cold*, will be flawed. He's burned out, empty. Usually heroes are not flawed. Robin Hood may have a little too much hubris, but he is not really flawed. Most heroes have a little hubris. Some have a lot of hubris. Samson had enough for the entire U.S. Marine Corps.

But after all, when you're Samson and you kill a thousand Philistines with the jawbone of an ass, or you're Robin Hood and you can split an arrow that's about a quarter inch in diameter at three hundred paces, or you're James Bond and gorgeous women are hurling themselves at you every time you turn a corner, you have a right to be a little swelled-headed.

Anyway, make sure your hero and villain are well orchestrated. It's not just important—it's critical to the creation of a damn good thriller.

■ Heroes for Our Sample Scenarios

Let's take a look at possible heroes for the sample thrillers we've been discussing.

In my workshops I've discovered that when writers are forming their stories, they are often too quick to settle on who will be the hero without first brainstorming the possibilities. You'll want a colorful character the audience will emotionally connect with that will charm the audience. Make your hero someone the audience will want to spend time with.

Let's start with *DXP*. This is the one about the the crusading pope being switched with his twin brother, the crooked cop. The suave and charming, absolutely ruthless and ambitious Henry Zink, the global tycoon, is the villain.

Who might the hero be? We know he or she has to fit the hero profile. Heroes will have to be courageous, clever, and good at what they do for a living, and they'll have a special talent. Heroes live by their own rules, so they are outlaws but still are self-sacrificing for others. They've been wounded.

It could be Father Dorfman, a young German priest who is the pope's appointment secretary. He suspects that something has happened: The pope is suddenly no longer arrogant and demanding.

It could be a cop hired by the pope's sister. She knows it's the twin brother; she could always tell them apart.

Maybe it's the American ambassador to the Vatican, Mike Connors. The real pope gave him some secret investigation papers on DXP that the replacement pope knows nothing about.

It could be the head of the Vatican's security team, an American woman, Elsa Fawn, who brings the real pope marijuana brownies that he eats to relieve a lifelong stomach condition. The replacement pope is allergic.

Okay, when you make up a hero, you want the hero to be fresh, to be a theatrical character and, if possible, memorable. Let's go with Elsa Fawn. Say she's sixty-two, a former FBI special agent who was forced out (the *wound*) when she discovered the FBI lab was getting convictions using junk science (good at what she *does for a living*). She did not go quietly (*self-sacrificing* for others). Wanting someone he could trust to head his security team, the pope picked her.

Say she's Jewish—that would be interesting, a Jewish woman who befriends the pope. Her father was a rabbi, say. She was in an accident as a kid that damaged her ovaries, and she could never have children.

She was married twice to older men: one, an agent killed in the line of duty; the other died of cancer. She's a crack shot, twice won the all-FBI shooting tournament (*special talent*). She spotted the problems in the lab, so she's clever, but getting kicked out makes her a sort of *outlaw*. She's well orchestrated with Henry Zink. Her ruling passion is to prove to herself that she's the best.

You get the idea. To really flesh her out, you'd need to do a complete biography, of course.

Who would be the hero for *Code Red* (where the mad president is about to toss nukes at Russia)? It could be a White House aide or a military adviser or the president's wife. She'd be worth considering. What's she like? What would her special talent be? In what way is she an outlaw? Suppose she's a former beauty queen who became a doctor. Let's say she loves the president, but she's savvy enough to see the telltale signs of madness in him.

Okay, that's the way it's done. Don't like the idea of the hero being the First Lady? Okay, ask yourself who might be the hero. How about we make the hero a woman intern and the president's secret lover? Say she was once an up-and-coming tennis star who was attacked by a goon working for one of her rivals and has had vision problems ever since. The wound. But she has great reflexes, her special talent. She's Korean-American, maybe.

If you keep brainstorming, you will find characters who appeal to you.

Day Three is about the former germ warfare scientist who disappears while on vacation in Florida. The hero might be a private cop his wife hires. He could fit the hero profile, be an ex–homicide cop who got shot and was forcibly retired because of a limp (a great wound). He might have a special talent for illegal wiretaps and breaking and entering. He's an outlaw, of course.

Or maybe the hero is the wife's brother, Larry Tweed, a con man who bilks only rich guys who bilk the public—his special talent. He's been in and out of jails and has at least five different identities. He might be a great hero, but his sister is the only person on earth he'd self-sacrifice for.

In *The Legend of Hungry Wolf*, the hero is the title character. He's old but still a great warrior, with all the heroic warrior traits hidden under his wrinkles. He rises up to defeat evil and is killed, but he wins in death.

The story of the space aliens hunting hunters in *Hunting Season* might be a challenge. The hero is a redneck hunter. Let's call him Frank Foxxworthy (nicknamed Dos Equis). He would be hard to create without making him a stereotype. We'd have to brainstorm a bit to find elements in his character not usually found in rural rednecks. He might be, say, a cowboy poet. Yes, they do exist: They have a big gathering every year in Elko, Nevada. He could be a poet and songwriter. And he could be a master gunsmith with a superior mechanical aptitude.

Often when writers try to break strong stereotypes, they end up with characters the audience does not quite believe. What? A redneck hunter is really a plastic surgeon married to a movie star? And he's a concert pianist? But if you keep brainstorming, you'll get on the right path and you'll find interesting dimensions of character that can be integrated into the character's physiology and sociology so that he or she is both fresh and believable.

The victim in *Shadow Self* would probably be the hero because she is under so much pressure and the audience would feel great sympathy for her. She's a brave soul, trying astral projection. She has an unfaithful husband, so she's wounded. Let's call her Linda Rank. Special talent? Maybe she's the concert pianist. The special talent, remember, does not have to be useful in the struggle with the villain.

The hero for the light comic thriller *The Hunt for Jethro Potts* is, of course, Jethro, who is blowing up TV stations because TV ruined his marriage, made him impotent, made his friends hate him, and gave him headaches—all great wounds for a comedy. He's a former U.S. Navy SEAL, so he's got lots of special talents. He's a comic Rambo. The audience suspects television is evil, so there will be no problem identifying with him.

And last there's Joe Smigelski in the broadly comic thriller *How Joe Smigelski Saves the World*. Joe is our hero, of course. Joe is a bungler, so he's not clever; he has no wounds that are not self-inflicted; and he mis-interprets clues and gets lucky—the opposite of a real hero. But Joe is just the right guy to save the world.

For a demonstration of how a hero is created from the ground up in detail, read on.

■ A Hero for *Peace Day*

So far in the creation of *Peace Day*, we have a villain, Josh Pape, whose dark mission is to get revenge on Mary Cathcart for exposing his best-selling book as a fraud, which brought on the ruin of his life. She is now organizing a group of young people called the International Association of the Sane to hammer out a peace treaty for the next generation and planning to do a documentary film about them.

Okay, first thing: For my hero, do I want a man or a woman? I created a female character, Shakti Boxleiter, as the hero in the mystery *Murder in Montana* that I made up for *How to Write a Damn Good Mystery*, and I created another female character, Garrett Holland, for the mythic story *The Blue Light* in *The Key*, so why not make the hero for *Peace Day* a man? To achieve gender balance. I live in Berkeley, you know. Gender balance is important here.

Now, how does our hero get involved with the kidnapping of Mary Cathcart? Let's say he's Mary's friend or maybe a relative. How about he's her uncle on her mother's side? Okay, our hero will be Mary Cathcart's uncle.

The only thing we know about him is that he will be well orchestrated with Josh. Okay, Josh is a big-time writer, well-known, sophisticated, worldly, smooth as petroleum jelly, and full of hate. Our hero needs to be the opposite. He's from a small town, let's say—not worldly, not famous, a private, quiet man.

We need a name. I have found that once you name characters, they will start to breathe and will come alive. How about Walter Butterfield? A good name for a guy from the country. The name is hardly heroic sound-ing, but I like it. The name sounds as if it would belong to an Everyman.

Now this hero of ours is going to be the character the audience will be identifying with and cheering for. We need to make him colorful and three-dimensional, so that even though he'll be larger than life—as all heroes need to be—he'll seem real as a rock. To make him real, he'll need (pay attention, class, this will be on the final)—that's right—a physiology and a sociology that will together produce his psychology.

Physiology: Let's say Walter is six feet tall, medium build, muscular—he works out every day and goes on hikes. He is now forty-four years old. He has thick, reddish gray hair. Born with a quick mind and prodigious memory, he has a serious, scholarly look about him. He's neat and well groomed, and he dresses more formally than is currently in style: suits and ties, a real Southern gentleman. No visible scars except for a couple of bullet wounds in the back; no defects or deformities and no tattoos.

He walks with an easy gait and always erect. There's something military about the way he moves with long, confident strides.

Sociology: Walter was never considered attractive to girls when he was a kid—too bookish. He had few friends. One problem was his high IQ, and another was his quiet, scholarly demeanor. But the few friends he did have were close. He and his friends were all into computers and tinkering with bicycles. His father—loving, but strict—was the elected local sheriff and encouraged his two sons to follow in his profession. Walter's older brother, Franklin, always wanted to be a cop, but not Walter. Walter's sister, Daisy, had a kid—Mary—at sixteen. Daisy lives with Walter.

Walter's parents were Southern Baptists, Truman Democrats, and they lived near the tiny town of Crooked Creek in the Cumberland Gap area of Tennessee. His mother, a small-time bootlegger, made and sold spirits to friends and neighbors to get what she called "egg money."

The egg money was enough to finance a free clinic in town that had volunteer doctors and a full-time nurse. His parents never got along and squabbled constantly, Walter's father being in law enforcement, his mother being a bootlegger. Walter's dad often swore he'd arrest her if he ever caught her red-handed. Luckily, he never went into the woods behind the house, despite the strong smell of the mash. (When you're doing the backstory, it's a good idea to make the character's parents well orchestrated with each other as well, I've found. It makes for an interesting background.)

Walter's brother was killed while working as a rookie cop in Philadelphia when Walter was twelve and Daisy was ten. Walter's mom never blamed Walter's dad for the death of their eldest, but Walter's dad blamed himself for pushing Franklin into a law enforcement career. His grief ate him up, and he died two years later. He just sort of faded away.

Despite being a bootlegger, Walter's mother, called by the townspeople "Mama Butterfield," was deeply religious and took her son's death as God's will, grieved, and moved on. She's a strong woman, large-boned, with flaming red hair now gone white. She's opinionated, boisterous, and full of good humor. She is now eighty-two and still deeply involved in local politics and still sits on the school board.

Walter followed in his mother's footsteps into bootlegging after college, where he majored in botany. He applied his scientific and fledgling computer skills to bootlegging and soon, in partnership with his mother, was making the best bourbon in the state.

Growing up, Walter had tried playing sports but was never any good at baseball or football, although he was a pretty good pool player. He could swim long distances and had a lot of endurance. He liked to hike in the mountains. Now, he loves the mountains and the highly individualistic people who live there.

He married Irma Ruth "Ruthie" Benner when he was twenty-three and she was nineteen. Knockout gorgeous, outgoing, popular, a social butterfly, she was everything he wasn't. She finished second in the Miss Tennessee pageant and was a great horsewoman. Walter was madly in love with Irma Ruth. She made him tongue-tied and weak-kneed, and he thought he was the luckiest man alive to have her as his bride.

It turned out Irma Ruth could not have children, which was all right with her. She wanted to party. They weren't married a year when she broke Walter's heart by having an affair. He got drunk for the first time in his life, forgave her, and the cracks in their marriage were plastered over but never repaired.

She married Walter because he was from a leading family that claimed ancestors back to the Revolutionary War and he spoke French. She hated the valley as much as he loved it. Walter tried to please the restless Irma Ruth by taking her on trips to the East Coast, to Florida every winter, to Europe from time to time.

While on a trip to Paris, Irma Ruth met a Wall Street billionaire and went off with him, aglow with promises of travel, glamour, big cities, and bright lights forever. She came back to the valley two years later, repentant. Walter burns for her, but he couldn't take her back, he was so deeply wounded. She has no permanent address and even at forty is still a beautiful woman. In between boyfriends, she blows into town every once in a while and taps him for money.

Since he's still married and can't bring himself to get a divorce, he never has any serious romances. He's bleeding badly from his wound.

In Walter's part of the country, bootlegging is a tradition, starting with the Whiskey Rebellion of 1791. He has been very successful at what he does for a living: untaxed, illegal booze. He also operates a legal distillery, supports the free clinic, and finances a visiting home nurse for the community. In the 1990s, he was in a feud with two other bootleggers; this became known as the Crooked Creek Wars. He won, and afterward he organized all the bootleggers into what is called "the distiller's union" to settle squabbles before the shooting starts.

A lot of marijuana is grown in the area, and there was always pressure on Walter to get into the business, but he didn't. And he didn't bother anyone who did, as long as they didn't sell it to the schoolkids. But in the 1990s, when the plague of crystal meth was spreading through the South, he put out the word that it would not be made or sold or used in the Crooked Creek Valley. A couple of meth labs were destroyed, and the guys who were selling it were found on the road out of town without their trousers and buggy whip welts on their buttocks. Some suspected Walter Butterfield of being behind this, but nothing was ever proved. In fact, in his nineteen arrests for bootlegging, the government has yet to win a single conviction.

Walter's *psychology:*

Walter loves to hike the mountains. He loves his town, his family, his friends. He loves to read, particularly about Civil War history and the Napoleonic era in Europe. He has a wry sense of humor. He's thoughtful and contemplative. He likes fine wines, never drinks bourbon. He gives talks at universities on the life of John S. Mosby, a behind-the-lines Confederate colonel during the Civil War who was his great-great-grandfather. I think of Walter as a sort of reincarnation of his ancestor.

His favorite game is poker. He plays every Saturday night in a game with a ten-thousand-dollar buy-in. He keeps track of his winnings and losses. Last year he came out eighty-four thousand dollars ahead.

Walter is into improving himself and his community: This is his ruling passion. He thinks the Internet is wonderful, making it possible for local young people to get a good education without leaving home. He sees great, positive family values in the country people; he wants to stop the exodus out of the valley. Most of the really bad things are brought in by outsiders, including Felix Blunt, a Bureau of Alcohol, Tobacco, Firearms and Explosives agent. They hate each other. Felix has made it his mission in life to shut down Walter's illegal distillery.

Walter is very close to his sister Daisy's daughter, Mary Cathcart. Mary's daddy was, in Walter's term, "a no-good womanizer" who ran off with a barmaid. Walter supervised Mary's homeschooling and helped her become a writer but could not keep her home. They're extremely close. She's like his child; he'd do anything she asks. And she worships him.

Except that he's still in love with Irma Ruth and can't seem to pry her loose from his heart, Walter is a contented man.

■ Walter Butterfield's Journal

The people around here call me "Professor," even though I'm not an academic. I should say "folks" around here. When I'm home, I speak in the local vernacular. I might say, "There's a slew of fokes yonder doan know nothin' 'bout football 'cept it's played on grass with a ball made from the backside of a hoag."

I love these people, love them for their loyalty to their families, their love of God, their love of country. You can count on them. Tennessee is the Volunteer State. They're great people. Most are poor, but hardworking. Family is the most important thing. Some are violent drunks, but not many. Most are honest, God-fearing, churchgoing. We don't like "outlanders," but we tolerate them. Outlanders are anybody from outside our valley. "Bricks," we call them, if they come from a city. My people find city people amusing. City people can get lost in a phone booth. They put soft drinks in their drinks. The men can't handle firearms or drive a tractor, and these inept incompetents think of us as hicks. And they all seem scared of us, even when we're trying to be friendly. They think we're all inbred idiots. I guess all they know of us is what they see on TV.

Clementine is the largest town in our valley; it only has twelve hundred souls.

I like it here in Crooked Creek County. I intend to stay.

I live on top of a mountain, where I read and play chess on the Internet and write e-mails to lots of people. I have a part-time housekeeper and a man who looks after the property, all ninety acres, and my two horses.

I have a business rival, Thadeus Jackson, over in Clementine. He busted up one of my stills once, pretending to be revenue agents. I was forced to take countermeasures in order that he modify his fiendish behavior. He still walks with a limp. And when we meet, he calls me "sir."

When Irma Ruth—who now calls herself "Nora" after some soap opera star—left me for Royal Summerset IV, I was unable to keep my cool. I was alone suddenly in Paris, walking the streets all night, not being able to sleep and drinking vast quantities of wine. I admit to you, my author, that I had murder on my mind. I come from people who don't back away, who see murder as sometimes necessary, and I've already admitted to you that I've sometimes had to resort to violence in my business. But I took no action in this case, though the impulse in me was strong. I *took a perverse kind of pleasure in planning the execution of Royal Summerset IV, but did not, for reasons that are obscure to me, carry out my exquisite plan.*

When I returned home, I buried myself in my work. I was in the middle of building a new barn and buying a couple of horses.

Then Irma Ruth came back two years later and wanted to reconcile. I loved her so much and seeing her made me burn with desire, but there was a tear in my soul and I couldn't bring myself to allow her back into my home. I've given her money from time to time, and we even had dinner once and I listened to her tell me how much she loved me and how sorry she was, that she was temporarily overwhelmed by unfulfilled longings. . . .

Okay, does Walter fit the hero profile? Let's see, he's *courageous*, that's for sure. He's *clever and resourceful* or he wouldn't have lasted in his chosen career. He definitely is an *outlaw*, living by his own rules. He *self-sacrifices* for his neighbors and relatives. He has a *special talent* for games, particularly poker. His *wound* is the love he has for his estranged wife. That wound might be partially healed by what happens in the course of the story. The wound will humanize our hero and help the audience sympathize with him and make a strong emotional bond.

You may get the impression that I just dreamed up this hero and his background for *Peace Day* bim-bam-boom. Not so. At various times, I had him older, really older, younger, facing a debilitative disease, a Buddhist, a prison inmate, happily married, unhappily married, with kids at home, with grown kids, with kids who loved him, with kids who hated him, with grandchildren and without. I once made him a cop, then a retired cop, then a disgraced cop . . . So my hero had many incarnations before I finally settled on this one.

I had some problems, but also a lot of fun making him up, and now

I am quite happy with the result. I hope you are, too. Walter is just the guy to bring Josh Pape down.

■

Okay, we have our three major characters: Josh Pape, Mary Cathcart, and Walter Butterfield. We'll add others as we develop our plot. First, we'll need to discuss the structure of a thriller plot.

7
■ All About Plot Structure

I advocate a character-driven plot—where a chess game is played by a well-motivated villain who has a dark mission and a hero who has a mission to stop him. It is the clever and resourceful machinations of the villain and the countermoves by the hero and other major characters that make the complications of the plot.

In a plot-driven approach to plotting that some creative writing coaches champion, the characters are puppets of the author, who follows a cookie-cutter design, one-size-fits-all, such as the so-called three-act structure.

Using this formula, the hero starts out on his mission on page 30 of a screenplay at the start of act 2, and act 3 starts on page 90. The screenplay is exactly 120 pages long. Some creative writing coaches advocate this three-act structure for novels as well as screenplays. Aristotle said all stories have a beginning, middle, and end, it's often said that he advocated the three-act structure. But Aristotle never said the beginning, middle, and end have a preordained length. He was merely saying that a drama has a beginning, middle, and end, as all things in nature do—a tree, a frog, a storm, day, night, you, me—everything. To Aristotle, it was important that art imitated nature: That was his point.

As you begin to design your story, the problem with the three-act structure comes when you try to decide where it is exactly that the beginning ends and the middle begins and where the middle ends and the end begins.

I know there are well-known writing coaches who advocate this scheme, but what if the beginning clearly ends on page 26? Do you then pack in four extra pages? It seems silly to think about story structure this way. It's so mechanistic and formulaic that it would suck all the life out of your story as you stuff in more pages here and cut them there to make everything turn out "right."

In *Casablanca*, Rick, the protagonist, as mentioned earlier, does not take on the mantle of a hero and set out on his mission to fight Nazis until about five minutes before the end of the film. If you see it as a three-act screenplay, this makes for a long act 1, a short act 2, and a five-minute act 3. Where is the three-act structure of the widely acknowledged masterpiece *Citizen Kane* (1941)? The film jumps around in time and place so much, you'd get a headache trying to stuff it into a rigid structure. The first plot point in *Spartacus* (1960) comes fifteen seconds or so into the film when the mine slave Spartacus hamstrings a guard with his teeth. Is this the end of act 1? So much for formulas.

Be wise, my friend—let your characters drive your story, not some predetermined plot design a supposed structure guru has set in concrete.

■ The Movements of a Damn Good Thriller

In *How to Write a Damn Good Mystery*, I divided mysteries up into what I called "the five-act design" because it was helpful to talk about mysteries this way. Most, but not all, mysteries would fit this paradigm:

> *Act 1: A body is discovered, and the hero accepts the mission to find the murderer.*
>
> *Act 2: The hero is tested and has emotional change and, in the pivotal scene, dies and is reborn, more determined to find the killer.*
>
> *Act 3: The hero is tested again and finally succeeds in discovering the identity of the murderer. This is the pivotal scene.*

Act 4: The hero traps the murderer.

Act 5: The reader is shown how the events of the story impact the major characters.

In a thriller there's a similar pattern, but beware, not all thrillers are so neatly arranged. Let's not call the sections "acts"—it's such a loaded term. Plays are divided into acts so the audience can get out of their seats and have a pee once in a while and buy an overpriced drink at the bar in the lobby. Instead of "acts," let's break up the damn good thriller into what we'll call "movements." The term is stolen from symphonic music, of course. We can think of our thriller as a symphony having five movements, rather than a play with three acts.

I. The gripping opening.

II. The evil plot gets under way and the hero, in terrible trouble, fights a defensive battle.

III. The turning point (often a kind of symbolic death and rebirth). The hero goes on the offensive.

IV. The hero confronts the villain, who almost wins but is finally defeated in a slam-bang climax.

V. Resolution. Tells what happens to the major characters as a result of the hero's victory or defeat.

Okay, let's take a look at some examples that seem to fit this scheme fairly well.

■ *Fargo*

I. **THE GRIPPING OPENING:** Jerry Lundegaard hires two scary psychotic thugs to kidnap his wife in order to squeeze forty thousand dollars in ransom from his father-in-law.

II. **THE EVIL PLOT GETS UNDER WAY AND THE HERO, IN TERRIBLE TROUBLE, FIGHTS A DEFENSIVE BATTLE:** The kidnappers snatch the wife and kill a cop while making their getaway. Our hero, Marge Gunderson, the local sheriff, casts around for clues as to who may have done this terrible thing. She guesses it was two men.

III. **THE TURNING POINT (OFTEN A KIND OF SYMBOLIC DEATH AND REBIRTH). THE HERO GOES ON THE OFFENSIVE:** When she finds Jerry Lundegaard is involved, he goes on the run. Now she can go after him.

IV. **THE HERO CONFRONTS THE VILLAIN, WHO ALMOST WINS BUT IS FINALLY DEFEATED IN A SLAM-BANG CLIMAX:** Marge catches the psychotic villain cutting up bodies in a woodchopper.

V. **RESOLUTION. TELLS WHAT HAPPENS TO THE MAJOR CHARACTERS AS A RESULT OF THE HERO'S VICTORY OR DEFEAT:** Marge is hailed as a hero.

■ *Alien*

I. **THE GRIPPING OPENING:** A spaceship receives a distress call and sends Warrant Officer Ellen Ripley, our hero, to investigate the source. It turns out to be a wrecked spacecraft. Ripley discovers the signal is a warning to stay away, but, gads, it's too late.

II. **THE EVIL PLOT GETS UNDER WAY AND THE HERO, IN TERRIBLE TROUBLE, FIGHTS A DEFENSIVE BATTLE:** The crew gets into really terrible trouble: They inadvertently take a murderous alien slime creature on board, and they fight a defensive battle.

III. **THE TURNING POINT (OFTEN A KIND OF SYMBOLIC DEATH AND REBIRTH). THE HERO GOES ON THE OFFENSIVE:** Ripley battles the alien and finally forces it into the airlock.

IV. **THE HERO CONFRONTS THE VILLAIN, WHO ALMOST WINS, BUT IS FINALLY DEFEATED IN A SLAM-BANG CLIMAX:** Ripley has a life-and-death battle with the creature and is nearly killed, but she manages to shoot it with a grappling gun and push it out the door into space.

V. **RESOLUTION. TELLS WHAT HAPPENS TO THE MAJOR CHARACTERS AS A RE-SULT OF THE HERO'S VICTORY OR DEFEAT:** Ripley, with Jones, the ship's cat, heads for Earth, victorious.

■ *Charade*

I. **THE GRIPPING OPENING:** An unidentified dead man is thrown off a speeding train. At a ski resort, Mrs. Lampert, our hero, meets a stranger who may be up to no good.

II. **THE EVIL PLOT GETS UNDER WAY AND THE HERO, IN TERRIBLE TROUBLE, FIGHTS A DEFENSIVE BATTLE:** Menacing people are after our hero for a fortune she must know about, only she doesn't.

III. **THE TURNING POINT (OFTEN A KIND OF SYMBOLIC DEATH AND REBIRTH). THE HERO GOES ON THE OFFENSIVE:** Our hero teams up with her love interest, and they go after the fortune. They are menaced by the villain, other nasty characters, and the police.

IV. **THE HERO CONFRONTS THE VILLAIN, WHO ALMOST WINS BUT IS FINALLY DE-FEATED IN A SLAM-BANG CLIMAX:** The heroes have a life-and-death battle with the villain and are nearly killed, but they manage to kill the villain and get the fortune.

V. **RESOLUTION. TELLS WHAT HAPPENS TO THE MAJOR CHARACTERS AS A RESULT OF THE HERO'S VICTORY OR DEFEAT:** The heroes bask in glory, turn the money over to the government, and go off to get married, victorious.

■ *The Hand That Rocks the Cradle*

I. **THE GRIPPING OPENING:** The hero, Claire Bartel, is sexually molested by her obstetrician. She reports him, and he commits suicide.

II. **THE EVIL PLOT GETS UNDER WAY AND THE HERO, IN TERRIBLE TROUBLE, FIGHTS A DEFENSIVE BATTLE:** The widow of the obstetrician, seeking revenge, hires on as the hero's nanny and menaces their child, kills a family friend, and secretly wreaks havoc on the family.

III. **THE TURNING POINT (OFTEN A KIND OF SYMBOLIC DEATH AND REBIRTH). THE HERO GOES ON THE OFFENSIVE:** The hero investigates and uncovers the villainy.

IV. **THE HERO CONFRONTS THE VILLAIN, WHO ALMOST WINS BUT IS FINALLY DEFEATED IN A SLAM-BANG CLIMAX:** The hero confronts the villain in a life-and-death battle and is nearly killed, but kills the villain instead.

V. **RESOLUTION. TELLS WHAT HAPPENS TO THE MAJOR CHARACTERS AS A RESULT OF THE HERO'S VICTORY OR DEFEAT:** The hero, victorious, happily returns to her normal life.

■ *Miss Congeniality*

I. **THE GRIPPING OPENING:** The hero, Gracie Hart, a tomboy FBI agent, is on the job, arresting some dangerous thugs.

II. **THE EVIL PLOT GETS UNDER WAY AND THE HERO, IN TERRIBLE TROUBLE, FIGHTS A DEFENSIVE BATTLE:** A beauty contest is threatened by a terror plot. Gracie has to go undercover as a contestant and requires a huge makeover.

III. **THE TURNING POINT (OFTEN A KIND OF SYMBOLIC DEATH AND REBIRTH). THE HERO GOES ON THE OFFENSIVE:** Our hero, left on her own, discovers the identity of the villain and the villain's plan.

IV. **THE HERO CONFRONTS THE VILLAIN, WHO ALMOST WINS BUT IS FINALLY DEFEATED IN A SLAM-BANG CLIMAX:** The confrontation takes place on the runway at the beauty contest. Our hero manages to save the day and bag the villain.

V. **RESOLUTION. TELLS WHAT HAPPENS TO THE MAJOR CHARACTERS AS A RESULT OF THE HERO'S VICTORY OR DEFEAT:** Gracie gets the recognition due a hero and finds love.

■ *Sleeping with the Enemy*

I. **THE GRIPPING OPENING:** Laura, our hero, is abused by her control-freak rich husband.

II. **THE EVIL PLOT GETS UNDER WAY AND THE HERO, IN TERRIBLE TROUBLE, FIGHTS A DEFENSIVE BATTLE:** She tries to appease the monster by complying with his every wish, but whatever she does is never good enough.

III. **THE TURNING POINT (OFTEN A KIND OF SYMBOLIC DEATH AND REBIRTH). THE HERO GOES ON THE OFFENSIVE:** Laura prepares for her getaway by learning to swim, then fakes her own death in a boating accident, which is a great death and rebirth.

IV. **THE HERO CONFRONTS THE VILLAIN, WHO ALMOST WINS BUT IS FINALLY DEFEATED IN A SLAM-BANG CLIMAX:** Laura has a new life, but her ex shows up, stalks her, and in a final confrontation, she shoots him dead.

V. **RESOLUTION. TELLS WHAT HAPPENS TO THE MAJOR CHARACTERS AS A RESULT OF THE HERO'S VICTORY OR DEFEAT:** The villain dead, the hero is finally free.

■

There are, of course, some damn good thrillers that do not conform perfectly to this pattern. The damn good western thriller *Hombre*, as an example, does not have a gripping opening. It's interesting, but hardly gripping. In the opening, the hero is living with Indians he grew up with. They're making a living breaking wild horses and selling them. The hero gets word that he's inherited a rooming house in town and goes there to settle the estate. It's later on the stagecoach, when it's held up, that the thrills begin.

Frantic, the 1988 Roman Polanski thriller, has a gripping opening in which the hero's wife vanishes from a Paris hotel room, and it has a high-energy middle, but although in the climax the hero does get his wife back, the cops and spies, and not the hero, shoot it out with the villains. It's a powerful ending, though, and Michelle, the hero's helper, is tragically killed in the gunfight.

In *Eye of the Needle*, the villain, a German agent in England during the war, is being tracked by heroic counterintelligence spies. Lucy, the hero, arrives late in the story, and she first falls in love with the villain, then kills him in the life-and-death struggle at the end.

■

Let's take a look at some of the scenarios that I've been crafting for this book to see how they might be structured.

■ Day Three

I. **THE GRIPPING OPENING:** The hero's husband is kidnapped while they are on a vacation trip to Disneyland.

II. **THE EVIL PLOT GETS UNDER WAY AND THE HERO, IN TERRIBLE TROUBLE, FIGHTS A DEFENSIVE BATTLE:** The hero tries to find out what happened to her husband. The authorities act weird. The hero can't even prove he ever existed.

III. **THE TURNING POINT (OFTEN A KIND OF SYMBOLIC DEATH AND REBIRTH). THE HERO GOES ON THE OFFENSIVE:** The hero gets a lead on the kidnappers and goes after them while the villain tries to kill her.

IV. **THE HERO CONFRONTS THE VILLAIN, WHO ALMOST WINS BUT IS FINALLY DEFEATED IN A SLAM-BANG CLIMAX:** The hero frees her husband and is almost killed by the villain but manages to kill her first.

V. **RESOLUTION. TELLS WHAT HAPPENS TO THE MAJOR CHARACTERS AS A RESULT OF THE HERO'S VICTORY OR DEFEAT:** The hero, victorious, is reunited with her husband. All seems to end happily—except, in a surprise twist, the hero's husband returns to the government secret project and, to protect her, severs all future contact.

■ The Legend of Hungry Wolf

I. **THE GRIPPING OPENING:** A vicious gang of outlaws takes over a train stop where a bunch of innocent people are waiting for the train.

II. **THE EVIL PLOT GETS UNDER WAY AND THE HERO, IN TERRIBLE TROUBLE, FIGHTS A DEFENSIVE BATTLE:** Our hero stoically takes the abuse as the villain's gang members insult him and smack him around. They rape and brutalize the other passengers.

III. **THE TURNING POINT (OFTEN A KIND OF SYMBOLIC DEATH AND REBIRTH). THE HERO GOES ON THE OFFENSIVE:** The gang rapes Hungry Wolf's granddaughter. He gets his granddaughter to safety, then turns into the warrior he once was. He takes on the gang, despite his age. With stealth and cunning, he kills them one by one.

IV. **THE HERO CONFRONTS THE VILLAIN, WHO ALMOST WINS BUT IS FINALLY DEFEATED IN A SLAM-BANG CLIMAX:** The gang leader almost kills Hungry Wolf, but Hungry Wolf manages, with the help of a blind gunfighter and a rancher's spoiled son, to defeat the villain in a slam-bang climax.

V. **RESOLUTION. TELLS WHAT HAPPENS TO THE MAJOR CHARACTERS AS A RESULT OF THE HERO'S VICTORY OR DEFEAT:** Hungry Wolf dies of his wounds. His granddaughter turns away from white man's medicine and returns to the tribe to carry on her grandfather's work.

■ How Joe Smigelski Saves the World

I. **THE GRIPPING OPENING:** The villain and his gang hoodwink an air force security officer and steal an atom bomb.

II. **THE EVIL PLOT GETS UNDER WAY AND THE HERO, IN TERRIBLE TROUBLE, FIGHTS A DEFENSIVE BATTLE:** Joe (the bumbling P.I.) is hired by the security officer to find the atom bomb before anyone knows it's missing. Joe stumbles blindly through the clues and suspects and gets nowhere.

III. **THE TURNING POINT (OFTEN A KIND OF SYMBOLIC DEATH AND REBIRTH). THE HERO GOES ON THE OFFENSIVE:** Joe stumbles on the villain and his plot by chance and goes after him.

IV. **THE HERO CONFRONTS THE VILLAIN, WHO ALMOST WINS BUT IS FINALLY DEFEATED IN A SLAM-BANG CLIMAX:** Joe defeats the villain with his stupid one-finger martial art and the chunk of armor plate around his neck.

V. **RESOLUTION. TELLS WHAT HAPPENS TO THE MAJOR CHARACTERS AS A RESULT OF THE HERO'S VICTORY OR DEFEAT:** Joe basks in his unearned glory. The atom bomb gets back in its rack and no one's the wiser.

■ Hunting Season

I. **THE GRIPPING OPENING:** Frank Foxxworthy and four of his friends are deer hunting when they encounter space aliens stalking a deer.

II. **THE EVIL PLOT GETS UNDER WAY AND THE HERO, IN TERRIBLE TROUBLE, FIGHTS A DEFENSIVE BATTLE:** Frank is horrified when one of his buddies turns up missing. He meets a strange woman who claims to be Kitty Apple, a waitress in a bar and an amateur ufologist. But he discovers the truth, that she's an alien.

III. **THE TURNING POINT (OFTEN A KIND OF SYMBOLIC DEATH AND REBIRTH). THE HERO GOES ON THE OFFENSIVE:** Our hero gets himself captured in order to rescue his friend and is then hunted and manages to turn the tables on the alien hunters.

IV. **THE HERO CONFRONTS THE VILLAIN, WHO ALMOST WINS BUT IS FINALLY DEFEATED IN A SLAM-BANG CLIMAX:** After he helps the woman alien get back the spaceship, she wants to vaporize our hero, but in a confrontation, he defeats her and saves himself and his buddy, and maybe all the Earth.

V. **RESOLUTION. TELLS WHAT HAPPENS TO THE MAJOR CHARACTERS AS A RESULT OF THE HERO'S VICTORY OR DEFEAT:** Frank returns to his job, a hero to the ufologists and thought a crazy by the rest of the world.

■ Shadow Self

I. **THE GRIPPING OPENING:** Linda Rank, a concert pianist, is the adventurous sort. She tries astral projection on a lark, hoping to catch her husband with his mistress.

II. **THE EVIL PLOT GETS UNDER WAY AND THE HERO, IN TERRIBLE TROUBLE, FIGHTS A DEFENSIVE BATTLE:** Linda returns followed by her doppelgänger, who is playing tricks on her. Linda can't figure out what the hell is happening.

III. **THE TURNING POINT (OFTEN A KIND OF SYMBOLIC DEATH AND REBIRTH). THE HERO GOES ON THE OFFENSIVE:** Linda, with the help of some kind of psychic, finally figures out that she's dealing with an occult phenomenon.

IV. **THE HERO CONFRONTS THE VILLAIN, WHO ALMOST WINS BUT IS FINALLY DEFEATED IN A SLAM-BANG CLIMAX:** She has a confrontation with her shadow self: They go into a room, and when the door is broken down, we find only one body, Linda's.

V. **RESOLUTION. TELLS WHAT HAPPENS TO THE MAJOR CHARACTERS AS A RESULT OF THE HERO'S VICTORY OR DEFEAT:** Her friends all think she was a suicide.

■

Okay. In general we have an idea how a thriller plot goes. Now there are a few things to decide before we can get down to plotting our story. First we'll have to discuss, for the novel writers among us, voice and viewpoint.

8

■ All About Voice and Viewpoint and Other Cool Stuff

Before you begin plotting, you'll need to make a few choices about viewpoint and voice that will have important consequences for how you go about plotting and drafting your thriller.

You are probably well aware that almost all thrillers—over 99 percent—are written either in first-person past tense or third-person past tense. We won't be discussing the other possibilities like present tense or a plural "we" narrator or "you" narrator because they are so rarely used and are artsy tricks that make the audience conscious of the technique and pull the audience out of the story world and wake them from the fictive dream every time.

■ First-Person Narrators

A first-person narrator is more suitable for a small menace thriller. I've never seen a big menace thriller written in the first person, though it is possible there could be one. Usually, first-person narratives are in the voice of the hero or the murderer protagonist, as in James M. Cain's damn good thriller *The Postman Always Rings Twice* (1934, film 1945, 1981). It begins:

They threw me off the hay truck about noon. I had swung on the night before, down at the border, and as soon as I got up there under the canvas, I went to sleep. I needed plenty of that, after three weeks in Tijuana, and I was still getting it when they pulled off to one side to let the engine cool. Then they saw a foot sticking out and threw me off. I tried some comical stuff, but all I got was a dead pan, so that gag was out. They gave me a cigarette, though, and I hiked down the road to find something to eat. . . .

Note how the author raises a story question about what will happen to the poor slob, gains sympathy because he's *poor*, and has wonderful empathy-producing details—about the joke, the smoke, the hay wagon—and our protagonist also has a goal the reader can identify with—to get out of poverty.

But who is this first-person narrator? Is it the guy who gets thrown off the hay truck? you ask. Well, yes, and no. It's the same character all right, but it's not the same guy we see here in the present of the story (sometimes called *the now* of the story). Instead, it's the same guy in the future—after the events of the story have already happened—and he's reflecting back on these events. In the case of *Postman*, it's after he's committed murder and after his lover is dead by accident and he's convicted of killing her. Any character transformation he's going to go through, he's already had. He's wised up, you might say. So when you say that the narrator in a first-person story is the character, it's not the same character as in *the now* of the story. In this case, the narrator is in the future, in a jail awaiting the gas chamber, and he's reflecting on the events that got him there.

Occasionally, first-person narratives are written in a voice other than the protagonist's. The Sherlock Holmes mystery series, as an example, was written using Dr. Watson as the narrator. The following is from a short story, "A Scandal in Bohemia" (1891), by Sir Arthur Conan Doyle:

To Sherlock Holmes she is always THE WOMAN. I have seldom heard him mention her under any other name. In his eyes she eclipses and predominates the whole of her sex. It was not that he felt any emotion akin to love for Irene Adler. All emotions, and that one particularly, were abhorrent to his cold, precise but admirably balanced mind. He was, I take it, the most perfect reasoning and observing machine that the world has seen, but as a lover he would have placed himself in a false position. He never spoke of the softer passions, save with a gibe and a sneer. . . .

Using another character who is not the hero for the narrator of a thriller is rarely done, mainly because it is far more difficult than the slick Sir Arthur makes it look. You might do this if you have an inarticulate hero and an erudite sidekick, but I can't think of any other reason you'd consider it, except for comic purposes.

■ The Pros and Cons of First-Person and Third-Person Viewpoints

I have seen many writers seduced by the music of their own voice who opt to write in first person. I've done it myself. We read the Sherlock Holmes stories, or *Postman*, or the Edgar Allan Poe Award winner in 2002, David Ellis's *Line of Vision*, and we think, Wow, that sure looks easy. But the truth of the matter is, it ain't.

Writing in the first person feels right. After all, we've been doing it all our lives, starting with the birthday present thank-you cards to Aunt Mildred and Uncle Wilbur. We write diaries in first person and notes to our friends and lovers—intimate, poetic stuff, right from the heart. That's what first-person narratives are: intimate, sincere, personal.

Because first-person narratives read like a personal communication between the author and the reader, they have a nice, friendly, welcoming feel and a kind of instant believability and immediacy—very much like what I'm writing to you right now.

So first-person narration does have its virtues, but it has snares and traps as well. For one thing, there's the difficulty of dramatizing scenes where the hero is not present. It can be done, but it's as tricky as thread-ing needles with your elbow:

> I was asleep at the time. Elrod must have come home late that night and, seeing her car in the driveway, thought something was up. Maybe he just wanted to surprise Millie and that's why he snuck up on her. But then when he saw Fred's pants over the chair, he must have flown into a rage. . . .

It would be hard to say just what Millie might have said or how she looked, that kind of thing, because the narrator wasn't there, so the au-thor has a problem properly exploiting the scenes for drama, sometimes even key scenes such as the climax. I went into this problem at some length in *How to Write a Damn Good Novel II: Advanced Techniques for Dramatic Storytelling*.

There are other problems with the first-person narrator as well. The reader may tire of the voice. There's often too much introspec-tion and interior monologues, even whining, in first-person narratives. I call it "the 'poor me' syndrome." Too many sentences begin with "I." An even more serious problem: First-person narration often lends itself to preaching. And your voice, despite how much you love it, may not appeal to as large a segment of the reading public as you hope it would. The first-person narrative voice calls for liberal use of meta-phor, and that means the writer needs to have the soul of a poet, and . . . well, if you want to know the truth, most of us don't have the soul of a poet.

If you've read what I had to say about narrative voice in *How to Write a Damn Good Novel II: Advanced Techniques for Dramatic Storytelling*, you might get the notion that I've changed my tune. . . . Well, *mea culpa*, I have. Although I still believe you can convey all the same fictive values using either first person or third if you're a skilled stylist, I've since seen how difficult it is for some writers, even those who can handle third person in a workmanlike manner, when they take a crack at first person. Often the prose gets slack and wordy and the metaphors become clichés or strained or not quite apt. Instead of snapping, crackling, and popping prose, we get beautiful-sounding word dribble with foggy meanings.

I would be remiss in my duty as a creative writing coach if I discouraged you from using first person when it might be right for you. You might be a natural like James M. Cain.

Now how would you know whether you're good or just think you're good? Writers, I've noticed, have an endless capacity for fooling themselves about the quality of their work. Me too.

One way to find out if you're kidding yourself would be to write a chapter with your first-person narrator and the same chapter with a third-person narrator, then have your readers—I mean fellow fiction writers—read both and give their opinion. The jury can't decide for you, but their input may help you make up your mind.

It's weird, but when you ask others to judge something like style, if everyone says, Hey, babe, this rocks, you might actually be pulling it off. But more likely than not, you'll get mixed results. If you fail to gain a lot of enthusiasm for your first-person voice, I suggest you go with third person.

In other words, if your first-person narrative voice is colorful, idiomatic, and chock-full of sensuous details and has a lot of fresh metaphors that leap off the page and sing and dance on into the night, then go for it.

Now then, you can write in third-person "objective" or third-person "subjective." In objective third person, you do not reveal the thoughts or feelings of the characters; you write as if you were watching a play and describing it. Sometimes a thriller writer will open a novel in third-person objective viewpoint, creating a suspenseful scene that raises a lot of story questions, and then switch to third-person subjective viewpoint later.

Let's take a look at *The Boys from Brazil,* which opens in third-person objective:

Early one evening in September of 1974 a small twin-engine plane, silver and black, sailed down onto a secondary runway at São Paulo's Congonhas Airport, and slowing, turned aside and taxied to a hangar where a limousine stood waiting. Three men, one in white, transferred from the plane to the limousine, which drove from Congonhas toward the white skyscrapers of central São Paulo. Some twenty minutes later, on the Avenida Ipiranga, the limousine stopped in front of Sakai, a temple-like Japanese restaurant.

The three men came side by side into Sakai's large red-lacquered foyer. Two of them, in dark suits, were bulky and aggressive-looking, one blond and the other black-haired. The third man, striding between them, was slimmer and older, in white from hat to shoes except for a lemon-yellow necktie. He swung a fat tan briefcase in a white gloved hand and whistled a melody, looking about with apparent pleasure.

Okay, the reader is being shown the scene, but the narrator never reveals any thoughts or feelings of the characters. It is as if the narrator were watching this scene and reporting what he sees but has no godlike knowledge of the characters' pasts or their inner lives. If he does have such knowledge, he's not letting on.

You will notice how this viewpoint, with its factual, plain, and direct narrative voice, creates an atmosphere of suspense, even though nothing has happened, really, that foreshadows trouble—except the two guys in suits look like goons who might menace someone. There are no bombs or guns or canisters of poison gas shown that would foreshadow violence. But readers have been trained by a hundred other thrillers they have read that when the narrator goes *objective*, there's terrible trouble about to happen. The style alone projects it.

In addition to the tone of the narration, though, there are subtle story questions skillfully being raised.

The odd guy in the white suit somehow does seem strange and vaguely menacing. What's he up to? What's in the briefcase? How come they went into a hangar to get into the limo? Levin makes us want to read on just by the skillful use of viewpoint and the subtle details. The audience is pretty much locked into the story world and dreaming the fictive dream, and we're only two paragraphs in.

This is an example of a sure-footed narrator, a master craftsman at the top of his skills.

Now then, how can this be done for one of the scenarios I made up for this book? Let's do the one called *Code Red* about rogue spies planning a preemptive nuclear strike against Russia. Okay, let's say this story starts with the murder of a small-time bureaucrat who has (in the backstory) uncovered something and has asked his boss about it. Word has gotten back to the conspirators, and they order the guy's execution, which turns out to be the point of attack; in other words, this would be the first scene in the book or in the screenplay.

Here's how that scene might start out in objective viewpoint:

A blue Mercedes slowly cruised past the house at 10 Westover Drive in Sandstone, California. It was early evening. A cool evening. In the upstairs window a young girl was playing the violin— badly. Beethoven's "Ode to Joy." Lights were on in most of the neat, middle-class, ranch-style homes along the street. The Mercedes continued to the corner and turned, went half a block, and parked. There was a high fence next to the street. Somewhere a dog yapped. The driver got out and looked around, apparently making sure he was alone on the street. He went to the trunk and opened it. Inside was a stainless-steel case.

The man paused for a moment and held his stomach, taking a couple of quick breaths. He opened the case with deliberation. The inside was felt-lined to protect the contents: a Pakistani-made 9 mm SMG PK submachine gun. Compact, with a fifteen-round magazine and a pistol grip. He picked it up and pulled back the receiver and put it under his coat, closed the trunk, and took a deep breath, once again looking carefully around. Then, with the air of sudden resolution, he crossed the street and headed back toward Westover Drive. . . .

Thoughts and feelings are shown indirectly: *The driver got out and looked around, apparently making sure he was alone on the street.* And: *Then, with the air of sudden resolution.* The narrator is writing as if he didn't know who the man is or what he's up to, so this narrator uses words like "apparently" and "with the air of" to indicate feelings and thoughts. Ira Levin does it in the previous section as well:

> He swung a fat tan briefcase in a white gloved hand and whistled a melody, looking about with apparent pleasure.

There are very few thrillers written completely in objective viewpoint. The overwhelming majority are written in subjective third-person viewpoint, which is discussed next.

■ Third-Person Subjective Viewpoint, Fully Omniscient and Limited Omniscient

In subjective viewpoint, the reader is seeing the events through the eyes of a character. We're seeing what the character is seeing, and this perception is being filtered through the consciousness of the character, so that the character's perception might distort or color reality, or at least flavor it.

If the author claims the right to go into *any* character's thoughts or feelings at any time, then the narrator is said to be *fully omniscient,* as opposed to a *limited omniscient* narrator, who claims the right to go into the thoughts and feelings of only *some* of the characters. Both fully omniscient and limited omniscient narrators can take the reader to different times and places at will and fill in the reader on the characters' backstories. And sometimes an omniscient narrator (either a fully omniscient narrator or a limited omniscient narrator) can go into the conscious mind of more than one character at a time. *The three ran up the hill. They all were thinking but one thought: Kill Frankie, kill Frankie.*

If only one character is selected, the story will read very much like a first-person narrative. In most thrillers today, the narrator has limited omniscience, written from the point of view of a few select characters, called *viewpoint characters*.

A viewpoint character is any character whose inner life, thoughts, and feelings are revealed. An omniscient narrator also knows the viewpoint character's past and everything about him or her. The narrator is an all-knowing god.

This all-knowing god can *describe* thoughts:

Joe was moody all day, his mind spinning with the horror of the previous night. He kept seeing the car going over the cliff in slow motion.

The narrator can also *quote* thoughts:

Joe woke that morning agitated. Holy moly, he'd really seen it. Damn car just flew off the damn cliff.

Holy moly and *Damn car just flew off the damn cliff* are thoughts in Joe's head. Thoughts he's thinking now. These are *quoted* thoughts.

When the narrator describes thoughts or feelings but does not quote them, we say this is a *distant* third-person narration.

When the narrator is quoting thoughts, it's said to be *close* third-person narration.

As you write using a subjective third-person narrator, you are constantly switching back and forth between objective narration and subjective narration, both close and distant.

Jack woke that morning, yawned, and rolled out of bed *(objective third)*. He was in a deep funk *(distant third)*. He remembered what that bitch had said to him *(part objective, then a switch to close;*

that bitch *is in his mind, not the narrator's*). Gotta do something about that wigger (*close*). He went to the closet and retrieved his hockey stick (*objective*).

■ The Visible and Invisible Narrator

It was common in days of yore to have a narrator that intruded on the narrative in what I call "the narrator's big mouth." This is sometimes termed *editorializing* and is considered a grave sin. The worst kind of editorializing is called *preaching*.

There's a lot of confusion regarding what is permitted and what is not permitted. Some creative writing coaches advocate the doctrine of *author invisible* and insist that fictional narrative should always be written without the personality or opinions of the narrator coming through. This is yet one more widely held pseudorule with no merit whatever. Your narrator can have an edge or an attitude and even a personality—it all depends on the genre of thriller you're writing and the story you're telling.

Okay, first you need to understand that the narrative voice you use is not you. If not me, then who? you ask. Well, the narrator is sort of a character you create to tell your story, although it's a character who is not *in* the story but simply telling the story as an observer.

Some narrators have a personality. Some don't. When they don't, they are said to be *invisible*. You might have an invisible voice such as Peter Benchley uses for *Jaws*. Here's the opening to chapter 5:

Thursday morning was foggy—a wet ground fog so thick that it had a taste: sharp and salty. People drove under the speed limit, with their lights on. Around mid-day, the fog lifted, and puffy cumulus clouds maundered across the sky beneath a high blanket of cirrus. By five in the afternoon, the cloud cover had begun to disintegrate, like pieces fallen from a jigsaw puzzle. Sunlight streaked through the gaps, stabbing shining patches of blue onto the gray-green surface of the sea.

Brody sat on the public beach, his elbows resting on his knees to steady the binoculars in his hand. When he lowered the glasses, he could barely see the boat—a white speck that disappeared and reappeared in the ocean swells *(switched into Brody's viewpoint)*.

Okay, this is very straightforward narrative in objective viewpoint switching to subjective. The narrator is invisible, not colored by the personality of the narrator. For *Jaws*, this is an effective narrative voice.

I used a similar narrative voice in a section of *The Legend of Hungry Wolf*, which I will show you more fully later:

The Great Spirit had not answered Hungry Wolf's prayers. His seventeen-year-old granddaughter, Mary Red River, was going through with her plans despite his entreaties and all his prayers and chants and fasting. As he came out of his tepee and into the early morning sun, Hungry Wolf could see *(switching to Hungry Wolf's viewpoint, putting the camera behind his eyes)* she was loading her bundle of clothing and the box of books the white missionaries had given her at the mission school into the wagon. How he hated those pious devils *(close third: Pious devils are what he, not the narrator, calls them)*. They were stealing the souls of his people *(close third)*.

In this example, the narrator is also invisible, but it is in both objective viewpoint and subjective viewpoint, both close and distant. Narrators commonly switch back and forth at will between objective and subjective points of view, and it does not disturb the reader an iota or pull the reader out of the fictive dream.

Let's take a look at an omniscient narrator used by a master craftsman, Elmore Leonard, in *Get Shorty* (1990, film 1995). Again, the narrator is invisible, and he shifts in and out of character viewpoint.

Chili asked Harry if he liked to sleep in. He said, "If you're going to sleep in and I have to sit around waiting, forget it. Anything I can't stand is waiting for people."

Harry acted surprised. He said it was only ten after ten. "I got back in bed and Karen wanted to talk."

That stopped Chili.

He wanted to know if Harry was putting him on or what. He couldn't imagine Karen letting this fat guy get in bed with her. But there was no way to find out if it was true.

He said, "Well, she was up, no problem. She dropped me off to get my car. I come back and have to sit here another hour."

Harry said the limo guys never go to their office before ten-thirty anyway.

Okay, let's look closely at the text. The narrator tells us:
Harry acted surprised.

Not *Harry was surprised.* If it had been *Harry was surprised,* it would have been a switch to Harry's viewpoint. Get it? The narrator does not tell us what is in Harry's mind because Harry is *not* a viewpoint character.

But Chili *is* a viewpoint character. So the narrator can tell us what's going on in Chili's head:

He wanted to know if Harry was putting him on or what. He couldn't imagine Karen letting this fat guy get in bed with her. But there was no way to find out if it was true. *(This is distant third: The narrator is telling us what Chili thinks but not quoting his thoughts exactly; if he did quote Chili's thoughts exactly, it would be close third.)*

■ The Opinionated Narrator

You're probably wondering, What if the narrator is not invisible? Ah. What if the narrator shows himself and has a viewpoint of his own? What if the narrator has a personality?

Giving the third-person narrator a personality might be one of the most important decisions you can make.

We've already seen two narrative voices of the scenarios that I've offered as examples: *Code Red* and *The Legend of Hungry Wolf.* Both are serious thrillers: one, a spy thriller; the other, a serious western thriller. For both of these stories, I've chosen an invisible narrator. I'd probably do the same for *Day Three,* the Hitchcock-type thriller, and *DXP,* about the plot to switch the pope with a twin.

But the narrator in *The Hunt for Jethro Potts* might not be quite so invisible. This is a comic story of a mad bomber blowing up TV stations. The narration might go like this:

> Jethro Potts, was, as you may have read in the paper, not exactly sane, clinically speaking. As some said, his elevator went to the top floor, but the doors did not open. He was rowing with one oar— that kind of thing. But to others he was a hero, a regular Saint George, the dragon slayer. And the dragon he was trying to slay was television. Which, really, if you think about, is not such a bad idea. . . .

This narrator, as you can see, is taking sides. He has a point of view of his own, apart from the characters'.

■

The narrator of the wacky *How Joe Smigelski Saves the World* would have a personality. This is the one about the stolen atom bomb. It might go like this:

> Joe looked across the clutter on his old oak desk at the young man in an air force uniform perched on the client chair chain-smoking Marlboro cigarettes, his glasses fogged. Joe cleared his throat and asked him to repeat what he just said about how he had lost a frickin' atom bomb. Joe managed to get the

words out, even though he was choking down a wad of panic the size of the San Francisco Airport. How was he going to explain to Mama that he had offered the company confidential services to a man who couldn't keep track of a sixteen-megaton atom bomb? Joe feared his mama more than, well . . . anything. She was one tough old broad who had once been married to Sam Shovel, the man Dashiell Hammett modeled Sam Spade after. Even though Joe was, as his ex-wife, Cindy Lou, continually reminded him, a pretty dim bulb—and he was—he knew he should be calling the FBI. The only thing that stopped him was the $870 the man was offering as a retainer.

The *and he was* is the narrator's opinion of Joe—that he's a dim bulb. There's nothing wrong with employing such a narrator. It adds color to the narration.

I hope you don't get the impression that an opinionated narrator should be used only for comedy. It's possible to use such a narrator in more serious works to good effect. As an example:

Alden Mears looked over the valley where he knew, in the morning, his men would be advancing, a force of a mere two thousand men, with no tanks and very little artillery, going against a force ten times larger *(distant third, so far)*. They're gonna eat us alive—we'll be mowed down like summer wheat *(close third)*. But Alden was a man of no faith and less courage, and little imagination . . . *(narrator's opinion)*.

Opinionated narrators with a lot of personality, such as this one, are not often used today, but it may be the right choice for some stories. The narrator could help the reader understand the historical or social context of the story.

Okay, once you've settled on your voice and your viewpoint, you can gct on with plotting your damn good thriller. I've decided to use a third-person, limited viewpoint in past tense for mine.

Now we're about ready to start making up the story *Peace Day*. We'll start with techniques to draw the audience into the story to dream the fictive dream.

9
■ How to Make the Reader Dream the Fictive Dream

The most important part of your thriller is the opening, because that is what the audience, the editor or producer, the editor or producer's reader, and the agent see first.

The first thing a reader reads when opening a novel is called *the point of attack*. It's the same in a film. Where you start the actions of your story is the point of attack.

All the techniques that you study and try to master are for the purpose of making the audience dream the fictive dream, that wonderful, dreamy state that allows us, when reading fiction or viewing a film, to live the lives of other people, to think what they think, to feel what they feel. This is the powerful magic of storytelling: It has the ability to transport the audience out of reality so that they become completely absorbed into the story world.

In *How to Write a Damn Good Novel II: Advanced Techniques for Dramatic Storytelling*, I went into some detail about openings and how you go about inducing the fictive dream the way a hypnotist induces the hypnotic state, bit by bit, sensuous detail by sensuous detail.

One powerful technique is to start with a strong *story question*. A story question is something that will make the audience curious: an action, a line of dialogue, a bit of foreshadowing. This should be done as soon as possible, even in the first sentence.

> Fred got up that morning with but one thing on his mind, that .357 Colt Python in his dresser drawer.

This audience wonders what he intends to do with his .357. Let's try a story question that raises another sort of curiosity in the reader's mind:

> Fred got up that morning with but one thing on his mind, that quarter-carat diamond ring in Hackensack's store window, propped up in the little red leather box with the heart on it.

This is a romantic story question, of course.

Great thriller writers are very good at raising story questions early. Carl Hiaasen opens *Skinny Dip* (2004) with this potent story question:

> At the stroke of eleven on a cool April night, a woman named Joey Perrone went overboard from a luxury deck of the cruise liner MV *Sun Duchess*. . . .

Peter Benchley opens *Jaws* with this:

> The great fish moved silently through the night water, propelled by short sweeps of its crescent tail.

It's a wonderful opening line. It's subtle, but chilling. What's more chilling than a hungry shark? William Peter Blatty opens *The Exorcist* with a little more heavy-handed story question:

> Like the brief doomed flare of exploding suns that registers dimly on blind men's eyes, the beginning of the horror passed almost

unnoticed; in the shriek of what followed, in fact, was forgotten and perhaps not connected to the horror at all.

The Day of the Jackal opens with a gripping story question:

It is cold at 6:40 in the morning of a March day in Paris, and seems even colder when a man is about to be executed by firing squad.

The adventure thriller *She* (1887, film 1965) by H. Rider Haggard, a book that has sold over eighty million copies, making it one of the biggest-selling books of all time, opens with a strong story question. Writers then were a bit heavy-handed, but Haggard certainly knew about raising story questions. The novel *She* begins:

In giving to the world the record of what, looked at as an adventure only, is I suppose one of the most wonderful and mysterious experiences ever undergone by mortal men . . .

■

What fiction writing is all about, one crafty old writing coach once told me, is making promises and then keeping them. A story question makes a promise that will need to be answered. Foreshadowing makes a promise that something is going to happen. Rising conflict makes a promise that the conflict will be resolved.

■ Connecting the Reader Emotionally

Okay, now that you've opened with a story question and have aroused your audience's curiosity, you should next try to get the audience emotionally connected to the story by making them feel sorry for a character. This arouses the audience's sympathy. In *Skinny Dip*, a hapless woman has been thrown overboard far from shore; in *Jaws*, a shark eats a woman swimmer; in *The Exorcist*, a young girl is possessed by the

Devil; in *The Day of the Jackal*, a patriotic army officer faces a firing squad.

Notice that the actions start in all these masterworks right from the beginning. Except for nineteenth-century H. Rider Haggard, who worked with the gaseous, melodramatic style of his day, these authors don't use a lot of ink "informing" the reader of the facts. The story starts unfolding at the point of attack. Characters are in conflict. There is terrible trouble. The authors are following one of the oldest and most important principles of creative writing: *Show, don't tell.*

Telling is like this: *Fred got up early and got his gun out.*

Showing is like this: *Fred got up and, blinking against the already blazing sunlight flooding into the room, opened the drawer slowly so as not to wake his snoring grandpa in the next bed. . . .*

■ God Is in the Details

"Showing" means giving specific details. Gustave Flaubert supposedly said, "God is in the details." If he didn't say it, he should have. There are different types of details you should know about.

Generic details. Details such as "he was tall and handsome" are considered weak because they do not individualize the character or the thing being described.

Specific details. "A polished mahogany Victorian dining table with reeded legs and brass casters" is specific. This makes a better image than the generic image.

Telling details. Telling details evoke a sense of the characters or the situation that generic details cannot: *Fred had deep-set eyes, the eyes of a cost accountant on audit day.*

Clincher details. A truly great telling detail that really nails down a character's character or gives a sense of place in just a few words is called a *clincher* detail: *Fred's Harley had a*

death's-head with glowing ruby eyes on the handlebars.
Clincher details are often memorable: *Make him an offer he
can't refuse.* It's worth the effort to find them. A clincher detail
has the power to absolutely convince the audience that the
author knows what he or she is talking about. Dirty Harry's
"Make my day" is such a detail. Clincher details are emblematic
of the character and help make the character unforgettable.

Sensuous details. These are details that appeal to the senses:
sights and smells and sounds and touch and taste, as well as
impressions that are often called "the sixth sense." They are
important for helping the audience dream the fictive dream.

In addition to details, be sure to have:

Active verbs. "To be" verbs are considered weaker than active
verbs. "He's on the couch" is weaker than "He's slumped on the
couch." Active verbs create images in the audience's mind that
"to be" verbs don't.

Conflict. This is the most basic principle of drama. It's a clash
of wills. One character desperately needs or desires something,
and another character—or some physical obstacle—prevents
that character from getting it. Remember: At all times in a damn
good thriller you will have a well-motivated character overcoming obstacles in pursuit of a goal. Overcoming obstacles (people
or some physical things) is called *dramatic conflict.* Sometimes
the conflict is inside the character and is called *inner conflict.* It
is a desperate need for something that the character has a
resistance to getting in his or her own psyche. Dramatic conflict
and inner conflict, if the stakes are high, can both be very
gripping.

*Emotion. Fiction writers often fail to note the emotion of the
characters, assuming that the audience will know from the*

context what the characters are feeling. Not so. Emotion needs to be indicated directly or indirectly. Directly: Fred felt, at the death of his son, a coldness creep over him, and an intense feeling of isolation, as though he were floating alone on an iceberg in the middle of a vast, arctic sea. Indirectly: Fred returned home from the funeral, went into his son's room, and picked up Andy Pandy, his stuffed bear, and held it tight, sitting on the edge of the bed, rocking and humming and whispering prayers he'd been taught as a child and thought he'd long forgotten. . . .

Emotional growth. This is a term long used in playwriting that refers to the emotional changes that come to characters as a result of conflict. Say a man accuses his wife of something, and they fight. He realizes he's wrong and begs her forgiveness. He "grows" from anger to repentance.

■

Like all damn good fiction, thrillers are written in three modes: scenes, half-scenes, and dramatic narrative. All three should have conflict, sensuous details, telling details, emotion, and emotional growth. There are exceptions, of course. You might have a scene with few details, say, or the emotions may not be revealed for dramatic effect or to raise story questions, but for the most part you will want all of these elements in all parts of your story.

■ Scene Writing in a Damn Good Thriller

The key to writing damn good scenes for your thriller is to meditate for a while on what the characters want before you begin drafting them. The more intensely characters want something, and the more intense the resistance, the greater the conflict. And conflict is the most important ingredient for getting your audience to dream the fictive dream.

At all times, you should have a motivated character overcoming obstacles in pursuit of a goal. This drive toward a goal is the character's agenda. You may also think about what the character's emotional growth might be.

You have not seen the step sheet yet, but this is one of the steps:

Back to Walter and Lori. We're at Lori's apartment. She's changed her clothes while Walter has been on his cell phone with his computer guy back home to get Feldt's address. We see that Lori has two dartboards full of darts. Each of the boards has a large photo of a different man. "Exes," Lori says. "I have one myself," Walter says. "I must get a set of darts immediately upon returning home."

I chose this step because there is no conflict indicated. But in a damn good thriller, every scene must have conflict. What to do, what to do? Okay, we need an agenda for each character. So after brainstorming, pacing around a bit, and watching an old *Perry Mason* rerun, here's what I've come up with:

They pulled up in front of a two-story Victorian in the Western Addition near the Golden Gate Park Panhandle, on Ashbury *(details to give credibility)*. Large oaks lined the street. The sky was darkly overcast *(generic detail—scene setting)*. It had been only a few minutes from the hospital to her place. On the way, Walter kept asking Lori to tell him again everything she saw and heard. The story hadn't changed. She told it to him again in the same monotone, just-the-facts cop manner she'd used in the hospital. The third time she went through it, irritation had crept into her voice. *(Emotional growth. You might wonder why I'm "telling" rather than "showing" the dialogue. I don't show him asking her the questions because they would have been asked in the previous scene and I don't want the repetition.)*

"I'm sorry to keep pressing you about what you remember, but I'm terribly worried about my niece. Please accept my apology if it seems rude. Some small thing might have been overlooked."

Lori said she understood, then added she needed only a minute to change. She asked Walter if he wanted to come up. He said he did. *(Notice that because there is no conflict in these lines, they are summarized rather than related in dialogue.)*

Lori wondered why he didn't wait in the car. He followed her around and up the metal staircase that was added onto the back of the house to access the three rear apartments. *(You'll notice that I've switched to her viewpoint. Some creative writing coaches preach that you should not switch viewpoints in the middle of a scene. You may follow that rule or not—it's up to you. In some stories I might follow the rule; in others, like this one with so many viewpoints, I would not.)*

At the top of the stairs, she paused, fumbling with her keys. For a moment she felt dizzy and tried to stay steady. Finally, the door creaked open. Inside, it felt closed up, a little musty, with the faint odor of old coffee grounds *(sensuous details)*. She'd been staying at the hotel the past couple of days in case she was needed for crowd control. The hotel had given her and six other officers luxury rooms.

But it felt good to be home *(emotion)*. It was a small one-bedroom, drafty, and cold in the morning when the fog was in, but she loved it. This had been her home for six years. The bookshelf that covered all of one wall of the living room was jam-packed with paperbacks, mostly mysteries and thrillers. A dozen of them were stacked on a table next to her funky but oh-so-comfortable reading chair. She was a junk fiction addict *(a telling detail)*. On another wall were two dart targets with large darts sticking out of them. On the bull's-eyes of each was the photo of a different man *(a clincher detail)*.

"My ex-husbands," she said.

Walter smiled and nodded. "A grand idea. I'll be getting a dartboard as soon as I get home, I have just the wall for it—and just the photograph."

She smiled. "You have an ex?"

"We're still married, technically. Well—I am, she is not."

"The South, they do have strange customs."

"An absurd number."

"I'll be just a moment." Lori went into the bedroom. Walter immediately started looking through her desk, her checkbook, her bills. . . . *(Note that I've switched to his viewpoint.)*

Suddenly the door to the bedroom swung open with a bang.

"What the fuck do you think you're doing?" *(Emotional growth.)* She had her 9 mm Glock in her hand, pointed not quite at him. He put his hands up, stepping back. She was wearing jeans and a bra. He thought she looked just fine like that, but he felt it best not to mention it.

"Where I come from a lady does not use such language," he said. "Except white trash."

"What the fuck are you looking for? And I'll use any language I damn well please *(emotion)*."

He felt himself blush *(emotion)*.

"Well, explain yourself," she said.

(This is all conflict.)

"You were protecting my niece when she was taken," he said. "I thought you might be in need of money and perhaps in league with the culprits."

She looked at him curiously, as if to ask if he was for real *(growth from her anger)*.

"I was hoping to find a checkbook, overdue bills, something of that nature—anything that might indicate your financial status. I can see, by the quality of the furnishings, you are not exactly flush." *(Now we see what his agenda was all along.)*

She stared at him for a long moment, then smiled. Then laughed *(emotional growth)*. "I'm not exactly flush—the damn divorce lawyers have about cleaned me out—but I don't work the other side of the street. I just work more overtime." She lowered her weapon. "It wasn't loaded anyway."

"I never thought you'd shoot," he said. "I am a fair judge of people. With your kind permission, I think it best I be leaving."

"I still haven't finished changing. I rarely go out in my bra, though it is a really nice Wonderbra—a gift from my rich and crazy aunt Mavis. I'll only be a moment."

She disappeared into the bedroom, leaving the door half-open.

"I had assumed my outrageous behavior would have caused a change in plans," he said.

"Nope, look all you want. Best if you eliminate me as a suspect. My computer password is 'supercop.' I do my banking online."

He went back to rummaging through her desk, with little hope of finding anything *(emotion change)*. He noticed she belonged to a judo club. He wondered why she was so easily knocked cold. When she came out, he noticed she seemed a bit unsteady.

"You better lay down," he said *(emotional growth: concern)*.

"I'm fine." Though she didn't look fine. She was having trouble keeping her balance.

"Maybe I should take you back to the emergency room."

"Maybe you should mind your own business. Look, I want to nail this son of a bitch as much as you do. He coldcocked me, made me look like an ass, took the woman I was supposed to be protecting. Let's get going."

"If you start seeing angels or hearing voices telling you to shoot somebody, you let me know."

"Fair enough."

Okay, lots of nice conflict. See how the characters come alive when they mix it up?

Now for a bit of spice in our soup, let's toss in some nice metaphors.

■ Controlling Metaphors

One well-used trick in literary fiction, *the controlling metaphor*, can work just as well in popular fiction.

A controlling metaphor works like this: Say you have a lonely woman who has a potted plant, a geranium, that she cares for, worries about, fertilizes, waters on schedule, and so on, but because of overattention—too much water, fertilizer, bug spray—it never does well. A lover comes into her life. She is swept off her feet. She neglects the plant: It flourishes. The lover leaves her. She is again lonely, only now she's bitter. She again gives the plant too much attention; again it does not do well.

See, it's not so hard to be literary. Academy Award winner *High Noon* (film 1952), from the short story "The Tin Star" (1947) by John W. Cunningham, certainly had a wonderful controlling metaphor: the clock. The camera kept showing it to the audience every few minutes as it ticked its way to high noon, when the villain was coming for the showdown with the hero.

The marshal's badge in *High Noon* is a second controlling metaphor. That's right, you can have more than one. Proud of it at the beginning of the film, the marshal throws it in the dirt at the end because the town he loved betrayed him. In *The Wizard of Oz* (1900, film 1939), the controlling metaphor is Dorothy's red slippers. *The Man in the Iron Mask* has a truly great controlling metaphor: the mask itself. When the mask is taken off the good brother, he is liberated from his cell and France is liberated from tyranny. *Miss Congeniality* has a controlling metaphor: the sparkling crown meant for the winner of the beauty pageant. *The Shawshank Redemption* has the girly posters that change with the times and mark the years.

To create a controlling metaphor, you simply need to have two things paralleling each other. Say in a man-against-nature story, the man's fortunes go bad as the weather goes bad. Or a CIA agent craves a medal of valor and does dirty deeds to get it. In the end, he's found out and disgraced, and (don't groan too loudly at this) he's shot down in a gunfight with his own people, taking a bullet through the medal that he's wearing under his shirt over his heart.

If handled well, the controlling metaphor can be a powerful device.

When you're planning your novel, something might strike you as being a possible controlling metaphor. It can be anything, as long as it parallels some other aspect of the story. If it works well, it might add another dimension to your story. It will certainly please the critics, who may even give you a pat on the head for writing a literary thriller.

■ Contextual Symbols, Pervasive Symbols, and Literary Symbols

The controlling metaphor has a single, clear meaning. A *contextual symbol*, on the other hand, can have many meanings, depending on its context. Perhaps the best-known example of this is the white whale in *Moby-Dick*, which symbolizes men's ambition, the power of nature, evil, death—lots of things. But all the time it remains a whale. Contextual symbolism applies only to the story being told. Whales are not symbols of evil in other stories.

Pervasive symbols such as the flag, a rosary, a religious statue, a wedding ring, a diploma, and so on are not contextual. They carry the same meaning regardless of the context.

An atom bomb, say, might be a contextual symbol in a story. It might symbolize men's folly, scientific power, military power—lots of things. Contextual symbols are not always perfectly clear. Characters might indicate something has contextual meaning just for themselves. In my story *Joe Smigelski Saves the World*, Joe might put his hand on the atom bomb and say, "Dang if it don't give me a hard-on."

Avoid metaphors and symbols that the author and the audience share but the characters don't. This is a cheap trick, even though it's considered by some to be damn literary. So you name a character Bellona, a Roman goddess of war, and the character is warlike, but the other characters aren't aware of the connection, and only those who read reviews in *The New York Times* know it. I call these *literary symbols*, and they are artifice and have no place in a damn good thriller.

■ Empathy and Identification

By showing sensuous, telling, physical, and emotional details, we create the reality of the emotions, and gradually the audience will begin to feel what the characters feel. This is empathy, and empathy is a powerful emotional magnet that draws the audience into the story.

To get your audience to identify with your characters, simply give your characters agendas that the audience will want to see them achieve.

Fred knew that Horace Greggs had brutally raped Ellie Mae. Hell, Greggs had practically admitted it, was damn near bragging on it. And he had walked because he was blackmailing that pig of a sheriff, Cullen Bates, who'd knocked up his sister. There was but one way for Fred to get justice for Ellie, Fred thought as his hand closed on the pearl-handled grip of the Colt, and it was up to him to stand up and be a man.

When you get your audience to empathize with your characters and identify with them, they are solidly dreaming the fictive dream.

Then, to get the reader totally involved, you create inner conflict, where the audience is pulling for a character to decide one way or the other.

Fred crouched down behind the manzanita bush just outside the cone of light from the window. There was Greggs sitting at his kitchen table not ten feet away, his bald head glowing in the light of the flickering fluorescent light over the sink. Fred raised the gun. How heavy it was. An image passed through his mind of Greggs's head exploding. Fred took aim. The gun would speak with a terrible roar. Would the McCoys across the way come running? Hell, guns go off a lot around Jessup—nobody gives a shit. Fred sighted down the barrel as his finger rested on the trigger, and he slowly started to put pressure on it. The image of Horace tearing Ellie's clothes off flooded into Fred's mind and he felt choked for a moment, his head dizzy. He knew that another eighth-of-an-inch pull on the trigger and Horace Greggs would be in hell and Fred's life would be forever changed. . . .

At this point, hopefully, the reader is living in the story world. Come on, Fred, pull the damn trigger! At this point, the audience may find themselves squeezing the trigger.

Or the audience may be pulling for him to not pull the trigger. Either way, when you hang your character out on the horns of a dilemma, you have the audience gripped.

Okay, so when we begin to draft our story, we'll keep in mind that we need to raise strong story questions, get the readers to identify with some character's agenda, use telling details, and exploit inner conflict (sooner or later). We'll need these elements no matter what incidents we begin with and what characters—heroes, villains, patsies, bystanders, victims—are involved.

Reading this, you may think, Wow, Jim, this is a hell of a lot of balls to keep juggling in the air. It's really not all that complicated or difficult. Inducing the fictive dream is easily accomplished. I told you in the beginning that thriller writing is as easy as smacking a beached banana fish, and it is.

Think of it this way: In your opening, you'll want to show a character, any character, in terrible trouble and struggling to get out of it. Or you'll want to show a nasty character inflicting terrible trouble on some sympathetic character. Either way, you'll want to open with a story question right away to gain the audience's curiosity. Show a heroic character carrying out an agenda so the audience can identify with the character or, if an evil agenda, identify with the character trying to stop the evil. Include the details so the audience can dream the dream.

To begin, you sit back and let your imagination run. You'll need a character with some agenda who is taking action and has obstacles to overcome. The most basic unit of good storytelling is showing a well-motivated character overcoming obstacles in pursuit of a goal. In every single part of your story, you should have a well-motivated character overcoming obstacles in pursuit of a goal.

In a film, of course, the camera shows the details, making the writer's job easier. I'll give you an idea of how it might be done in the thrillers

I've been making up as examples in this book. Let's start with *The Legend of Hungry Wolf.*

Okay, it's 1888, Arizona. Some bad guys are going to take over the train station where an old Indian, a former warrior and now an apprentice medicine man, is taking his granddaughter so that she can learn white man's medicine at a nursing school. Where to begin? I want a character in terrible trouble. Well, if a man feels he's losing his beloved granddaughter to another culture, a culture he hates, that would be terrible trouble. I could start back at the reservation like this:

> The Great Spirit had not answered Hungry Wolf's entreaties. His seventeen-year-old granddaughter, Mary Red River, was going through with her plans despite his entreaties and all his prayers and chants and fasting. *(Right off the bat we have a story question: What's she up to?)* As he came out of his tepee and into the early morning sun, Hungry Wolf could see she was loading her bundle of clothing into the wagon and then her box of books the white missionaries had given her at the mission school. How he hated those pious devils *(emotion).* They were stealing the souls of his people. *(He's well motivated to stop her.)*
>
> Hungry Wolf was wearing buckskins, stiff and cold now, in the morning. He never wore white man's clothes. He pulled on his antelope moccasins and walked to the well, pulled up the oaken bucket, and washed his face in the cool water. He felt weary this morning, and his many old war wounds were causing stiffness deep in his bones *(sensuous detail).* His knee throbbed even more than usual. He had been shot with an arrow while hunting deer in the high country when he was yet a boy *(hopefully gaining sympathy).*
>
> Around him stood wood shacks and old tepees, patched and weather-beaten, and worn tents on raised platforms. The smoke of wood fires drifted across the ground, and beyond were corrals for a dozen ponies and a dried-up cornfield. Next to the village was the fort, with barracks for the twenty-five troopers, the mission school, the Indian agent's office, a storeroom. This was it: the reservation.

His world for the past twenty-six years. It was a jail for two hundred and eight Chiute Apaches, the last of a once proud nation. He hated the reservation. The white men believed in hell. It was in their religion, and they had made one here *(creating more sympathy by the obvious poverty and the oppressive conditions).*

He walked over to his granddaughter. She was wearing a blue, flowered dress, and her hair was not braided as their customs for a young maiden required. It was loose down to her shoulders. How could she degrade herself like this? He had raised her from a cub, taught her the way of her people, and now she scorned these ancient ways. His anger burned in his belly. He held his tongue in check.

An old woman was helping his granddaughter hitch up the horses. Gray Elk's widow, Little Raven. Gray Elk was a great warrior who died at Crooked Creek in the Summer of Blood a hundred moons ago. Many blue-coat scalps were taken that day, he remembered with a flush of pride *(details to build the story world, to create empathy).*

His granddaughter was already seated on the buckboard seat, the reins in her hand. Little Raven was just climbing aboard. Hungry Wolf stopped her.

"Hungry Wolf will take her," he said.

She nodded and backed away. She did not speak. He was a medicine man now, and none of the old women would speak to him unless he asked a question. A matter of respect.

"What if I don't want you to take me?" his granddaughter said in that sharp tone he hated.

"It is my horse and my wagon. . . . Would you rather walk? It would take you two days and you would miss the white man's train."

"Do I have to hear any more of how I'm deserting my people? Being a nurse and bringing them white man's medicine is hardly deserting them. I will cure many sick people." *(Conflict. The first rule of fiction writing: conflict, conflict, conflict. This is a product of the conflicting agendas.)*

"Your spirit is sick," he said. "You should be in the sweat lodge chanting the purifying chant, speaking to the spirits of your ancestors to get their forgiveness."

"You aren't supposed to be off res without permission," she said.

"I have a paper signed by the colonel. I am too old to go raiding, so they let me go."

"Then let's get going, Grandfather, but I won't listen to any of your stupid arguments or your stupid superstitions. . . ."

Okay, so that's how it might begin by raising a story question, gaining sympathy, empathy, and identification. I could have exploited some inner conflict in the old man about whether he should take her. I think this is a good demonstration, although it is a rough draft and in need of a rewrite. I need to paint a better picture of the reservation, for one thing. I'd have to do some research to make it more real.

I could have started the story at the train station, at a point before Hungry Wolf and his granddaughter arrive. You, of course, don't have to start with the hero. Let's say I decided to start with the train station before the hero arrives. I'd start with a minor character, say the guy who runs the train station:

Seth Duggan noticed the horses were edgy *(raises a story question)* when he went out to feed them just after sunup. Maybe there was a big cat prowling around. Something. He kept his hand on the butt of the .44 in his belt.

Maybe it was a storm coming *(quoted thought—close third)*. He went into the corral *(objective)*.

He kept the relay teams for the Butterfield express that ran from Jackson Hole to Paradise. Six bits for the whole trip, including a lunch his wife made. Beans with a little pig fat and cornbread. Filling, and mighty tasty *(details, creating the story world)*.

Daisy, the old mare, seemed particularly upset. She was bobbing her head and refused to eat. He thought she might be coming down with the bloat. Or maybe there was a big cat snooping around. He'd shot one of the sons of bitches just a month before, right after the shindig over in Apache Butte on the Fourth of July. It got a four-month-old colt and a milk cow that belonged to the schoolmarm (*described thoughts*). He felt the hairs on the back of his neck tingle (*sensuous detail*). There was something in the air (*the sixth sense*).

Couldn't be redskins, he thought. They was whipped, staying on the res for maybe twenty years now, behaving themselves. Some even got Christianized, real Baptist Bible believers, and settled down planting corn and raising pigs (*quoted thoughts, close third-person narration*).

Then he remembered the flyer on the Slade gang (*backstory*). He hadn't figured on them coming north; everyone said they'd be heading for Sonora, down Mexico way. But what if they had come north? He felt his throat close up.

If the Slade gang was heading his way, he and Cindy Lou better get the hell into town, he thought.

He started back to the house that served as a train station. He was running now. The Slade gang. Jesus. The house was a long and low adobe building with a flat roof and wood-shuttered windows. A curl of gray smoke came up the chimney. . . .

Let's say he goes inside and the Slade gang is there molesting his wife. Seth draws his gun and is shot down. That's a pretty good opening, I'd say.

As you can see, you can get the reader involved in the story through story questions, sympathy, empathy, and conflicts, starting with various characters, even though Hungry Wolf is the hero. And it all begins with well-motivated characters overcoming obstacles in pursuit of goals.

So which one would make the better opening? The first one involves the hero and the granddaughter; the other is perhaps more tense and has more menace. How do you choose?

Lots of these kinds of choices for the writer are subjective. I decided in this case to start with the train stop, showing how damn dangerous these guys are, and then switch to Hungry Wolf, knowing he and his granddaughter are heading for terrible trouble.

10

■ Hook 'Em and Hold 'Em

Various Gripping Openings to Consider

You may think that I'm focusing a lot of attention on the opening of the story. The reason is that it is the most important part. If you do not have a gripping opening to your thriller, it is unlikely that you will dazzle an agent and woo an editor.

Years ago, I knew a wonderful writer, Irma Ruth Walker, who wrote sci-fi, mysteries, romances, and half a dozen best-selling mainstream novels. She told me she thought openings were so important that 20 percent of the time she spent writing a novel was on the first fifteen or twenty pages.

At the time she told me this, it staggered me. But now I see how vitally important it is that the audience be drawn into the story immediately. A gripping opening is not simply a good thing for your story: It's absolutely essential

These days, creative writing coaches call the opening of a story *the setup*. In the past, it was called *the hook*. I prefer hook because that's what you want to do in your opening sequence: hook the audience good, so they will stay hooked right to the end.

In chapter 4, I discussed how thriller writers such as the authors of *Blood Diamond*, *Serpico*, *Dr. Strangelove*, and *The Constant Gardener* are often concerned with social injustice. These are writers on a mission. I am now going to suggest that creating a situation of injustice of some kind is crucial to the creation of a damn good thriller.

The situation of injustice does not have to be an attack on a social injustice, such as trading in illegal diamonds, corrupt police, the threat of nuclear war, or killing people with bad drugs. But the hero's quest to correct a situation of injustice of some kind is at the heart of every damn good thriller.

Hardly seems possible, does it? Every one? That's right, my friend, every damn one of them. So when you're plotting your thriller, keep in mind how important it is for you to create a situation of injustice that your hero will be determined to make right by foiling evil. And the sooner you present this situation to the audience, the better.

In *Jaws*, the unjust situation appears right from the start, when a young woman is attacked by a shark. In *The Day of the Jackal*, the injustice is an attempt on the life of French president Charles de Gaulle as the story opens. In *High Noon*, as the credits roll, the villain's henchmen are joining up to ride into town for a showdown with the marshal. In *Absolute Power*, an innocent man (even though he is a burglar) is framed for a murder committed by the president's men. In *Alien*, it's the injustice of a slime creature murdering people. In *The Boys from Brazil*, it's the murder of all those innocent adoptive fathers—and the eventual coming of age of a reborn Hitler.

Okay, you say, but it's not always possible to present a situation of injustice right away. Well . . . true. In *Hombre*, as an example, the situation of injustice does not appear until the outlaws hold up the stage and leave the passengers to die of thirst in the desert, about a third of the way into the film. Sometimes the delay in presenting the situation of injustice is done deliberately on the part of the author, as in *Invasion of the Body Snatchers* and *Alien*, where the slow buildup to the takeover of the villains is calculated to tease the audience a bit and foreshadow what's coming. However you do it, make the reader want to see an injustice corrected and you've gone a long way to creating a gripping thriller.

There are any number of situations of injustice you might present to the audience by way of a gripping opening that raise story questions, start conflicts, and create sympathy, empathy, and identification. You can create the situation of injustice many ways using various strategies. Here are some examples of the most common ones.

■ The Villain's Dark Mission Opening

You might open with the villain carrying out his dark mission. This can be a great way of opening with powerful story questions and getting the audience worried about what may happen even before the heroes know there's terrible trouble afoot. One great example of this working well is in *The Day of the Jackal*. We see the Jackal going about his business— stealing passports, having a sniper's rifle made, and so on—and the situation of injustice is well formed way before the hero ever knows about the threat to the president of France.

But it does not always work out so well. There are pitfalls.

The problem comes when the hero arrives and seems like an idiot because he or she can't figure out what's going on, while it's all perfectly clear to the audience. The audience then becomes impatient, waiting for the hero to catch up.

One example is *The Invasion*, the 2007 remake of the 1956 master-piece *Invasion of the Body Snatchers*. *The Invasion* opens with the vil-lain, an alien, funguslike crud, clinging to a space shuttle when it returns to Earth. This crud infects people, who become mindless automatons. A great situation of injustice indeed. But the audience knows all this before the hero, Carol Bennell, comes on scene, and the audience has to sit though long, dreary scenes of her figuring out what the audience already knows.

Okay, say we are going to start *Peace Day* with this kind of opening. You might recall our villain is Josh Pape. Let's have him getting ready to kidnap Mary Cathcart. Remember now, this is the beginning of the story; the reader knows nothing of the plot behind the plot. I've already decided on a limited omniscient narrator, third person.

Here's how this type of opening might look:

■ The Villain's Dark Mission Opening for *Peace Day*

He was a careful man. His planning and execution had to be meticulous, precise. There would be legions of law enforcement against him with their laboratories and computers and armies of technicians, and all he had was his own genius.

Yes, that was what gave him the edge. He could outthink all of them.

He was at the moment in a shabby hotel above an adult bookstore called the Desire Palace. His room was rented under the name of Ali Kabali, who the clerk would remember as a Middle Eastern man with dark, blotchy skin and a deformed nose. A shy man who hid behind dark glasses and spoke broken English. He knew he played that part perfectly; he had practiced long and hard. One thing he'd learned playing Arabs: People looked at them with contempt in their eyes. When they showed that look, you knew you had them fooled.

He'd never been in the room without wearing gloves. He'd shaved his head and body so there would be no hairs left behind. They would not find a single fingerprint of his, but they'd find others on the bottles he left in the room. Bottles he picked out of Dumpsters. There were a dozen bottles; who knew how many sets of prints? He'd have them chasing their tails all over the world. He'd gotten some of the bottles out of trash cans at the airport, and all the hair and fibers he was leaving behind he collected in the trash at a hair salon that catered to Arabs. The carpet fibers came from everywhere, many from a Persian rug store that bought their carpets in Turkey.

Thinking of it, he chuckled out loud. The FBI would have hundreds of leads, but none that would point to him.

How could they point to him? He'd been dead for eighteen months. A suicide in New York, his body burned beyond recognition in a Viking funeral and buried in a pauper's grave. Forgotten.

He wondered what they'd do to the real Ali Kabali, who made

a living as a diesel mechanic and taught Arabic at a local mosque in the evening. Poor Ali.

A siren sounded on the street below. Always sirens. He loaded his 9 mm Glock and his .32 Beretta and put on a bulletproof chest protector. Now he put on the blond wig, padded bra, lipstick and eye shadow, and a red dress. In the mirror he looked great. He'd practiced walking like a woman for weeks. He had padded his hips and knew he had to have the right sway—that was the key. He got a large red suitcase on wheels out of the closet. He'd bought it at a thrift shop for forty-two dollars with a credit card in the name of Timon el Malik. They would find him to be a ghost who lived in a mailbox.

It was time to pick up his date; the party was about to start.

Okay. You will notice that I did not mention who the villain was. That would put the reader too far out in front. Withholding his identity, even though we're in his viewpoint, would bother some purist creative writing coaches. But readers don't mind, and editors don't either, because we are solidly in the fictive dream and we understand that this sort of withholding is a time-honored convention of storytelling. The author has made a contract with the reader that the narrator would go into the character's mind somewhat but leave his identity to be revealed later. This is not cheating, because I am not putting things in the villain's mind that throw the reader off in any way. I am only denying access to his identity because it would spoil all the fun otherwise.

So what is the situation of injustice? The reader knows the villain is going to commit some sort of crime, but not what crime specifically. The reader is more than willing to read on to find out.

Now let's take a look at another type of opening.

■ The "Minor Character in Terrible Trouble" Opening

The James Bond film *Octopussy* (1983) is a good example of this kind of opening. It starts out with British Agent 009 dressed as a clown being chased through the woods by a couple of villainous knife-throwing assassins. He manages to make it to the British consulate, crashes through the window, and a Fabergé egg rolls out of his hand, all of which create story questions. Why was he dressed as a clown? Why a Fabergé egg? The death of a patriot is a situation of injustice, and it's a damn good opening for a spy story: lots of fast action, high stakes, death.

Jaws, of course, opens with a minor character: a beautiful young gal who goes swimming and is eaten by you-know-who. Nice job. It kept millions of people out of the water for several years and brought lots of seaside resorts to the brink of bankruptcy.

Thrillers sometimes open with a scene involving characters who are remote in time and place from the actions of the story. This is often done because the start of the story in the present—the now—lacks strong story questions or strong emotions or enough action. A remote opening can be a way of foreshadowing the terrible trouble that is to come or setting the tone or establishing the genre.

The Exorcist has such an opening, involving an elderly Catholic priest, Father Lankester Merrin, on an archaeological dig in Iraq. He uncovers a statue of a demon, and then there's a cave-in. It's all very horrible, as befits a horror story. This is quite remote from the rest of the actions of the story, which pretty much all take place in Georgetown near Washington, D.C., and involve an actress, Chris MacNeil, and her twelve-year-old daughter, Regan, who becomes possessed by the Devil.

Such openings may raise story questions and set the tone, but as a general rule, it's best to avoid them. Why? Because you have spent a lot of screen time or ink getting the audience interested in a character or a set of characters and their problems, and then you jerk the audience away and start all over again with another set of characters who have problems unrelated to the previous scene, and then the story questions from the first scene begin to fade. This is not true in *Octopussy* or *Jaws*, because their first scenes lead directly into the story.

The Exorcist opening might be more effective if the remote scenes were connected directly to what comes next. Say the priest finds the statue of the demon, then comes to a bad end. A thief steals the statue and comes to a bad end after he sells it to an antiquities dealer. Then when we switch to Georgetown, the statue has just been purchased by one of the characters in a curio shop. That way, the opening sequence of scenes would be remote but tied to the main characters of the story.

Okay, if I were to start *Peace Day* with actions involving a minor character, how might I do it?

■ A "Minor Character in Terrible Trouble" Opening for *Peace Day*

Herman the Weed was careful after he bought his evening libation—a bottle of Harvest Select premium red table wine for $3.99—and he was keeping his eye on the little old Japanese car that was following him.

Part of him thought that it wasn't possible anybody'd give a fig about him. But yet, when he turned the corner and looked back, there it was coming slowly up the street in front of the moving company warehouse. He started to hurry, the soles of his worn-out shoes flapping on the sidewalk.

He was in Armstrong Alley now. It felt better passing by all the Dumpsters and trash cans with the stink of the garbage from the Arab restaurant. It was, he always said, good stink. This was close to home, his territory. This is where he'd been sleeping for—what was it now? Three years? Ten? Dammit, but keeping track of time was a tricky business. A year could wiggle away without you even noticing it.

The little car did not follow him when he turned up the alley. It just vanished. Just like that. Poof, into thin air. He unscrewed the metal cap and took a couple of slugs of wine. It felt good going down, and a moment later he felt the warm quiet flooding over his body.

The old parking garage, long out of business, was at the end of the street, all boarded up. He slid past the ramp at the end and pulled back the plywood board over the entrance and squeezed in. It was dank and cold inside. This was his place. Nobody knew about it. Not his friend Crazy Maggie or his old pal Bold Bill, who was at the moment taking the cure because he saw spider men after him and went screaming into the 45th precinct police station.

There was a shelf of concrete where the old ticket booth used to be. He slid up on it. Here were his blankets and some cardboard, and in a moment he'd be toasty warm. The place smelled of old shit and piss from the slobs on the upper floor, but, hell, a few more swallows and he'd forget all about the stink.

Then, a weird sound. A rat. Damn rats.

In the shadows, there . . . somebody in the shadows!

"What ya want?" he blurted out.

No answer. For a moment he thought it might be a cop . . . or worse, a frickin' social worker wanting to drag him to a damn shelter. He wasn't hurtin' nobody, why the hell can't they leave him to hell alone? Then again, it might be one of them damn Christian Bible thumpers again, come to preach about the kingdom of God and that piddley.

He reached for the piece of pipe he kept handy just for an emergency. It might be somebody coming for his goods.

"You ain't gettin' none of my libation. I got to warn you, I'm armed and dangerous."

"So am I," said whoever the hell it was. Herman could hear his heart pounding at his temples.

"You a bluefoot?"

"A cop? Hardly."

"What ya want? I can yell mighty loud."

"Are you Herman Volker?"

Nobody'd called him that for what? Since the elevator company job. "I used to be him," Herman said. "Now they call me Herman the Weed."

"You are six foot one inch tall?"

"About. What the flip ya want?"

"You weigh one hundred and eighty pounds?"

"About." He took a few gulps out of his bottle. The guy must be one of them celestial beings been pokin' around. Dark angels. Shadow men. That, or a damn social worker.

"You gonna tell me who you are, or do I go into attack mode?" Herman said.

"I'm your friend."

"You been following me in a car?"

"Yes."

"Why?"

A light came on. Herman squinted. "What the flip you want?"

"I need your services."

"Me? For what?"

"You're going to be a very important part of a very big plan."

"What plan?"

"A secret plan."

"That black guy, he president now?"

"Has been for some time."

"Just asking. Trying to figure out if I can trust you."

"I have some clothes for you, new clothes. Your clothes."

The man stepped closer and put a bundle of clothes next to him.

"I ain't puttin' on them clothes."

"Why not?"

"I don't like brown."

"How about I pay you?"

"My services come high."

The man slid a bottle over to him. Hennessy cognac.

Herman looked at it for a long moment before picking it up. He turned away from the light and read the label.

"Baby, come to daddy," Herman the Weed said, opening the bottle. He poured the cool, sweet liquid over his tongue.

"The taste of heaven," he said. And then the room started to move around, and for one crazy moment he thought there was an earthquake, but there ain't no earthquakes in New York, any mo-ron knows that.

That's when he fell forward into the darkness and felt himself sinking into eternity. . . .

In this case, the minor character in terrible trouble dies, creating a nice situation of injustice the audience wants to see corrected. Of course, it wouldn't be too much further into the story that Mary Cathcart will be kidnapped and threatened with death, and that will be an even bigger injustice. You don't have to stop at just one.

■ The "Hero in Terrible Trouble" Opening

In the wonderful comic thriller *Stakeout* (1987), the hero, Chris Lecce, is working in his everyday world as a cop and gets the crap beat out of him in a wonderfully exciting opening. The fight takes place in a fish-processing plant long before he gets the assignment to go on the stake-out, where he will have some terrible trouble when he falls in love with the suspect he's supposed to be keeping under surveillance. This open-ing is all fast action, bim-bam-boom, but all this action has little to do with the core plot or the dark mission of the villain.

The comic thriller masterpiece *Miss Congeniality* (2000) opens the same way, bim-bam-boom, as our female hero FBI agent is making a drug bust. She tries to save one of the bad guys from choking, which leads to a lot of fast action and terrible trouble back in the office.

Sometimes the actions in the world of the everyday may be exten-sive, going through many complications with lots of damn good con-flicts. The melodramatic, overly sentimental, and jingoistic war thriller *Sergeant York* (1941), supposedly based closely on a true story, is mostly about the hero trying hard to avoid being a hero. He does not go off on his mission to end the evil of World War I until far past the halfway point of the film. Despite its slobbering patriotism, I like it, principally for the moral struggle the pacifist, Bible-believing hero faces when he's drafted into the military. The conflict in the world of the everyday—the romantic courtship, the working night and day to pay for a farm—is absorbing and makes the war action more involving for the reader because by the time the shooting starts, we identify strongly with the hero. That is the point of this kind of opening: The audience becomes intimate with the hero before the hero is given the mission to foil evil.

In *How to Write a Damn Good Novel*, I referred to this part as *the status quo situation*, which seems to imply to a lot of readers that there isn't much going on. In the mythic paradigm that I wrote about in *The Key: How to Write Damn Good Fiction Using the Power of Myth*, this part of the myth is called *the world of the everyday*. That, too, seems to many readers to imply there isn't much going on. A better way to say what I mean is that the opening should show the hero in terrible trouble in his everyday life, in what I earlier called *the gripping opening*. That's more like it.

This terrible trouble can be any kind of trouble, as long as it's truly terrible. It might be love trouble or it might be trouble on the job or with family. The stakes can be, say, life and death, a man's honor, a situation of embarrassment, anything. Let's take a look at the terrible trouble Walter Butterfield might have in his everyday world in *Peace Day*. Remember, the aim here is to get the audience to feel sympathy and empathy for the hero and to identify with him before he ever heads for New York and gets involved with the plot of *Peace Day*, where his heroic mission will be to rescue his kidnapped niece.

■ An Opening of *Peace Day* Involving the Hero in His Everyday World

Cory Dixon didn't understand country people. Why, as an example, did this old coot Okra Bean want Walter Butterfield beat up?

Cory and Okra were meeting at Bean's auto body shop down by the creek to settle the deal. The place had room for only half a dozen customers' cars, Cory noticed. It was dirty and cluttered and smelled like bondo dust and paint. The only customer's car in the place was an old Chevy, a '98 or '99, with the door bashed in. Cory thought the work being done on it was sloppy, amateurish.

Okra spit some tobacco juice and ground it into the floor with his old boot. They were by a workbench littered with parts and tools. Cory was thinking he'd never get his car fixed in this dump.

Okra was saying: "And I want both his legs broke. Break 'em good."

"Be easier to kill the fucker."

"I ain't buyin' no murder. I want him beat bad, and both his legs broke, but you're to leave him breathin'."

Cory never did understand yokels. "You mind me asking why you're doing this?"

"He's been uppity."

"That's it?"

"We been at war, his family and mine, since forever. I'm gonna end it. You been checkin' him out?"

"Yeah."

"It's like I said—he's mostly alone at that big old house of his at night, ain't it so?"

"He's alone at night. Just him and a dog. He keeps the dog in the yard."

"You gonna get him tonight?"

"He's supposed to talk about his great-granddaddy the Civil War general tonight at the Elks Club in Beaver Forks. He'll be home at midnight. I'll be waiting on him."

"He weren't no general. A colonel. And he was a Republican after the war, the snake. Are you gonna kill the dog? I don't know . . . I like dogs."

"I got a gas to make him sleep. I don't kill animals unless they got their teeth in my leg."

"Okay, good. They say you got a lot of army trainin'?"

"Two tours in Iraq, special forces. You want to see my medals?"

"I want to see Walter Butterfield a mess a blood and crippled good."

"And I want to see four thousand dollars." Cory held out his hand.

The old man gave him an envelope. "Just see to it you do it right."

"I'll do it right. Weren't for this economy, I'd be wanting a whole lot more, I want you to know that."

"Times is tough all over."

■

Cory rode his Harley up the winding dirt road after ten that night and laid it down under a pine tree on the side of the road and camouflaged it well with pine boughs he cut off another tree. Damn tree was sappy. His hands got sticky.

He was wearing all black and had a shoulder bag packed with a pine board and a ten-pound sledge, Ace Hardware heavy-duty duct tape, a flashlight, a Jungle-mate combat knife with a serrated edge, night-sight binoculars, and horsemeat laced with barbiturate for the dog. Under his shirt he had a black 9 mm Glock stuck in his belt and a lock-picking kit he got from a guy he met in the Jamestown jail who knew locks like a magician knows rabbits. He had actually never been in the military, but his uncle Bennie had, and Uncle Bennie had taught him a lot.

Cory had done his homework on this guy Butterfield. He was on the school board, dressed good, drove a new Acura, and was an authority on the Civil War and gave lectures and had written a couple of books on it. But everyone in the damn town knew he was really a bootlegger, the biggest in the whole state. He even sold a legal bourbon called Lightning in a Bottle to tourists along the Mississippi. Rumor had it he had the sheriff and the state attorney in his pocket. Cory had heard the story of how the feds raided Butterfield's place eight times in one year and never found a single drop of illegal booze. Butterfield got his lawyers to go after the feds for malicious prosecution, and even though a judge threw the case out, they left him alone after that. The barber in town had told Cory Butterfield was putting the sheriff's kid through college and he bought a new Lincoln for some prosecutor's wife every two years.

Supposedly Butterfield makes his scratch as a milk wholesaler, everybody said with a wink, but it was just a cover. It's supposed to be a big mystery how he gets his booze to Memphis, where he distributes it. They dismantled some of his milk tankers and found no evidence they ever had any corn liquor in them.

Cory admired the guy. He was sorry he had to break his legs, but business was business. Two grand a leg. Not bad for an evening's work.

He sat in the trees and watched the road. It was a pleasant night. Cool. He had a leather jacket on and was quite comfortable. It was April and had rained early in the day, and everything smelled fresh. He wished he could have a joint, but that would have to wait till the job was done. He was feeling that supergreat tingle of excitement in his toes he always felt before a job. He loved his work.

He sat there for over an hour before he heard a car leaving the main road below. Must be him: After the turnoff, Butterfield's was the only place on this road. Cory checked his watch. He was right on time.

Cory stayed low in the grass and watched the car go by and turn up the driveway. The garage was attached to the house. The garage door opened and the car went in. The garage door closed. Lights came on inside. He heard the dog barking. A moment later a light came on in the backyard. He was putting the dog out in his little house. Perfect.

Cory made his way around the hill, sticking close to the trees. There was a quarter-moon that ducked in and out of the clouds. He moved steadily and slowly, keeping low. He kept telling himself, Be patient, boy. Patience was one of the most important things about being an enforcer. That's what he called himself, an enforcer. It had a neat ring to it. Cory Dixon, the enforcer.

Here he could make his move on the house without being seen by anyone from any window. He took out his National Geographic Night Vision Binoculars with 3-power and fourteen-degree field of view and slowly checked in every direction. Nobody. For a guy who was supposed to be smart, this Butterfield was really a chump. Living way out here by himself with just a dog, he was asking for it.

Cory made a dash across the open ground for the corner of the house, then stopped and folded himself into the shadows. Slowly, he peered around the corner. There was a fence around the backyard, and there, not ten feet away on the other side, was the dog. He was sitting, just looking at him, with his big old tongue hanging out. The damn dog didn't even bark.

Cory went into his pack and brought out the meat with the sleeping drug in it and tore the cellophane off and hurled it over the fence. The dog went over and sniffed it, then trotted off. Cory watched him disappear into his kennel. Cory didn't move. He'd used this trick a half dozen times before; the dog always took the meat and had a nice sleep. What the hell was wrong with this one? Or was he just well trained? He'd heard about dogs like that. German shepherds. Dobermans. But this one was just a goddamn mutt. That kind of training cost a bundle. What jackass would waste it on a mutt?

He was beginning to lose all respect for Walter Butterfield.

He stood there for several minutes, waiting to see what the dog had on his mind. But he didn't come out of the kennel.

Okay, the hell with it. If the dog attacked him, he'd slit the damn thing's throat.

The fence around the yard was barely four feet high. No problem. He put his pack on top so he wouldn't get spiked and rolled over it. He came up on his tingling feet. His heart beat fast now.

He crept up to the back door, looking for lights or movement in the house, keeping an eye on the kennel. He had a narrow-beam flashlight in one hand, his knife in the other. He climbed the back stairs, keeping his weight on the ends of the stairs to keep the noise down. Quiet as a cobra.

At the top of the stairs, he knelt and put down his flashlight. He was about to get out his lock-picking kit, but he touched the door-knob, and what do you know, the door swung inward.

A buddy of his, a real second-story man of the old school, once said the scariest thing on earth was an unlocked door.

Now his heart was really pounding, and the tingle in his feet was turning to an itch. Could the yokel be this dumb? He'd heard people in town say Crooked Creek was the kind of place where folks didn't have to lock their doors at night. He didn't believe it, but what the hell, maybe it was true.

He stood up and stepped inside, shining his flashlight down a hallway. Along the walls on both sides were hooks to hang jackets. The hallway was empty, clean as a hospital. He stepped in, and in half a second he knew he'd made one of the biggest mistakes of his life. Bigger than marrying that bitch Cindy Ann, and that was a whopper.

A sliding metal wall suddenly shut behind him and another in front of him, bam-bam, and goddamn, he was trapped.

He drew his gun, waiting for . . . for what? He thought he might just fire through a wall, but then what if it bounced off? He'd be like in an armored personnel carrier when a shell comes in and bounces around. He felt dizzy for a moment, then managed to get his breath. And stop shaking.

"Okay," he said, trying to be as cool as a 007. "You got me. I'm stupid as a chicken."

A drawer slid out from the wall. "Please be a gentleman and put all your weapons in the drawer," a voice said.

"I may be a little on the dumb side, but I ain't crazy."

"All right."

He heard the hiss of gas.

"Hey, what are you doing?"

No answer.

"Hey! What's that?"

"It's an odorless, tasteless gas. You'll be dead in a hundred and twenty seconds."

Fumbling, Cory put the gun and the knife in the drawer. The drawer closed. Then a door at the end of the hallway opened.

He went through the doorway into a nice, bright kitchen. Modern, lots of stainless-steel-and-copper pots, granite counters. Butterfield was in a thick bathrobe with slippers and had a big revolver in his hand. An antique, maybe. Cory had seen Butterfield a couple of times before, but never up close. He had a handsome face that reminded Cory of the actor who played Batman once. He had a calm expression, yet there was intensity behind his eyes. You didn't have to ask if he could kill you; one look at those eyes told you he could.

"Won't you join me in a drink? I think you may need one." The old southern gentlemanly quality. He'd heard the guy was a throwback.

Cory moved farther into the kitchen. "What about the gas, do I need a doctor?"

"It was just air. Funny, isn't it, the power of suggestion?"

Cory sat down at the table. Butterfield remained standing. He looked at Butterfield's eyes, the big revolver, and measured the distance between them. He'd jump the bastard if he had half a chance.

"You're thinking of attacking me. You might make it, but I practice with this a lot." Meaning the revolver. "It makes a hell of a hole in a man."

Cory said nothing. He was quick as a cat when he had to be. It wasn't but a few feet. Suddenly Butterfield's hand twitched and the gun exploded. Cory felt a sting in his earlobe. The kitchen was half-full of smoke.

"Christ, you coulda blown my head off!" He touched his earlobe—blood.

"I apologize for frightening you, but I could see you did not appreciate the precariousness of your situation. Now . . ." He poured a half glass of bourbon for each of them. "I have a few questions to ask you."

"I will not give up the man who hired me."

Butterfield smiled. "I gave you credit for more brains than that."

"I won't do it. I have my principles. Torture me, kill me, you can pull my nose off, I will not squeal. There's no one lower than a squealer."

"You should know I am perfectly capable of pulling your nose off. But I do not think that your recalcitrance will force me to perform such an unpleasant act."

He took out a stack of hundred-dollar bills and put them on the table. "There's ten thousand dollars here, Cory Dixon."

"You know my name?"

"Of course. I don't do business with people I don't know."

"What kind of business?"

"The man who hired you . . . what did he have in mind?"

"That I break your legs and beat you to a pulp . . . but not kill you."

"Ah. Well, since you bungled the job, I suppose you will no longer be working for him. So you are unemployed."

"I work strictly freelance."

"Ah, yes, the enforcer."

Cory blinked.

"I pride myself on my intelligence network," Butterfield said.

"You are to be congratulated. What do I have to do for that ten thousand dollars?"

"Without sacrificing your integrity by revealing the identity of the vermin, I want you to do to him what he had in mind for me. It's called an eye for an eye among biblical scholars."

Cory let the right of it slide around in his brain for a few minutes. "Well, if I'm working for you . . . okay."

"Finish your drink. I'd like to be getting some sleep."

Cory picked up the money, his knife, and his gun. "It's been a pleasure meeting you, sir."

Butterfield walked him to the front door. "Give my kind regards to Mr. Okra Bean, will you, please?"

Cory stopped and turned to him. "You knew?"

"I wanted to know if you are truly a man of character."

"What's he got against you?"

"When dealing with the truly stupid, it is always difficult to tell."

"An honor to know you, sir."

"The honor is all mine, sir," he said.

I like this opening. It shows my hero to be clever and resourceful and a good dramatic character and, I hope, fresh. *Peace Day* is a "fish out of water" story. A common motif in Hollywood films.

Okay, it's the next morning that Walter gets his call to action and becomes involved in the plot, the kidnapping of his niece. I think this beginning would work just fine, but as you'll see later, when designing the plot, I picked another one for reasons I'll explain at that time.

■ The "Hero Already on His Mission to Foil Evil" Opening

You might start with an opening involving the hero already on his or her mission to foil evil. This opening is rarely used. Hemingway used it in *For Whom the Bell Tolls*. Despite having the hero already on his mission, the story has a rather slow beginning as our hero, Jordan, meets the partisans who are going to help him perform his mission of blowing up the bridge. Hemingway is interested in character and language more than plot, so this is why he chose this opening. If you had a bim-bam-boom opening, the audience would assume it was another kind of story.

If you use the "hero already on his mission to foil evil" opening, you're asking the audience to get interested in the mission without having witnessed a situation of injustice, and that's a problem. The audience often fails to connect emotionally as soon as you'd like.

■

Okay, how might this hero already on the mission be done in *Peace Day* ? Let's say in the backstory the hero, Walter Butterfield, has been told his niece has been kidnapped, and he has flown to New York. So we pick up the story there.

■ The "Hero Already on His Mission to Foil Evil" Opening for *Peace Day*

Walter Butterfield was forty-four, tall, blue-eyed, fair-skinned. He stood upright and had what many said was an easy way about him, a certain graceful manner of walking—straight, almost military.

He approached the door. There was a man standing in front of it, a young man in a suit and tie, with a plastic ID that said he was Special Agent Bayless.

"Crime scene," Special Agent Bayless said.

"I need to talk to the man in charge. Who might he be?"

"She."

"She?"

"Special Agent Alice Dorn."

"I wish to speak to her, if I may, on a matter of some urgency."

"She's very busy right now—I'm sure you must have seen the gaggle of media downstairs. State your business."

"I will be conducting a search for my niece, and I wish to solicit Agent Dorn's assistance in my effort."

Special Agent Bayless suppressed a smile. "We have at the moment perhaps at least a hundred agents and another hundred police officers looking for her. Are you in law enforcement?"

"What I do for a living is not your concern."

"If you'll give me your name and number, I'll have Special Agent Dorn contact you."

"You must be a person of low intelligence. I told you why I must see her. You are to tell her immediately or I will alert that gaggle of media downstairs that she is an incompetent oaf."

This is not a strong opening. It's possible that some strong opening could be found that would work wonderfully well with the hero already on the mission, but I haven't been able to dream it up. Structurally, it's a poor way to start anyway, because it's putting the point of attack too late in the chain of events.

■ The Flashback Opening

The flashback opening works like this: You pick a spot toward the beginning of the climactic sequence quite late in the story and put that up front at the point of attack, and then you tell most of the story in one huge flashback.

One well-known example of this type of opening is in the film version of James M. Cain's novella *Double Indemnity* (1945, film 1944), widely regarded as a classic. It starts off with Walter Neff, the protagonist-villain who has been shot in the gut, returning to his office, where he works as an insurance agent. He turns on a recording machine and relates the story we're about to see.

Using the flashback opening is sort of an admission that what you have at the beginning of your story (in the *now* of the story) is dramatically limp.

In the novel upon which the film is based, author James M. Cain did not use the flashback device. He structured *Double Indemnity* as these femme fatale stories are usually done: He showed the shazam moment when the poor sap first meets the femme fatale, and then he showed how the poor sap gets tangled up with the femme fatale and her murder scheme. This was done in *The Postman Always Rings Twice* and, as discussed previously, in *Fatal Attraction*, *Play Misty for Me*, and *Body Heat* (1981). Almost all femme fatale stories have the same pattern—the shazam moment, followed by infatuation, love, passion, insanity, murder, capture, and a tragic death, usually in a shootout with the cops, execution, or a suicide.

Cain begins the novel *Double Indemnity* like this:

I drove out to Glendale to put three new truck drivers on a company bond, and then I remembered this renewal over in

Hollywoodland. I decided to run over there. That was how I came to this House of Death, that you've been reading about in the papers. It didn't look like the House of Death when I saw it. It was just a Spanish house, like all the rest of them in California. . . .

Notice how he sneaks in the foreshadowing—*this House of Death*—so you'll know something terrible is going to happen, but that's about all there is until Walter Huff, the villain-protagonist (Walter Neff in the screen version) and the femme fatale start discussing murder. The screen flashback version was written in part by the great Raymond Chandler, so who am I to criticize? You make up your own mind. This flashback way of telling a story has been used repeatedly in films by copycat screenwriters, and most of the time, the films would be better off without the flashback or the voice-over narrator that draws the audience out of the fictive dream.

Okay, now that you've been warned about the flashback opening, there's no reason for me to show you my version of the flashback opening for *Peace Day* because I'd never even consider it. It kills too many story questions dead as roadkill.

Nor would I consider using what I call the "turbid" opening, turbid meaning "muddy." Please never use it, but you ought to know what it is.

■ The Turbid Opening

This is designed to raise story questions by showing stuff happening, but not indicating the context of the events shown to the audience.

One of my colleagues, whom I shall not name because I don't want the moron suing me, is promoting the turbid opening as a great way of starting a dramatic story, including thrillers.

This turbid technique is spreading like the plague, and the otherwise really bright people who produce *Law & Order* on TV have been using it to open their *Criminal Intent* stories for some time and lately have been using it on their original series *Law & Order* shows. Whoever decided confusing the viewer is the way to get an audience involved in a story should be pink-slipped without delay. It's a pity that keelhauling is no longer allowed by the articles of war.

One reason the turbid opening may be used is that it seems artsy, and God knows every writer, director, and script boy wants to be thought an artist. Here's how it works: You show a bunch of various characters involved in conflicts, only you don't tell the viewer what the conflicts are about. What's wrong with that, Jim? you ask. Aren't you supposed to raise story questions?

Yes, of course you're supposed to raise story questions. You raise story questions to create curiosity in the audience at the same time you get them to connect emotionally to the story. The audience cannot connect to a story emotionally if they do not know what the hell is going on. The audience cannot identify with characters and their missions, cannot empathize with them, if they don't know what their agendas or missions are or why they're in conflict.

A turbid opening might go like this:

1. Two guys are arguing about loading a box into a truck.

2. New scene: A man and a woman are drinking tea, and he finds it suddenly hard to breathe.

3. New scene: A guy on a bike delivers a package to an office.

4. New scene: One of the guys in the first scene is taking a train and gives a newspaper to a woman in a red dress.

5. The woman in the red dress sits down next to a blind woman with a Seeing Eye dog.

Gads, if this were the opening of a thriller film, I'd be on my way to the ticket office for a refund.

This does not mean you should avoid an action opening such as *Octopussy*, discussed earlier. As long as the audience understands the situation and can become emotionally connected to the story, it's okay to leave the details for later. What you want to avoid is confusing the reader about the situation, as they do in *Law & Order: Criminal Intent* openings showing scenes of muddled conflicts.

■ The "Thrilling Climax to Another Story" Opening

In the opening of *Thunderball* (1965), James Bond is watching the funeral of one Colonel Jacques Bouvar, who had murdered two double-0 agents, Bond's colleagues. This is the end of a previous story, a story the audience doesn't know anything about. Bond notices that Bouvar's "widow" refuses the assistance of a limo driver in opening the door, so Bond concludes this is not a woman. He goes to Bouvar's mansion, and when the "widow" comes in, Bond attacks and manages to kill Bouvar for good in a bim-bam-boom opening.

The Spy Who Came in from the Cold also opens with the end of another story. It opens with our hero, British spy Alec Leamas, in West Berlin waiting in the night at the crossing point from East Berlin for one of his colleagues to cross over, bringing information from the Communist East. Leamas watches helplessly as his colleague is brutally murdered.

■ The "Thrilling Climax to Another Story" Opening for *Peace Day*

Walter Butterfield was ready that very night to tell Catherine Thornberry that he wanted her to come and live with him at Monteverdi, his stately home atop Morgan's Hill, overlooking the valley of the Crooked Creek. This meant he had to tell her that the rumors about him were true . . . he was indeed, well, a bootlegger. Only premium, well-made, 86-proof hooch, of course, not that stuff boiled in a pot and condensed in an old car radiator. No sir, his product was as fine a Kentucky bourbon as there was on the planet. It just did not move to market graced with a federal tax stamp.

His family had been in the business a long time, going back to the days of the Whiskey Rebellion in the late eighteenth century.

He had not known Catherine long. They'd been dating only four months, but he was extremely fond of her. She was a stock analyst who lived in Clementine, the county seat, and loved hiking and bike riding through the mountains as much as he did. She was originally from Arizona and grew up on a ranch. He had her checked out, of course, by one of the best P.I.'s in the business, Steve Brown in St. Augustine, Florida. He knew she had some kind of stress breakdown in New York when the market crashed and now wanted only the solitude of the country. She was well educated, and they shared a love of travel and classical music, as well as hiking in the mountains.

Still, Brown said he had more checking to do. Walter decided maybe he'd put her to the test.

They were having drinks on the veranda when the housekeeper, Mrs. McAferty, came out to announce that he had callers. She whispered in Walter's ear that it was his estranged wife and her lawyer.

Walter stood up and straightened his tie. "If you'll excuse me, Catherine, an emergency has come up. Unwelcome guests, I'm afraid. I will deal with them and return as soon as possible."

But it was already too late. His wife stormed in, not with her lawyer, but with Sam Muldoon, a competitor in the whiskey trade.

Though her complexion had paled from too much drinking and smoking, Walter noted, Irma Ruth was still a strikingly beautiful redhead. He was feeling the same powerful attraction to her, like a man addicted to drinking battery acid.

"Well, I see you have guests," she said, giving Catherine a nasty look. "Has he told you how he makes his living?"

"I know how he makes his living," Catherine said evenly. Of course, it was well-known in the community. Walter admired her calm.

"Has he told you how many times he's been arrested? Nineteen."

"No convictions," Walter said. "Did you have to bring this trash into my home?" he said, indicating Muldoon.

"He said he wanted to see you and you wouldn't agree to meet with him."

"I spend as little time with garbage as I can. I'm sure you can understand. The smell never bothered you, but I have a highly tuned olfactory system."

Sam Muldoon's face reddened. He glared at Walter but didn't say anything.

"How much did he pay you?" Walter asked. "For you to bring him here?"

"You are so sure of yourself, aren't you, Butterfield? You got a nice place here," Muldoon said. "But you can afford it, now that you've got 90 percent of the product coming out of the valley. After you squeezed me dry."

"Catherine, I apologize. I never conduct business at my home."

"Has he told you he's married?" Walter's wife said to Catherine. "He hates me, but he won't divorce me. He pays me five thousand a month so I won't divorce him."

"The subject of my matrimonial status was on my agenda for this very evening," Walter said. "I thought our relationship had progressed to the point where absolute honesty is required." He turned to his wife. "You would not understand that word, Irma Ruth, honesty being alien to your nature."

"The name is Nora."

"I knew you were still married," Catherine said to Walter. "You don't think I'd date a man I had not checked out? Just as, I'm sure, you checked me out."

"The fate of modern man—all his secrets are soon known," Walter said.

"I've got one," Muldoon said, pulling a gun.

"My, this evening has taken an ugly turn," Walter said.

"What's going on here?" Irma Ruth. "Guns were not in our agreement."

"Apparently you do not understand the nature of evil, my dear," Walter said. "As I always suspected."

"My grandpappy should have wiped out you Butterfields long ago. I'm simply correcting an error of history. I'm sorry, Nora, and you too, ma'am, that you have to be collateral damage, but this is war."

Walter's wife shrank back in terror.

Muldoon raised his gun and pointed it at Walter, turning his back to Catherine.

Catherine shouted: "Drop it!"

She, too, had a gun. It appeared in her hand, apparently from a holster in the small of her back.

"Federal officer!" she yelled.

Muldoon dropped his gun.

"My, this is an evening for surprises," Walter said, shaking the man's hand. "Thank you, my friend, for the fine performance."

"What is this?" Catherine said.

"You mean he's a friend of yours?" Irma Ruth asked.

"I apologize, Nora, for giving you a turn. But after all, you did take the man's money, thinking he was going to spoil my evening."

Catherine was blushing. She put away her gun. "I was warned you were sneaky."

"An apt description. My great-granddad was Colonel Mosby, as you know, perhaps. Sneakiness is in the genes."

"You could have scared me to death," Irma Ruth said.

"I think you're built of stronger stuff. Perhaps you could come by tomorrow and we could discuss our marital relations, Irma Ruth."

"Can you give me a ride down the hill?" Catherine asked Muldoon.

"No thanks, I don't care much for feds."

He left. Irma Ruth went with him.

"Please, Catherine, Mrs. McAferty has prepared a most delicious dinner. I was hoping you'd stay. Let us not throw away a beautiful evening like this. I was about to open a bottle of a really fine Cabernet from my vineyard."

"Do you have any idea how much the ATF has spent setting up my cover story?"

"It's no wonder income taxes are so high, money being spent on such foolishness."

They were still on the terrace after sundown, finishing their after-dinner aperitifs, when they were interrupted by a phone call. It was Walter's sister, Daisy, sobbing:

"Mary's missing. The Arabs must have her . . . terrorists."

"Simmer down now, tell me exactly what's going on. . . ."

And this is where our hero gets the call to adventure, and off he goes to New York. The above scene has a large hole in it, of course. You probably noticed. Walter could not rely on Catherine not shooting Muldoon dead, so this would not be a good plan. It would not be in his *maximum capacity* to do this. Except in comedy, the characters should be operating at maximum capacity at all times. This means they don't do stupid things at the behest of the author, like leave clues or go into dangerous places without adequate motivation. The famous "idiot in the attic" motif is an example of the characters being at less than their maximum capacity. This motif appears in cheap horror films. It goes like this: A beautiful woman in a filmy nightgown, hearing strange noises in the attic of a spooky house, goes to investigate, carrying a flickering candle for light, with no gun, knife, or club for protection.

If you discover your characters are not at their maximum capacity, you will have to rewrite to make them operate at their maximum capacity. Oh well, good writing is rewriting, no?

■ A First-Person Version

All of the previous openings were written in third-person viewpoint, past tense, from the viewpoints of various characters. I did this to demonstrate not only the different kinds of openings, but also writing in various viewpoints. I have not demonstrated any of the *Peace Day* sections in first person. Just to show how it could be done, I'll do a first-person scene. Let's say Walter gets the news by phone early the next morning after the kidnapping.

Here's the opening in first person:

I'd been up late working on my tortuously difficult-to-write book about my forebear, the Gray Ghost, Colonel Mosby, of the 43rd Battalion, 1st Virginia Cavalry, during the War Between the States, and so did not answer my phone when it rang at six in the morning. My message machine is in the kitchen, but I could still hear it—my sister, Daisy, was screaming something about her daughter—my beloved niece—Mary being kidnapped.

She was still screaming when I picked up the phone a moment later.

"Daisy, how nice to hear your voice."

"They got her, them damn Arab terrorists, they got her . . . took her out of her hotel. It's all over the news. The federals called this morning from Washington. . . . You got to do something, Walt, you know damn well the FBI can't find its zipper in the men's room. . . ."

Anyway, getting a phone call is not a very dramatic way of starting a story. In fact, it's weak. I don't like it much as an opening, but it's in the voice of the protagonist, so if I were to write in first person, this is the voice I'd use.

■ Openings to Avoid at All Cost

Writers often choose to start a story with a dream sequence. This is a bad idea. Lawrence Sanders, the great mystery writer, said the surest way to lose your reader is to start with a dream sequence.

The comic romantic thriller *Romancing the Stone* starts with a sort of dream sequence—a fictional narrative of the end of a western romance that the hero is writing at the moment. It's meant to be funny and exciting and is presented as the credits roll. It's effective because the audience knows it's not in the *now* of the story.

Butch Cassidy and the Sundance Kid opens with a herky-jerky silent-era film showing the Hole-in-the-Wall Gang robbing a train. The screenplay was written by legendary screenwriter William Goldman, his first feature film. The silent film opening sets the comic tone of the story. It's artsy, but I believe it distances the audience from the story and is not effective. The story that it shows is another version of the train robbery we're about to see, and it takes the audience out of the story world as they think about the differences. You want the audience absorbed in the events in the *now* of the story; you don't want them sitting there analyzing what they're looking at.

■

Plotting your thriller is a joyride. Since you know what the villain is up to and you know your hero and the other major characters, all you have to do is start the chess game, figuring out the moves. This is where, as a creative writer, you can really get creative.

We're now going to plot *Peace Day*, a contemporary urban thriller. You'll see that plotting it is still a step-by-step process and as easy as smacking a banana fish flopping on the beach.

Oh. My lawyer says I need to say no banana fish were injured or killed in the making of this book.

11

■ How to Plot a Damn Good Thriller Step by Step by Step by Step

The Gripping Opening of Peace Day, Movement I and The Hero in Terrible Trouble, Movement II

In my classes, I press all my students to plot out their stories with a step sheet. I know making a step sheet can seem like a daunting task. The first time my mentor, Lester Gorn, showed me how to make one and encouraged me to try it, I balked. I thought, Gee, this is going to put me into a straitjacket and curtail my creativity, blah, blah, blah. I was new at the writing game and into thinking of myself as an artist who created out of a vast well of genius, and I really didn't need to learn all this step sheet diddle, which would only stifle my genius.

But I gave it a shot because my mentor insisted it was a great tool. The first time I tried it, I found the process difficult. But I kept hacking at it. The more I fumbled around with it, the more I could see what a powerful technique it was. After a while, I could actually see the story unfolding in my mind as I made the step sheet, and I could quickly change the step sheet if I got a sudden burst of inspiration. That's why you make a step sheet: You can change the story, and when you do, you can see the reverberations that the change makes. Without a step sheet, you don't discover the effect of an ill-considered change until you write a dozen or a hundred pages, and then, uh-oh, you have a mountain of rewrite to do.

I recently met Jeffery Deaver at a writers' conference. He's the author of a bunch of damn good mysteries, including *The Bone Collector* (1997, film 1999). He says he spends months making his plot plans, which run to two hundred pages. He said he knows all the intricacies of the plot before he ever drafts a single scene.

The more you practice making step sheets, the better you get at it. Without a step sheet (call it a summary or synopsis if you prefer), your first draft will not be well planned and will not be well crafted, and you will have to do a second draft and maybe a third, and you'll still be spending weeks and months patching holes in the plot that could have been worked out in a step sheet in a few hours.

As I make this plea, I hope you can see my tears on the page, tears for all those step sheet–less writers who are still suffering through long, turgid drafts as they shape their stories. Writing a thriller without a step sheet is like ordering a meal without a menu, building a bridge without a blueprint, or surfing the Web without Google.

If you get good at writing step sheets, you will, in your lifetime, be able to write twice as many damn good thrillers as you would if you do not master this technique. That's right, my friend, step sheets are a productivity tool, sort of like a good word processor.

Okay, so far in this book, I have urged you to do the following:

First, find a damn good germinal idea that excites you, that sets your blood on fire.

Next, create a damn good three-dimensional thriller villain with a *physiology*, a *sociology*, and a *psychology* that fits the villain profile. This character will be the author of the plot behind the plot. Write a journal or a diary in the villain's voice, so that you get to know this vile character intimately. Once you know the villain down to the bone, find his or her dark mission and make a step sheet of the dark mission: This is the plot behind the plot.

Then create a damn good three-dimensional hero with a *physiology*, a *sociology*, and a *psychology* that fits the hero profile. Write a journal in the hero's voice so that you get to know your hero intimately.

Now you start your step sheet, creating other characters as you go. Making a step sheet is some of the best fun you can have writing. Just don't get too committed to anything. Any step you create is not set in stone; it's subject to change at any time. And remember—every good dramatic scene has this: a well-motivated character overcoming obstacles in pursuit of a goal. Keep reminding yourself of the seven pillars: high stakes, unity of opposites, seemingly impossible odds, moral struggle, ticking clock, menace, thriller-type characters. You can't keep all this in your mind as you go, of course, but you can keep checking back to make sure you have all or most of these elements in your plot.

To simplify things, I'll break up my step sheet for *Peace Day* into the five movements we already discussed so that it will be easier to follow.

I. The gripping opening.

II. The evil plot gets under way and the hero, in terrible trouble, fights a defensive battle.

III. The turning point (often a kind of symbolic death and rebirth). The hero goes on the offensive.

IV. The hero confronts the villain, who almost wins but is finally defeated in a slam-bang climax.

V. Resolution. Tells what happens to the major characters as a result of the hero's victory or defeat.

■ The Gripping Opening to *Peace Day*

Of all the scenarios I developed earlier for this book as demonstrations— *DXP*, *The Legend of Hungry Wolf*, *Code Red*, *Day Three*, *Hunting Season*, *Shadow Self*, *The Hunt for Jethro Potts*, *How Joe Smigelski Saves the World*, and *Peace Day*—I decided to use *Peace Day* to make a demonstration step sheet, not because it's the easiest of all the scenarios, but rather because it is the most challenging.

I set out in this book to show you how to create a damn good thriller, and many thrillers are complex. Creating a thriller is supposed to be fun, and it can't be fun if you get overwhelmed by the complexity of the plot that you're developing. Even a complex thriller plot is developed through simple steps, one at a time.

So let the fun begin. The story will take five days. It begins on a Monday and ends on Friday, except for the brief resolution some days later.

Movement I: *The gripping opening.*

1. *Peace Day* opens in objective viewpoint: A mysterious man is cleverly bypassing security to get into the International Association of the Sane conference at a hotel in San Francisco (raising story questions). He's short, with a hawkish face, and nervous. He's a high-energy person who darts from place to place, staying in the shadows. For all the audience knows, he may be a killer. He cleverly knocks out a security camera or two (we may not know what he's up to, but we clearly have a well-motivated character overcoming obstacles in pursuit of a goal).

   I have not figured out how he cleverly knocks out the cameras or bypasses security, but that's okay. This is a flexible step sheet; it is not set in stone. I'll figure it out later. Especially in the early drafts, there's no need to figure out these technical things, as the scene may be cut or radically changed and I'd have wasted a lot of time on it.

2. The mysterious figure gets to a railing on the second floor, looking down on the foyer of the lavish hotel packed with media types, cameras, lights. Protesters are jamming the doorways. There's a press conference under way. The cops are manhandling some protesters who managed to get in. Our mystery man might have a gun—but no, it's a camera. We switch to the mysterious figure's viewpoint (distant

third) and find out he's HARRY FELDT, a 26-year-old freelancer who sells to supermarket tabloids and Internet blogs (I wrote a full bio for him, journal and everything, because he's a major character). He starts taking some pictures. His main interest is in MARY CATHCART, 28 (I did a full bio of her as well), the conference coordinator and publicity director. She's bright and witty and speaks enthusiastically about what they intend to do at this conference: create a peace treaty for the future so that both Jews and Arabs may live free and prosper. This is a moral struggle. Using world opinion, they intend to shame their elders into signing the treaty.

Harry is jealous of Mary because of her success, which he imagines she did not earn. He thinks the whole idea of the peace conference is absurd (close third). Harry angles his camera toward one of the other reporters—apparently an Orthodox Jew, with ringlets, long beard, and a long black coat. It looks as though he's got something hidden under his coat . . . a gun? (Strong story question.) Harry shoots a quick couple of photos, then races downstairs to find a cop. He has a chance, he thinks, to expose a terrorist and get on the evening news. Harry would die to get on the evening news.

3. We're still in Harry's viewpoint, switching to objective. There are catcalls, shouts, chaos, and pushing and shoving from protesters, both anti-Israel and anti-Arab. A few bottles are tossed; a window is broken. Mary and her assistant, TOMMY ACRE, 35, a PR guy, a smiley-faced, glad-handing slime, try to keep control (wonderful conflict).

Harry frantically tries to get a cop's attention (conflict). He overhears the cops telling Mary of a message they just got: *Those who oppose the word of Allah will be punished. Mary Cathcart, take heed* (raising more story questions).

Mary dismisses the message with a smile and a laugh. Harry hates her for her damn bravado. Harry tells the cops he's spotted a reporter with a gun. He shows them his photos on the screen on his camera, but they can't make out a gun. The cops say the Orthodox Jewish reporter has press credentials—by the way, where are Harry's? He has none. The cops escort him out. He protests vehemently that they might have a terrorist in their midst (conflict). Harry is the excitable type.

> *I like this better as an opening than the others I played with. Here I have a well-motivated character overcoming obstacles in pursuit of goals, and at the same time there are strong story questions being raised and we get right into the conference, which is the vortex of the storm in this story. It may not be as gripping as the opening of Jaws, but I think it will be effective.*

4. As the cops are hauling Harry out, they bump into DANIEL LAP-POR, 24, a Jewish protester. He has hold of one of the Jewish members of the association, DAPHNE ZINE, 23. He's screaming at her that it's against God's will to give up land for peace with the Arabs and that she's fraternizing with the enemy (very nice conflict). NABIL YASIN, 26, an Arab member, gets Daniel to unhand her. She's grateful. Daphne and Nabil have a brief moment together amid the hubbub. She thanks Nabil but is wary of him. He is, after all, the enemy.

5. We switch viewpoint to Nabil. He leaves the chaos and meets secretly in an alley with ACHMED SALMI, 30, who is the head of a pro-Arab protest group (political, but nonviolent). This group is determined to see the conference fail. Nabil assures Achmed that everyone thinks that he, Nabil, is an idealistic, wide-eyed peacenik. He is going to be on the planning committee that will make the decisions about speakers and so on. Achmed is delighted. They plan to have Nabil denounce the Jews as Zionists and the Arabs who thought they could deal with these evil Zionists as fools, putting an end to this stupid peace movement (more story questions).

> *There is not much conflict in this scene. It is foreshadowing conflict and would definitely hold the audience's attention. On rewrite, I may be able to find some conflict. When the kidnapping*

*takes place, the audience will suspect that Achmed is involved—
and later the FBI will, too.)*

6. Back to Harry. He's on the street. He has been released by the cops and follows the Orthodox Jewish reporter through the crowd. Harry loses him but finds a wig and fake beard at the spot where he vanished (more story questions). Harry turns back to give the wig and beard to the cops and sees Mary being escorted by police officer LORI KELLY, 29 (tentatively the hero's lover/sidekick in the future—I did her bio as well), who is going to take her home. Harry tries to get Lori interested in his suspicions (more conflict). She says she'll turn the wig and beard over to the detectives, and she hopes that he didn't get his DNA all over them. Harry, the intrepid reporter, pesters Mary with questions that she sidesteps with humor. Mary and Lori leave in a patrol car. Harry follows stealthily on his battered old motorcycle.

*At all times I've tried to have a well-motivated character—
mostly Harry—overcoming obstacles in pursuit of a goal. The
secret of holding the audience's attention is to keep the conflicts
going, one after another after another. You should resist the temptation to have a boring, sit-down conversation full of a lot of
facts or philosophy you might want the reader to know. Through
the conflicts, the audience will learn everything they need to
know.*

7. Harry follows Mary and Lori. Using a clever come-on, he pesters Mary to give him an interview, but to no avail. She has the doorman block his entrance when she and Lori go in. Harry broods as he paces on the sidewalk, hoping to find a way in. He never gives up.

8. Later, Harry is still pacing out in front of Mary's apartment building and sees a large blond woman (Josh, the villain, in disguise) come out, pulling a large red trunk on wheels. He helps get the trunk into a cargo van. After the van leaves, he goes into the building and finds the doorman moaning on the floor, blood gushing from his head.

Realizing what's happened, Harry clicks a couple of photos, then races outside, jumps on his motorcycle, and chases after the van.

Mary is in the trunk: She's been kidnapped. This is the first plot point. A plot point is an event that sends a story off in a new direction. The first plot point, the one that takes the story out of the world of the everyday, is called the inciting incident. *The kidnapping of Mary is the inciting incident of* Peace Day. *Up until this point, the conflict had involved pesky protesters and reporters, a few vague threats, and a mysterious man disguised as an Orthodox Jew. Now suddenly, with this kidnapping, the stakes are much higher, and the story takes a new direction. In* How to Write a Damn Good Novel, *I referred to this rise in stakes as taking the story up to another* plateau.

If you're the sort who likes the three-act structure, this would be a good place to mark the end of Act 1, even though the three-act structure guys might say, Hey, we're not thirty pages into our screenplay yet. More like maybe ten or fifteen pages. So what do you do if you're following that formula? Stuff in some more pages? Gads, I hope not. You should add pages only when you need to exploit the scenes you have or you want to add complications that will exploit other conflicts. You don't add pages simply to satisfy some arbitrary page count.

The practice of dividing stage plays into acts was for the purpose of selling drinks to the audience back in the days when plays were competing with the bear baiting down the street for the audience's entertainment shillings. It has nothing to do with the integrity of dramatic structure. That a story has a beginning, a middle, and an end, I guess, creates the illusion that there are three acts, but sometimes you start a story in medias res *(in the middle of things), as in* For Whom the Bell Tolls, *and leave off the beginning. Other times (rarely done, but at times effective) you might cut off the end—or part of the end—for dramatic purposes, as in* Butch Cassidy and the Sundance Kid.

9. Harry, weaving in and out of traffic, follows the van through the streets of San Francisco. He clicks his lights off and follows through the dark streets to an abandoned factory. He watches as Mary in the trunk is unloaded, his devious black heart racing with excitement.

10. Back to Mary's apartment. Lori is tied up with tape, her head bleeding. She struggles with her bonds and manages to summon help. She's mad as hell at herself for being so stupid as to get whacked in the head and tied up.

11. We're in objective viewpoint. Josh (in the woman's disguise) takes the unconscious Mary out of the trunk inside the abandoned factory, down a labyrinth of dark hallways, and into a cell, where he chains her up.

12. In Harry's viewpoint—outside the warehouse—Harry watches as Josh, still in drag, drives away. He uses his lock-picking kit to stealthily get into the building, then finds his way down a bunch of hallways to Mary's cell. Through a crack in the door, he sees her chained to the wall. Giddy with delight, Harry goes back out and locks up after himself. He knows this kidnapping is going to be huge in the media. When the media frenzy hits its peak, he can say he just heard from an anonymous source where she's being held, and he'll be hailed as a hero and maybe even get a Pulitzer. And, as a bonus, that bitch can stay chained up for a while; it'll be good for her, teach her a little humility.

13. Later. Mary in her cell. She groggily comes awake and thinks that her kidnapper may hide from the FBI, but he'll never hide from Uncle Walter . . .

> *Okay, we have a gripping opening, lots of story questions raised, nice conflicts, lots of action, and gripping suspense. We've got a lot of thrills in our thriller. We have Mary Cathcart, a pure-hearted idealist, cruelly kidnapped and chained to the wall of a dank cell, creating some very powerful story questions about what will hap-*

pen to her. This is a situation of injustice the audience will want to see made right. So far, the story has been constructed on the seven pillars: high stakes, unity of opposites, seemingly impossible odds, moral struggle, ticking clock, menace, thriller-type characters. The clock is ticking only in the sense that Mary is in the hands of a villain, so there's a sense of urgency. But the ticking will get much louder later when Josh announces that he intends to decapitate her. The last line is a nice bridge to the hero, who is to be introduced next.

■ Peace Day Step Sheet Continues

Movement II: The evil plot gets under way and the hero, in terrible trouble, fights a defensive battle.

1. It's late in the afternoon, still on the first day. We're at the home of our hero, WALTER BUTTERFIELD, 38, in Crooked Creek, Virginia, in the Smoky Mountains. Walter is out riding with CASSIE THORN, 34. She's supposedly a former investment banker from New York who lost her job in the meltdown and moved to the country for her health. They're having a great time, jumping hedges, racing each other. She tells him she knows he's a bootlegger, kids him about it, says her granddad was a bootlegger and would love to see his still (he resists, so there's mild conflict). He plays it coy.

   Suddenly they're confronted by Walter's ex-wife, the lovely siren NORA (Irma Ruth), 36, who is with her latest boyfriend. Nora wants more money and uses her considerable flirtatious charms to get it. Walter's on fire for her but knows she's poison. He gives her what she wants. When she leaves, Cassie, seeing how much pain Nora causes him, consoles him.

   The conflicts here are not as intense as in the opening of the story, but there are still strong story questions operating because we know that terrible trouble is just around the corner for Wal-

ter. There is intense conflict with Nora, but the conflicts with Cassie are mild and what might be termed "happy conflict." This should work well: It would be good scene orchestration, contrasting the happy conflict with the horror of the kidnapping.

2. Walter takes Cassie to a cleverly hidden cave, and they stand at the entrance. He says the whole hill is hollowed out and he has a distillery inside that can manufacture five hundred gallons of illegal bourbon a day. Unfortunately, there are men working in there, and he doesn't want them to know he'd give away the location—it's supposed to be a secret.

   She whips out a badge and a two-way radio and calls in a swarm of ATF agents hidden in the nearby woods. She tells Walter she's sorry, but he's under arrest for violations of the Federal Alcohol Tax Act. She cuffs him. He offers no resistance. In fact, he handles the whole situation with wry humor. Like Samson, he moans, brought down by a woman.

   The agents swarm into the cave, but, alas, there's no still, no booze, no hollowed-out place, no men. Walter chuckles; the ATF guys are peeved. Cassie takes the handcuffs off Walter. She's crestfallen. Has he any idea how much the agency invested in this operation? As a taxpayer, he's shocked at the waste.

   The agents evaporate. His old nemesis is there, ATF AGENT-IN-CHARGE FELIX COLDIRON, 56, who swears they'll get him yet. He rides off, leaving Walter and Cassie alone.

   Walter, always the gentleman, tells Cassie there's no reason she can't stay for dinner as planned. He's serving barbecued ribs and cornbread and a really nice Cabernet Sauvignon from his own vineyard. She says okay, why not—her promotion has gone with the wind anyway.

3. As they ride to Walter's stately home, Walter's sister, Daisy, who lives with him and manages his household, comes riding toward him with the news that Mary's been kidnapped. She's frantic. She's certain

Mary's old boyfriend, Stewart Clark, has something to do with it. Walter calls one of his buddies, who has a plane to take him to New York.

I've changed Walter's backstory to fit developments in the story. Walter is now a horse breeder who loves to ride. He no longer plays chess. His passion for horses will fit perfectly with his other passion—Civil War history. The scene with him out riding with Cassie is an important one—the "introduction of the hero" scene. It's a pain to write because you want to show the audience what the character is like in his or her everyday life, but your hero has not yet gotten involved in the terrible trouble of the story. It's often hard to find drama in the hero's everyday life. What I have tried to do is to introduce Walter with a lot of nice conflict—the kind of conflict (involving his illegal business and Nora) that he would have in his everyday life. Frequently when key characters are introduced there is little conflict like real life when your daughter's new boyfriend drops by for an uneasy chat. When you create the introduction of the hero, remember that you don't want to just introduce a character; you want to introduce the character in a dramatic way, with conflict. What I have planned here should work fine. These scenes have conflict, they reveal what Walter is like and what his life is like, they have surprises, and hopefully we will sympathize, empathize, and identify with him. These scenes, too, are a good contrast to the kidnap sequence that comes before, making good scene orchestration.

4. Mary's apartment in San Francisco. LT. MORTON LAFARGE, 57, and INSP. RALLY JONES, 35, of the SFPD show up. The lieutenant is an old-time cop, beefy, intimidating, shrewd. The inspector is single, a fit and trim runner, a womanizer, vain, and political. He loves to get his picture on TV. Lieutenant LaFarge is disgusted with the way the world is going; all he wants to do is make captain and retire. Inspector Jones thinks what they have here is a first-class PR debacle for

the department, what with the press crawling all over his case and the FBI sure to be called in. He can't stand those assholes.

They're grilling Lori, who is hopping mad about blowing it and getting beaned. She tells them about Harry and the blond woman who hit her. They have the paramedics take her to the hospital, against her will. The cops start canvassing the area. Suddenly FBI agents are swarming all over the place with their lab guys and expensive equipment. It's not known who called them (turns out it was Josh, claiming to be the November Jihad). To the FBI, it looks like a pro job; the surveillance system at the building had been knocked out. The FBI team is headed up by SPECIAL AGENT ALICE DORN, 40.

LaFarge says, "The circus has come to town."

Jones says, "Ain't it grand?"

5. We're with Tommy Acre, the PR guy, at the hotel. You may recall that he's Mary's assistant. He's trying to settle some squabble among participants over the shape of a table when the police tell him of the kidnapping. The Jews blame the Arabs; the Arabs blame the Jews. Chaos reigns. An e-mail arrives: *We've got Mary Cathcart. She will pay for her crimes against Islam.* It's signed, *November Jihad.*

Tommy immediately sees what a bonanza this is for his career. He calls a press conference.

6. We're with Mary Cathcart. She's in her little cell, blinded by bright lights, being photographed by Josh. She spits at her kidnapper and swears at him. "You're going to be a TV star," he says in a disguised voice. "Everyone in the world will soon know your name."

She thinks it over after he's gone. He was disguising his voice. Why? Because she knows him! She thinks he must be one of the people at the conference, or one of the protesters, or maybe Stewart Clark, her old boyfriend.

She starts making a mental list of who it might be as she returns to work on getting the chain out of the wall.

■ A Note About the Process of Making a Step Sheet

In the course of working out the plot, as I said, you will find yourself changing your mind about things, such as Walter's newfound passion for riding. When I first planned the kidnapping, Harry Feldt was going to be killed on his way out of the place where Mary was being held prisoner. Now I see that Harry's keeping his discovery a secret would be very suspenseful, so I let him live. As you make your step sheet, don't be in a hurry. Keep looking for interesting twists and turns; keep brainstorming and you'll find them.

A good thing to do is make a few lists and keep referring to them.

- Make a list of characters. Refer to the list often and ask yourself what these characters are up to. I ask myself, What is the FBI doing now? What are the San Francisco cops doing now? What is Josh doing now? What is Daisy doing now? What is Mary doing now? What is Stewart Clark doing now?

- Make a list of possible clues.

- Make a list of possible complications, twists and turns in the plot, and surprises.

- Make a list of things that need to be followed up. As an example, the FBI will surely check out the e-mail message sent to the conference that made the threat on Mary Cathcart and try to track it back to the sender.

Okay, I ask myself about what the characters are doing offstage at this time. Here are some answers:

- Josh is planting clues to lead the FBI to an innocent Arab.

- Walter is flying to New York.

- At the conference: The Arab protesters think this is a plot by the Jews to make them look bad.

- Lori's at the hospital getting treated.

- At the conference: The Jews blame the Arabs.

- Harry Feldt is getting his best sport coat cleaned so he'll look good on TV.

- Stewart Clark, Mary's old boyfriend, thinks he'll be a suspect because they had a terrible fight that got physical. He knows the story of Mary and Josh, so he thinks Josh might be involved. He has not heard that Josh died, supposedly, in a fiery suicide. Stewart now puts the picture of Josh on his blog and sends out thousands of e-mails to gamers telling them to be on the lookout for this guy. Josh has software that scans the Internet for his own name and intercepts this e-mail. Josh tracks Stewart down and kills him.

When you meditate on what all the characters are up to, you often find little nuggets of plot gold you didn't know were there.

■ *Peace Day* Step Sheet Continues

7. The FBI is at Harry Feldt's apartment. They grill him and check out his camera; there are no photos in the memory. They take his laptop. He screams about it: freedom of the press, blah, blah, blah. He doesn't really mind; it isn't his real laptop. He doesn't tell them that he followed the cargo van, of course.

   THIS SCENE HAS BEEN OMITTED. *At times you will make a step and then later realize that you don't need it. Harry can tell Walter and Lori when they show up that the FBI agents have grilled him. There's no point in showing this scene to the audience, as nothing happens in it that advances the plot.*

8. It's morning of the second day, Tuesday. We're at Mary's apartment. The FBI is still there, finding lots of clues, fibers, hair, while the two

bleary-eyed San Francisco detectives look on helplessly. Walter shows up. The FBI guys patronize him, deny him any info, tell him to leave it up to the pros. The FBI profilers think they understand November Jihad perfectly (Josh has done his homework). But Walter sees what the FBI does not see: that the villain has deliberately left clues, including the piece of pipe used on Lori. He does not tell them about Stewart Clark; he doesn't want them spooking him. He thinks federal officers are a bunch of incompetents. He finds out from Inspector Jones and Lieutenant LaFarge what happened and that Lori is in the hospital, also that this November Jihad is a previously unknown group. (A lot of nice conflict here: Walter pushing for what he wants, the FBI resisting.)

9. At the hospital, Walter finagles his way into seeing Lori (exactly how he does this is still to be worked out). Lori, remember, is to be the sidekick/lover for Walter in this thriller—at least that's my plan. I hope they like each other. Oh, that's right. I'm playing God. I'll make sure they like each other, even though they're far different.

At first she's a little put off by his too-smooth southern charm. She's a hard-bitten Brooklynite. She's got her "Brooklyn up," she says, about being blindsided by a bimbo. She tells him to go back home: The fibbies (FBI) won't like him getting in the way and could throw him in the lockup for obstruction if he blows his nose wrong. Besides, these terrorists are dangerous people, and since he's an amateur, he could get hurt. He says he's come to find his niece, and by God, he intends to do just that. Lori finds herself liking him but sees him as naïve. Walter sees her as crude. He prefers a "womanly" woman. He gets her to tell him about Harry Feldt—including what happened at the press conference. Walter calls a good-ol'-boy computer guy back home, who will get him Harry's address in no time. Even though the docs want to keep Lori for observation, she leaves with Walter. She says she wants to stop by her place and get some civvies.

*As you can see, now that we're in Movement II, the hero is sort of ·
at a loss, grabbing at straws. This is what I mean by "fights a*

defensive battle." In this movement, the hero is fumbling for clues; he has no idea who the villain is and has no solid leads to follow.

10. Back to Walter and Lori. We're at Lori's apartment. She's changed her clothes while Walter has been on his cell phone with his computer guy back home to get Feldt's address. We see that Lori has two dartboards full of darts. Each of the boards has a large photo of a different man. "Exes," Lori says. "I have one myself," Walter says. "I must get a set of darts immediately upon returning home."

> *This is the scene that was written in chapter 9 as an example of how the scene would look taken from a step in the step sheet. In this step there is very little conflict indicated, but in the scene there was a lot of conflict. The steps keep you on the beam plotwise. You still have to work out the conflicts and emotions of the scenes.*

11. We're with Mary in her cell. She's determined that the voice she's hearing is on a tape and she's hearing the same conversation over and over again.

12. Change of viewpoint to the villain, Josh, who sees Mary scratching away through a hidden camera and is much amused. He's enjoying this.

13. We're at the FBI headquarters. There's been a one-hundred-thousand-dollar reward announced, and leads are flooding in. Walter and Lori arrive, summoned by the FBI because they have a break in the case. FBI agents are grilling an Arab-American suspect whose fingerprints were found on the piece of pipe used to clobber Lori. He says he has no alibi because he goes to work at two in the morning and he was asleep at the time of the kidnapping. He saw the piece of pipe in the hallway of his apartment building and picked it up and put it in the trash, but he didn't hit anyone with it. Yes, he has been arrested at pro-Arab demonstrations, but that does not make him a terrorist,

blah, blah, blah. They keep pressing (all nice conflict). News comes that a search of his apartment reveals that he's linked to a terrorist group. No matter how much the FBI pressures him, he protests that he doesn't know where Mary is, never owned a gun, and has no idea how one got in his house. But the FBI guys are sure they have their man and are basking in media glory. They won't let Walter speak to him. Walter has his doubts and tells them so. People this smart don't leave pieces of pipe around with their fingerprints on them. The FBI guys tell him he's crazy—crooks are always leaving fingerprints around, and terrorists are notorious amateurs who make all kinds of mistakes. This man fits the Arab terrorist profile perfectly. Walter says he knows when he's being conned. He and Lori leave for Harry Feldt's place.

14. On the way to Harry's place, Walter takes a detour and goes to where Stewart Clark, Mary's old boyfriend, works as a computer game programmer. Stewart is not in, and nobody's seen him. When he heard about the kidnapping on the news, he became distressed, his boss says. He had cleaned up his life after Mary threw him out, and he was apparently still mad about her. Lori flashes her badge to get his home address.

15. In the car again, Walter is excited. Stewart Clark is just the kind of guy who could pull off something like this and might get a thrill out of playing cops and robbers with the feds. Lori gets a cell phone call. Her detective buddies have checked out Walter: They tell her he's a bootlegger with nineteen arrests. "No convictions," Walter tells her.

16. We're at Harry Feldt's place. Walter and Lori grill him and get descriptions of the blonde and the fake Orthodox Jewish reporter. It could be Stewart Clark. Walter is really excited now. Harry can't stop whining about the FBI taking his computer (that occurred offstage in the scene I cut out). From the description of the way the blonde walked, Walter thinks it might have been a guy. Walter notices that

Harry is getting spiffed up and wonders why. Walter leans on him and he does shake a little, but he sticks to his story.

17. Walter and Lori go to Stewart Clark's place. His car is in its parking space. Walter and Lori get into his apartment. There are all kinds of medieval weapons and torture machines scattered about. We've got our guy, Walter says. But then they find Stewart dead on the floor with a Roman sword through his belly as if he'd fallen on it. On the computer screen there's a video playing of a cartoon figure that looks like Stewart, taking money from cartoon Arabs, who put a woman in a trunk and drive off with her. Walter wants to get a computer genius there to dig into these hard drives, but Lori insists on calling the FBI. It's part of their investigation—she's duty-bound. Walter calls his computer guy to find out what he can about Stewart. He connects the guy through to Stewart's computer so he can download the entire contents of the hard drive if he can get past the password. The computer whiz says he'll give it a try. Lori says this can get them a long stretch in Leavenworth. Walter wants to know if she'd be his cell mate. You're not my type, she says. She doesn't go for men with criminal minds, even well-mannered ones.

Josh got there first, obviously, and killed Clark and left the bizarre cartoon.

18. Soon, the FBI guys show up. In the room full of weapons, Walter notes there are at least ten better ways to kill yourself than falling on your sword. Stewart must have known that Roman noblemen slit their veins and sat in a hot bath—almost painless. Walter realizes now that Stewart is definitely not the guy who kidnapped Mary, but he could have helped with the planning. When they discover the computer's firewall has been breached, the FBI tells him to leave. He loses his temper with them. It's his niece, damn it!

19. In the car, Lori tries to cool Walter down. He says he hasn't lost his temper like this since he was in high school. She sides with the FBI. They are a bunch of arrogant assholes, she says, but they do get results.

Walter remains dubious. Why, if she thinks he has a criminal mind and the FBI is doing a great job, is she going along with him? To keep him out of trouble, she says. The San Francisco Mayor's Office has a campaign calling on all San Franciscans to be nice to visitors during the economic downturn.

20. Harry Feldt is watching Josh's hideout from a neighboring rooftop. He sees Josh come and go and takes pictures of him. He sees some kids slip through the fence once in a while. He tells them the police are watching the place and no trespassing is allowed.

21. We're in the cell with Mary. There are kids playing somewhere in the building. She calls to them, but they don't hear her.

22. At the conference, there's a lot of hubbub, but the participants vote to carry on. The TV news folks are crawling all over the place—lots of nice excitement.

23. At a workshop at the conference, the program continues. Jews are role-playing Arabs, and Arabs are role-playing Jews. Nabil has his turn: He has to pretend he's an actual Jewish person whose father is killed in a suicide bombing. A Jew is playing a man like Nabil's grandfather, who lost his orchard when the Jews took over. (Lots of conflict to be exploited here. Also, we'll see how hard it is to crack through all the hatred, even among well-meaning people who desire peace.)

24. Achmed, who has no connection to Josh or any real terrorists, gives Nabil some incriminating, handwritten diagrams of the conference hotel and Mary's apartment to plant on the Jews, making it look as if they are involved in the kidnapping. Nabil tries to get out of doing it, but Achmed leans on him.

25. Though Nabil's conscience bothers him, he sneaks into a Jew's room to leave the incriminating evidence. Daphne catches him in the act. Nabil tells Daphne his story: An out-of-work teacher, he was recruited by activists to participate in the conference and then disrupt it, but

now he believes in it. He thinks there's little hope of success, but it's better than no hope at all. The Jewish people he's met don't seem to be the monsters he was always told they were. Daphne doesn't turn him in. Nabil is relieved and grateful.

26. Nabil meets with Achmed and tells him he's quitting their group. He can't live with this hatred his whole lifetime. Somebody has to stop it, and here and now is a good place and a good time. Achmed beats the crap out of him.

27. Harry Feldt gets pictures of this beating. He loves it. The more combat, the better.

28. Walter and Lori meet with the FBI chief and plead to be allowed to talk to Arab Suspect A. There was a beer can left at the scene of Stewart Clark's place, and the prints on it belong to an American living in Saudi Arabia. Walter says that's odd—there was no beer in the fridge. No booze at all in the house, and the dead man was cleaning up his act, according to his boss. More evidence that the FBI is being led around by the nose. Since they've gotten nowhere with Suspect A, they let Walter talk to him as long as the man's lawyer is present.

    Although you and I know who's behind all this and what is really happening, please keep in mind that the audience at this point will think this is a story of Islamic terrorism—or Jewish terrorism—so it is possible Stewart is involved, just as the FBI say he is.

29. Interview with Arab Suspect A. Walter wants to know if the suspect has had any problems with his fellow protesters or if anyone else might be framing him. How did the evidence get planted? He says his sister did see someone coming out of his apartment. . . .

30. Walter and Lori interview Suspect A's sister, who says she got a good look at the intruder and his distinctive Oakland A's jacket. They get her to work with the police sketch artist. The facial features are different, but Walter thinks it could be the same guy who was posing as

an Orthodox Jew—and maybe even the blonde. They are all the same size.

31. At Lori's place, Lori and Walter try to find someone among the photos the police took of the protesters and the people at the conference who might be this guy. Special Agent Alice Dorn shows up. She wants info on how they got the drawing of the guy in the Oakland A's jacket. Walter says he'll tell her only if she'll let him talk to the man first when they find him. She agrees (but doesn't, as we'll see). She takes the drawing and photos and says she'll be right back. Walter and Lori crash from need of sleep.

32. It's the third day, Wednesday. Lori wakes Walter. Alice Dorn is on TV. They've arrested the man in the drawing. He's Arab Suspect B with ties to the blind sheikh convicted in the Twin Towers bombing in 1993.

33. Walter and Lori visit the FBI to congratulate Alice Dorn for arresting Arab Suspect B, angry that she lied to them about letting Walter interview him first. Walter wonders if they're any closer to finding his niece. She says they're working on it. Just then word comes that on Friday at noon, when the group is to sign the treaty of love, Mary will be beheaded. Walter is stunned. He unloads on Special Agent Dorn for wanting publicity but not giving a damn about results, and for being inept and not that bright. Walter is escorted out.

34. Outside, Walter is perturbed with himself. He never loses his temper. Lori says he's her hero. They have no time to waste on nonsense. He talks of his fond memories of Mary (exploiting emotions). The two detectives call: They want to meet Lori and Walter at Lori's place.

34A. The detectives have been digging into Mary's career and discovered she coauthored a book that got a dentist sent up for sexual abuse. After he got out, the chief witness against him disappeared. Lori gets his address. This feels right to Walter; this is the kind of fellow who could do it: smart, educated, highly motivated.

You'll notice that I added a 34a. to the steps when I thought, Gee, Mary's a reporter, surely she would have enemies. This will have to be handled cleverly. The FBI would be pursuing suspects—I'll have to dream up some reason the police got this lead first. Maybe the FBI has an all-points out on the guy and the San Francisco detectives have arranged for the dentist's parole officer to have the wrong address for him in the file by mistake.

35. Harry Feldt is at home practicing his spot on TV after he announces that he knows where Mary is. On TV, there is hot coverage of the promised beheading. Tommy Acre, the Sane conference PR guy, is getting a lot of time on camera. Harry is flush with excitement. Soon it will be him on camera; maybe he'll even be on *Good Morning America* and *60 Minutes*.

35A. Walter and Lori find the dentist sitting in a park near his home. His mind is gone.

36. Walter and Lori go to her place. The two SFPD detectives show up and report to Walter and Lori on what they know about Arab Suspect B. He's an anti-Israel Palestinian who has spent time for throwing rocks during the first intifada, then lied on his visa application and snuck into the United States under the radar in 1991. But since then, he's been a deli owner, paid his taxes, and behaved himself. Walter wants to know whom he loves and who loves him. Arab Suspect B's daughter and son-in-law died in a car accident, and he's the sole support of his granddaughter.

37. Walter and Lori meet with Tommy Acre, the PR guy. Walter wants to know if he's behind this—after all, it's made him a media star. He swears he's not involved.

Offstage, Tommy Acre has been meeting with Achmed to work out details of how they can make a bigger protest, get more press, and grab more airtime for Tommy. When the cops follow Tommy, they'll think they have a hot lead, but their bosses turn over this info to the FBI.

38. Walter persuades Special Agent Dorn to let him talk to Arab Suspect B. In the interview, Walter shows him pictures of the granddaughter and tells him to imagine how he'd feel if she were to be beheaded, that he feels the same about his niece as Arab Suspect B does about his granddaughter. Arab Suspect B tells him that he knows people who know people who might know something about the November Jihad. He is no terrorist. He wants to be a good American. He tells Walter there is an imam who might help him if he (Arab Suspect B) gave him a note, which he does.

39. Walter and Lori visit the imam, who agrees to see them only because Walter has the note. No one he knows is involved with this, and anyway it's impossible: He never heard of this November Jihad. He's absolutely convinced that the Jews are making up all this November Jihad stuff to make Muslims look bad, that Jews are monsters capable of any crime. Walter has never seen a man so full of hatred but believes him when he says there is no such group as the November Jihad.

40. Walter and Lori visit the Jewish protester Daniel Lappor. No Jew would do this. Look for a single incident where a Jew threatened to cut off someone's head. It's not what a Jew would do. Lori, who's been madly reading the files, reminds him of the Jewish terrorists at the formation of Israel and the Jewish Defense League. That's all true: The hatred against the Jews has provoked this even among the religious Jews, whose entire lives are devoted to becoming righteous. A Jew who beheaded a helpless hostage would be expelled from the community and shamed forever. Walter believes him, too.

41. Walter and Lori are at her place, going through photos, police reports—all kinds of stuff—and they're totally frustrated. Lori argues that it has to be terrorists; who else would do something like this? Walter doesn't know. He wanted it to be Stewart Clark or the mad

dentist. They're running out of time. Lori has hope the FBI will break it wide open. Walter says he brought up his niece to be strong; he hopes she can die with dignity.

This is the dark moment, where it feels absolutely impossible that the evil will be foiled.

12

■ Avoiding the Muddle in the Middle

How to Create a Damn Good Climax

You will notice at times that thrillers will have a gripping opening, then begin to sag. They become lethargic and seem to run out of gas. This might be the fault of creative writing coaches who hammer home the point that a story ought to have a gripping beginning and a smashing climax; but what about the middle? It's sometimes thought of as a sort of bridge between the exciting spots. Often this bridge sags under its own weight, and even more often, in an attempt to be clever, the plot gets overly complicated and muddled, and a small army of characters keeps marching through the scenes, leaving the audience wondering who is who and who is doing what to whom.

Writers, when they sense their stories are sagging, have a tendency to pile on the subplots.

Although a story comes at the audience in waves of excitement, even the troughs in these waves should have conflict and powerful story questions operating. The story movements are, as in a symphony, made up of a series of crescendos of rising excitement, one after another, after another, after another, from the gripping opening to the smashing climax. There should be no sag, no letdown. In *Peace Day*'s Movement II, the hero is fighting a defensive battle because he really doesn't know or understand the terrible trouble he's in. So far, there is no sag because the hero is engaged in conflict at all times and there is terrible trouble aplenty, with the promise of more to come.

Okay, this is extremely important: In a damn good thriller, there should be rising conflict at all times. There is never a moment (except during the resolution following the climax) where there is not a well-motivated character overcoming obstacles in pursuit of a goal. In *How to Write a Damn Good Novel*, I proclaimed that the three great principles of drama are *conflict, conflict, conflict*! Don't forget these three great principles.

To help you avoid midstory sag, let me tell you a few things to keep in mind. I've discovered after over twenty-five years of teaching creative writing and running fiction writing workshops that much of what passes for "knowledge of craft" is actually "writer's attitude." What? you say. But how can that be?

Let's say I'm going to teach a beginner how to write dialogue. One of the first things I'm going to teach is that dialogue is not just conversation. Dialogue is conversation in conflict. So to understand the difference, a writer needs to know what conflict is: Conflict is a dramatic presentation of an opposition of wills. Conversation without conflict is boring; dialogue with conflict is gripping. Well, hopefully it's gripping.

Most beginner's writing books, such as *How to Write a Damn Good Novel*, will go into greater detail on the subject. Here's just a tiny example of conversation:

> "Good morning, dear," Mildred said.
> "Morning," Edgar said in return.
> "Have a good sleep?"
> "Fair. You?"
> "Fine."
> "That new mattress we got is great."
> "Indeed it is. Air support, nothing like it."
> "Did you see them clouds? It's going to rain today."
> "Is it?"
> "That's what the paper says."

That's enough. I can't bring myself to write another line of this dreck. Okay, now let's take a look at what a little conflict does to conversation:

"Morning," Mildred said.

"Don't 'morning' me," Edgar said. "That goddamn mattress you bought has put my back into a corkscrew."

"Mattress I bought? What the hell are you talking about? You're the one who wanted this goddamn air mattress crap. My side was but half-inflated last night."

"Okay, then you won't mind if I take it back."

"That's so like you, to take a mattress back, tied with my clothesline to the roof of our poor little Volkswagen in the rain. . . ."

So much for my little melodrama. It's clearly more absorbing with conflict. Now then, for a writer, infusing a scene with conflict is not a difficult thing. Characters who want something, who have a will to go after something, and other characters or physical barriers that prevent it from happening, create an opposition of wills, and that is conflict. Is it difficult? No. Does it take a vast knowledge of craft? No. Then why, as a creative writing teacher, do I see scene after scene with no conflict in it?

It is because the writers of such scenes have not made a decision to write scenes with conflict. Their intent is to write scenes that mimic real life, which is chock-full of boring conversations.

So it is not a matter of not knowing craft; it is a matter of having made bad decisions. Good vs. bad decision making is a matter of attitude.

Before you write any scene, ask yourself, What do these characters want? Give all the characters an agenda, something they want to get. Let's say that Walter and Lori want some information from a neighbor of Suspect A, to find out whether he's seen anything suspicious. If you spend a few moments thinking of who this neighbor is and what he might want from Walter or Lori, you might have much more conflict than if you think only of what Walter and Lori want.

■

The following is a sample scene where only Lori is canvassing the neighborhood and wants some information. This is the kind of scene I often get from beginning thriller writers in my workshops. In fact, when I first started taking workshops, I wrote many scenes like this:

> "Hello, sir," Lori says. "I'm a police officer, and we're checking to see if you might have seen anything strange going on at your neighbor's house. You know, people coming and going at all hours, maybe."
> "No, I have not seen anything like that."
> "Any strange noises?"
> "No."
> "Political meetings?"
> "No."

This kind of dialogue is called *back-and-forth-ing* and is quite dull, even if it is sort of in conflict. You will see it sometimes in published novels or in thriller films. Let's give the neighbor an agenda of his own and see what happens:

> "Hello, sir," Lori says. "I'm a police officer, and we're checking to see if you might have seen anything strange going on at your neighbor's house. You know, people coming and going at all hours, maybe."
> "Gee, would you like to come in?"
> "No, we just have a few questions."
> "Would you mind answering a question for me?"
> "What?"
> "Have you been saved?"
> "I'm here to ask you about what's been going on next door."
> "You should be more worried about your soul."

You can see how this would lead to a lot of nice dramatic conflict. Or maybe this instead:

"Hello, sir," Lori says. "I'm a police officer, and we're checking to see if you might have seen anything strange going on at your neighbor's house. You know, people coming and going at all hours, maybe."

"Well . . . hello . . . are you really a cop?"

"Yes."

"Would you like to come in? Want some coffee? What are you doing tonight? I've got a couple of great show tickets."

You can see how this, too, could develop into some nice conflict, as each tries to get something from the other.

Back-and-forth-ing might be bad, but *informational dialogue* is even worse. In fiction, it's unforgivable. In film there may be a need for a tiny amount, but when I say tiny, I mean tiny—not more than a line or two.

In fiction, informational dialogue goes like this:

Lori put down the phone. Walter was looking at her. "Well?" he said.

"That was Lieutenant LaFarge. He says that he's checked out Stewart Clark. He was born in Ohio, June tenth, 1975. He has a juvenile arrest record: joyriding and making copies of copyrighted software disks. His mother was a Presbyterian minister, and his father was a math teacher and something of a chess prodigy. They moved to New York when he was ten. He won a scholarship to Purdue University, where he studied computer graphics and won a prize in a computer graphics contest when he was a junior. He's worked in the software industry all his adult life. Those who know him call him a supergeek."

As you can see, there is no conflict in this dialogue. Reading the phone book would be more fun. Now, say there is information that you must get across to the audience. How do you do it without using informational dialogue? You can use dramatic narrative:

> At about ten o'clock at night, Lieutenant LaFarge called and excitedly told them that they had tracked down Stewart Clark. He was born June 10, 1975, and had a juvenile arrest record for joyriding and making copies of software disks. This, the lieutenant found amusing, and he also thought it was funny that Stewart was the son of a Presbyterian minister mother and a math teacher father who was something of a chess prodigy. . . .

You get the idea. Information in dramatic narrative is easier to read than informational dialogue.

To write dramatic conflict dialogue and have information conveyed in it is not all that difficult. You just need to give characters an agenda. You do it like this:

> Lori put down the phone. Walter was looking at her anxiously (let's get a little emotion in here). "Well?" he asked.
>
> "That was Lieutenant LaFarge. He says that he's checked out Stewart Clark. He was born in Ohio, June tenth, 1975—"
>
> "Hold it. Did he say anything important, anything we can use?"
>
> "Not really. He has a juvenile arrest record."
>
> "For what?"
>
> "Joyriding and making copies of copyrighted software disks."
>
> "Hardly terrorist activities. Anything else?"
>
> "LaFarge said his mother was a Presbyterian minister, and his father was a math teacher and something of a chess prodigy. They moved to New York when he was ten. . . ."
>
> "Christ, is this what cops do, dance around with twiddle like this?"

You get the idea.

It's all a matter of your attitude. Give every character an agenda and put conflict in every line, and you'll avoid the muddle in the middle. And everyone will say you're a master of the craft.

Okay, back to *Peace Day*.

■ *Peace Day* Step Sheet Continues

Movement III of the story shows the actions from the turning point in about the middle of the story to *the obligatory scene*. The obligatory scene is where all the story questions are answered with the exception of the most important one, and that one is, "Will the evil be foiled?" That question keeps the reader turning the pages. It will be answered in the showdown with the villain at the climax.

The story questions that have already been answered are questions such as "Will the hero get the helpers he or she needs?" "Will the hero uncover the villain's evil plot?" "Will the hero get the weapons he or she needs?" "Will the hero be betrayed?" "Will the hero be able to find out who's the villain?" and so on.

In *High Noon*, the obligatory scene is when the marshal faces the fact that he's not going to get anyone to help him in the showdown with the villain, and he writes his will, loads his guns, and goes out into the empty street while the whistle of the noon train is heard. The only story question left is the showdown. Sometimes, following the showdown scene, there's a surprise. In *High Noon*, the surprise comes when his pacifist Quaker bride, who said she was leaving, stays and fights.

In *The Day of the Jackal*, the obligatory scene is the day of the planned assassination, when the hero and his minions go out to see if they can stop the Jackal from killing President de Gaulle at the Bastille Day celebrations. The obligatory scene is a short one. It's when the hero discovers that the Jackal, impersonating a disabled veteran, has penetrated the security lines and is in the apartment from which he will shoot de Gaulle. The surprise comes when the villain gets his shot and misses. The hero shoots him before he can get off a second shot.

In *Goldfinger*, the obligatory scene is when Bond realizes that Goldfinger's secret plan is to nuke the gold in Fort Knox, but he is unable to get help because he's been taken captive. The surprise comes when Pussy Galore switches sides and calls in reinforcements.

Movement III: *The turning point (often a kind of symbolic death and rebirth). The hero goes on the offensive.*

1. It's the early hours of the fourth day, Thursday. Mary is in her cell, working her gag loose. She hears somebody outside and gets excited. It's somebody stealing copper wire cable running down the side of the building. She yells to whoever it is that she's Mary Cathcart—call the cops! Tell Uncle Walter! She's knows he's looking for her; he would not leave it up to the cops.

2. Josh, asleep in a room near Mary's cell, is awakened by an electronic device monitoring Mary. He sees the copper thief running toward his truck. Josh races into the street, jumps in his van, and takes off after the thief but loses him.

3. The crook stops a police car. He demands the reward—he's found the missing woman!

4. Inspector Rally Jones has been summoned to the neighborhood police station. The copper thief seems to be telling the truth, but Rally doesn't want to jump into anything and maybe get somebody killed. He listens to the crook tell where he heard Mary scream. It's just one more crank, he thinks, but they can't afford not to check on it. But then the crook says he heard the woman say, "Tell Uncle Walter," and Rally knows it must be Mary Cathcart. He calls his bosses. He's going to need plenty of backup. They tell him they must call the FBI; it will have to be a joint operation.

5. We're at Lori's place, early morning. Lori is sleeping at a table with her head on a mountain of photos and papers. Bleary-eyed Walter is still trying to find photos that fit the guy wearing disguises. Lori gets a call. The police think they found Mary!

6. Harry Feldt is getting dressed so he'll look good on TV. He's got his TV set on: Breaking news . . . Mary Cathcart may have been found! There are photos of cops galore surrounding the factory. Harry is devastated.

7. Walter and Lori arrive at the factory. Alice Dorn is there all bent out of shape because the SFPD blew it—the perp took Mary and got away. Alice is hogging the camera, as usual. Walter looks at the cell. There's all kinds of stuff in Arabic, some of it handwritten, left behind. There are fibers and fingerprints galore, enough to keep the FBI labs busy for years. Mary, sometime during her incarceration, had scratched messages on the wall, but Josh had obliterated them. Walter keeps looking and finds marks on the bottom of the cot that say, "MYBT." It's inside a horseshoe shape. A message for him, he's sure. Only he has no idea what the hell it means.

8. Walter and Lori go to the horse stables in Golden Gate Park to think things through. It's about dawn. The early morning riders are there. Walter has no idea what "MYBT" means, and neither does Lori. He calls Daisy. She says years ago when Mary was working on the exposé of the crooked writer, she called it her "breakthrough," which she shortened to "BT" when she referred to the project. That would be Josh Pape, Daisy adds, who everyone knows is dead.

9. Harry Feldt installs a listening device at Lori's apartment.

10. Walter and Lori meet with the two San Francisco detectives. They ask the detectives whether it's possible Josh Pape could still be alive. Lt. LaFarge has contacts in New York. He says he'll check. Meanwhile, Lori and Walter go through everything they have on Josh Pape.

11. When Josh Pape first got into drugs, he was into rock and roll, with a talent for playing drums. He was a showman and a perfectionist. This fits perfectly, Walter thinks, with this whole show he's making of the kidnapping. The more they look at Josh, the more Walter is certain.

Alice Dorn comes by to tell them they have lots of leads brought in by the promise of the reward, and they are broadcasting on TV photos of the men they think are in the November Jihad. The reward is now two hundred thousand. Walter tries to tell Alice that it's Josh Pape, but as she's taking down the info on Josh, LaFarge shows up. He tells them the New York cops checked the DNA of the body that was burned up in this Viking funeral, as the tabloids called it—it was Pape for sure. In his suicide note, Pape said he wanted a Viking funeral. He shot himself after setting on fire the car he was sitting in, the seats soaked with gas. The guy is double dead. Alice Dorn gives Walter an "I told you so" look and leaves.

The ticking clock is ticking loudly: There's twenty-four hours to go.

Josh's being into rock and roll will need changes in his backstory, and when it's actually written, more changes might be made.

12. After Alice Dorn leaves, Walter calls his computer guy, who has been going over Stewart Clark's computer files. He reports that the day before he died, Stewart sent an e-mail with a photo to users of his games asking if anyone had seen the man in the photo. He got four responses, all saying the guy was dead. His name was Josh Pape. The computer guy says Stewart checked and found the guy was dead, so it didn't make much sense to send out his picture anymore. It looks as though Stewart also sent what seemed like a good-bye letter to all his fans shortly before the time of his death. After he hangs up, Walter says that settles it, Josh Pape is alive. Lori and the two detectives are astonished that Walter would come to this conclusion. Look, Walter says, Stewart sends out the e-mail with Josh Pape's photo. Stewart was a geek, probably never read the news and didn't know Pape was reported dead. Pape must have been scanning the Internet with spy software and saw his photo going around. That must have given him a jolt. He figures Stewart is a threat, so he kills him, making it look as though he fell on his sword.

Lori says it still does not explain how the DNA matches. DNA does not lie.

Where do they get the DNA to use as the sample? Walter asks. A hairbrush? A toothbrush? Pape knows how they investigate. All he had to do was leave hair on his comb or brush, hair from the guy he burned up . . . the FBI believes its science can't lie. Josh Pape is having fun with them. It's Josh Pape, I'm certain, now all we have to do is find him.

13. The FBI swoops down on Achmed, the protester. Josh has left fibers that the FBI found at Mary's place matching Achmed's sweater, and an anonymous tip led them to him. In the abandoned factory where Mary had been held, they find Achmed's writings, along with directions to Mary's apartment and lots of correspondence to other members of the November Jihad. They find bomb-making equipment in his car and a whole lot of explosives in his cupboard that he swears he never saw . . . and they have a witness, Nabil, who says that Achmed tried to frame a Jew and ruin the conference.

14. Alice Dorn holds a press conference and announces the arrests—they have broken the back of the November Jihad.

15. We're with Mary and Josh. No point in keeping his identity a secret from her anymore, her life expectancy being so short. Josh is enjoying himself. He knows the FBI computer guys will soon find that the e-mails he sent in Achmed's name were plants, and the FBI will have egg all over their faces and the media will have fresh meat to chew on. Mary is trying to show sympathy and apologizes for what she did to him, trying to understand him. He thinks she has Stockholm syndrome, and that delights him. He plays along. Then his software that scans for his name on the Internet finds that Harry Feldt put out a streaming video on his blog that identifies Josh as the kidnapper and Stewart Clark's murderer. He shows dozens of photos of him.

Josh gags Mary, puts on a hasty disguise, and leaves hurriedly.

16. Josh kidnaps Harry as he leaves an interview with the media, where he's been having a great time basking in media glory.

17. Alice Dorn meets with her team. They just got a tip that a man, possibly Josh Pape—though she doesn't believe it's him—has rented a sound studio. They have a warrant and they're going to check it out.

18. Walter and Lori are taken to the sound stage—it looks just like the TV studio where Josh was exposed, only there's an executioner's block and a headsman's ax. Alice Dorn has to admit that this is possibly the work of Josh Pape. All they have to do is wait for him to show up, Alice says, and they will have him. And hopefully rescue Walter's niece. They've been careful not to alert the kidnapper that they've found the place, and they have found no hidden cameras or microphones.

19. Walter does not believe this is the place; he thinks it's just one more of Josh's ploys. Alice Dorn and her team of idiots don't get it, he tells Lori. The guy is a master strategist, a real magician. He opens the doors for the FBI to walk through, and they do every time. The trouble is, Walter doesn't know what Josh will do either, or where he is, and the clock is ticking down.

This is another dark moment. There can be more than one.

20. We're back with the horses in Golden Gate Park. Walter and Lori just don't have enough people to look at all the places Josh might have rented over the last month or two, especially since the police are forbidden from helping and the FBI won't help. This is when Lori gets a brainstorm. There are two thousand people at the conference; maybe some of them would like to help.

21. Walter and Lori go to the Sane conference. They ask everyone to help out. Lori has recruited some volunteer cops to help as well—anything to poke the FBI in the eye. The idea is to comb the real estate agencies that handle rentals and go through old newspapers to find where Josh might have gotten an apartment or commercial space. Walter says they should look for somebody about Josh's shape. Better check sales, too. Josh could have put down a small deposit to

get a place. Walter tells the volunteers what kind of place they're looking for: remote, isolated. Josh could use a generator, so it doesn't even need electricity. Each team has a Jew and an Arab—they don't trust each other.

22. Walter handles the nerve center, along with a few volunteers. He's picking out the most likely places. Lori and the cops check out the suspected places as they come in.

> *Here's a place where change in the story is needed. I'll have to go back and make changes in the step sheet timeline. I have to move the deadline to six P.M. for both the signing of the peace treaty and Mary's planned execution. I might even have to change everything so that the conference starts on the previous Sunday or even the previous Saturday to make the time work out right. But that's okay, that's why you do step sheets; reordering and resizing are not problems. There are other changes that I know already need to be made, and I'll discuss them at the end of this draft of the step sheet.*

23. Nabil is with a Jewish lad, checking out a shoe store recently rented and now being stocked. The two are formal and standoffish with each other, but efficient.

24. Daphne is working with a young Arab woman. They have hit it off. But they stick to business. Both are committed to peace and want to find Mary desperately. They find Americans weird.

25. Achmed, released from jail, offers his services to Walter. His entire group wants to help. Walter accepts the offer.

26. With three hours to go, they still have found nothing. Walter is beside himself, but he presses on. Then he gets info that someone has taken an option to buy an old Orthodox Jewish slaughterhouse that killed animals in a ritualistic and humane way. It's out of business. Walter thinks this would be a place Josh would pick: The symbolism would appeal to him. Time is short.

27. Walter gives Lori a slip of paper—a place to be checked out. While she's gone, he'll stay and man the phones, he says. He's exhausted and fears he may collapse. He pauses for a moment to tell her how much he's appreciated her help, and even though she's not his type, he says he's grown quite fond of her and would love, someday, to take her to dinner, should she ever find herself in Crooked Creek, Virginia. She says he's not her type either, but she'd go to dinner if it was a really great steakhouse and she didn't have to wear a dress and have her hair done. This is the obligatory scene, the end of Movement III.

Movement IV: *The hero confronts the villain, who almost wins but is finally defeated in a slam-bang climax.*

This part of the story takes us from the obligatory scene up to and including the climax itself. This is *the climactic sequence*. It leads up to the climax itself. In the climactic sequence, you often have scenes where the hero is preparing for battle with the villain or is closing in on the villain, sometimes battling the villain's minions. There is mounting tension here and fast action. The clock is ticking like mad.

The climactic sequence leads directly to the climax, which is almost always a showdown between the villain and the hero. Often in the showdown there's a dark moment when it looks as if the villain might win, but fortunately the villain is almost always beaten and very often killed. Sometimes there's a dual-climax design, where the villain escapes and there's a second showdown. *Fatal Attraction* has a famous dual climax, when the villain, thought drowned, arises again. *Goldfinger* has a dual climax as well. There's a wonderful clock-ticking atom bomb scene inside the gold vault at Fort Knox. The villain, Goldfinger, escapes and there's a second showdown between the hero and the villain on the plane, where Goldfinger's gun goes off, a window is blown out, and the rapid decompression sucks Goldfinger out to his death. Very nice.

In the case of man-against-nature thrillers, the climax is the scene where the hero survives the earthquake or volcano or fire or triumphs over some large animal, as when the hero kills the shark in *Jaws*.

In *High Noon*, as an example, the obligatory scene comes after the last deputy walks out on the marshal. The marshal loads his guns and makes his will at the start of the climactic sequence and then goes out into the street to face Frank Miller and his three gunslingers. In *Misery*, the obligatory scene is when the villain kills the sheriff in the basement. The climactic sequence that follows involves the hero, Paul, cleverly tricking the villain, Annie, by asking for champagne, then killing her in the climactic confrontation. In *The Adventures of Robin Hood*, the obligatory scene is the arrival of King Richard the Lionheart. In the climactic sequence that follows, the heroes march to Nottingham Castle wearing monk's robes to have the showdown with the villain, Prince John, and his minions. In *The Adventures of Robin Hood*, the villain does not almost win, but it's exciting anyway.

Okay, let us begin the climactic sequence that will take us to the climax.

■ *Peace Day* Step Sheet Continues

1. Walter is in his rental car, racing toward the showdown. We're almost at the deadline. Lots of strong story questions and fast actions, racing against the clock.

2. Walter is in the Outer Mission district in an old industrial block that is slated for the wrecking ball. Around the corner he meets the Jew/Arab team from the conference that had called in the lead. They tell Walter there's a new satellite dish on the roof, and they can hear a generator going. He tells them to give him twenty minutes, then to call the cops. He sends them away. He doesn't want the cops storming the place until he gets his niece free. Okay, this is it: the showdown with the villain, the climax of our story.

■ The Making of a Damn Good Climax

The opening of the story is the most important part, but the climax is the most exciting. A great climax (and the resolution that follows it) will leave the audience feeling satisfied. The climax of a thriller should be thrilling.

Okay, what makes a thrilling climax?

- In almost all damn good thrillers, the hero is nearly killed in the climax but then manages to kill or capture the villain and to foil his evil plot. Audiences find this motif satisfying, even if, at times, the hero does not overcome the villain personally, such as in *Thunderball,* where the hero's lover does it for him.

- In the climax of a damn good thriller, good prevails over evil. Audiences love this, too. In fact, this is one of the oldest conventions in storytelling. The knight always slew the dragon. Good will prevail over evil in nearly all thrillers, except literary thrillers such as *The Spy Who Came in from the Cold*. Often in literary thrillers what's good and what's evil gets muddled, and that, I guess, is what makes them literary.

- Damn good thriller climaxes have surprises. In *High Noon*, it's a nice surprise that the marshal's Quaker bride shoots one of the villain's men. In *Samson and Delilah,* our hero looks doomed: He's weak and chained, but then, surprise, he gets his super-strength back. Even though he's blind, he's able to bring the temple down and kill all the enemies of his people. In *Bunny Lake Is Missing,* there's a terrible surprise in the climax: We discover the maniac who has kidnapped Bunny and wants to kill her is the heroine's beloved brother.

- The climax of a damn good thriller is not just more of the same old stuff we've seen before. When crafting the climax, you have a considerable challenge. The confrontation with the villain should be done in a fresh, innovative way. There are many tens of thousands of thrillers, almost all ending with a direct confrontation between the hero and the villain. It's difficult to find a fresh way to handle this situation, but it can be done. In *The Boys from Brazil,* the climax involves a battle between the hero and the villain, each badly bloodied, and then one of Hitler's clones sics his dogs on the villain and kills him. Very fresh, bloody, and gripping. Often when attempting to be fresh, writers go for something gimmicky, which rarely works well. Gimmicks are often implausible. I was tempted to go for one in *Peace Day,* but I resisted. I was going to have Josh use a mechanical ax set to a timer and then have him fall under it just as it went off.

- Often in a damn good climax the hero discovers something about himself or gains insight into the human condition. Leamas, in *The Spy Who Came in from the Cold,* blames himself for his girlfriend's death and chooses death for himself as well. Eleanor, in *The Haunting,* discovers she prefers the company of spirits to the loneliness she suffers among the living. John Russell, the alienated antihero in *Hombre,* learns to be a self-sacrificing hero when he sees nobility in others. All three of these personal revelations lead to great surprises as well as tragic death.

- Sometimes a hero experiences a loss at the climax, as with Brody's loss of his grizzled sidekick, Quint, the shark killer in *Jaws.* Ripley, in *Alien,* loses her entire crew. Lucy, in *Eye of the Needle,* loses her good friend and neighbor.

- Sometimes the hero dies in the climax, as in the case of Jordan in *For Whom the Bell Tolls,* Leamas in *The Spy Who Came in from the Cold,* and Christine (a suicide) in *The Bad Seed.*

■ *Peace Day* Step Sheet Continues

3. Walter, with the help of the two young men from the conference, loosens the fitting on the satellite dish, hoping to draw Josh outside.

Walter waits, holding his two Confederate Colt .44s. The clock is ticking: only a few minutes to go.

4. Meanwhile, in another part of town, Lori discovers she's been sent on a false errand. She goes back to the conference center. She uses threats of arrest for obstruction of justice to try to find out where Walter has gone, but the threats don't work on the staff, whom Walter swore to secrecy. She then breaks down emotionally, and for the first time she realizes how much she cares about Walter. Damn it, she doesn't really even like the guy. Seeing her distressed, the staff tell her where he's gone.

> *I have not focused on the Walter/Lori relationship in this step sheet except to note Lori's objections to Walter's searching her apartment in the scene that I drafted and showed you in chapter 9 and a few instances where they disagree on strategy. This is a first draft, and the nuances of their relationship will be worked out in subsequent drafts and during the actual writing of the story. I know that at first Lori thinks Walter is a male chauvinist, which is somewhat true (after all, he's a nineteenth-century southern gentleman), and he thinks she's rather unfeminine, which is also true: Her role model is Dirty Harry. But, yes, I intend for them to fall in love—because they come to know each other's sense of honor and courage and willingness to self-sacrifice, and their smarts, cleverness, and insights into human character. They are two heroes who are drawn to the heroic qualities in each other. I do not intend this to be a romantic comedy, though the story might have comic moments. All damn good stories do.*

5. Lori is stopped in traffic. Frustrated, she drives around the obstruction on the sidewalk.

6. Josh comes out of the old slaughterhouse to fiddle with the satellite dish. Walter creeps inside. It's dimly lit. Mary's tied to a post. She sees her uncle and gives a big smile.

7. Walter is heading for Mary to free her when Josh gets back. Josh opens fire, driving Walter under cover. A bullet hits the concrete next to Walter's head, and chips of concrete and dust go in his eyes. His vision is blurry, but he returns fire with an old Colt that sounds like a cannon going off, driving Josh under cover. Josh congratulates Walter on finding him. Walter, hoping to anger him so he will lose his judgment, says it was not all that hard, sort of like finding a rabid fox that's been molesting his chickens. Josh says Walter should have brought an army of cops. Walter says his Colts are enough to do the job.

8. Lori arrives outside and puts on her Kevlar vest. Hearing the shots fired, she calls for backup. She sneaks inside. She's armed, of course.

9. Josh, using Mary as a shield, puts a gun to her head. Walter offers Josh the chance to have an honorable duel. Josh passes on the offer. He tells them that the cameras are rolling, that this is going out to all of America. Lori draws a bead on him with a laser sight and tells him to drop his gun. It looks as if he's about to do it when he suddenly whirls and shoots Lori. Despite the vest, she's wounded. Walter resists the impulse to go to her. He realizes at this moment how much he cares for her. He's still frantically trying to clear the debris from his eyes.

10. Josh, still using Mary as his shield, is inching toward the door. Walter tells him that if he harms Mary, he will make him suffer a horrible death. Josh wants to know where the FBI is. Walter says the FBI wouldn't cut him a deal, but he will. If he leaves Mary, he can go. Walter says he's a man of honor, and his word is good. He tells Josh how much he admires the way he's played law enforcement for the fool. And that he has done the same thing for years, as did his pappy and his grandpappy and his grandpappy's grandpappy, back to the Whiskey Rebellion. But Josh will not hear of it. He's not finished with Mary.

Walter finally clears his vision. He tells Josh that he can't hide behind Mary—she's not big enough. Walter has a tiny part of Josh's shoulder for a target, about a square inch, and he's thirty feet away. Walter shoots Josh, and his gun goes flying.

Mary ducks for cover, struggling like crazy to get her hands free.

Josh pulls a second gun and starts spraying the place with bullets. Walter returns fire.

Walter turns back the barrel on one of his revolvers. Click. Click. The other is empty. Click. Click. Click. Click. Josh says, "Ah, you need time to reload? I think not." And he charges, firing like mad. Walter fires twice and hits Josh in his Kevlar vest. Josh goes down, rolls, and gets back up, continuing to fire, but the impact of the bullets has taken his breath away and broken a couple of ribs. Josh advances, firing automatic weapons. Walter retreats, reloading, and is just about cornered when Mary, her hands still tied, throws herself into Josh. He falls backward.

Lori has managed to get to her feet, wields the ax, and chops Josh's head off. It rolls over to Walter's feet—all on streaming video. So the nation gets its bloody show.

This is the climax.

■ Rewrite Notes on the Climax and the Story as a Whole

It's strange how, when you create a story, themes emerge that were not part of the author's intent. When I started this step sheet, I had no idea that one of the themes would be how reality is shaped by fantasies created by the media and how institutions, public and private, both manipulate the media and are manipulated by it.

On rewrite, I'll exploit the FBI's manipulation of the media and how their investigation in this case is driven by a desire to look good in the public eye. I wouldn't want to make Alice Dorn a media glutton cartoon, but I could definitely exploit her desire to create a good image for the FBI and herself. She's a martinet, after all, a careerist whose concerns go far beyond just Mary's case.

Josh's desire that Mary's murder be on streaming video on his blog and be broadcast to a huge audience could also be exploited. I think the public's thirst for blood could also be one of the major themes. Harry Feldt's role in this could be exploited as well.

And there is a dark side to the media. They often make deals with the villains of this world in their never-ending quest to give all points of view. I might be able to show, as an example, more of the deal Tommy Acre might make with Achmed. Or maybe even with Josh.

I did not exploit how the reward and the effect of the promise of reward would impact the events, including the overwhelming number of false clues the reward would generate.

To research this book, I took a trip to Israel and interviewed a few dozen Jews and more than a few dozen Arabs. One of the things I learned was not only do Jews and Arabs mistrust each other, but they are totally oblivious to each other's motives, hopes, desires, and worldviews. All of these misunderstandings could be exploited, as could the most important factor in this dispute, the fact that the leaders on both sides, and the leaders of other nations such as in the United States, both Republican and Democrat, are making a lot of political capital out of the misery this conflict generates. The more polarized things get, the more power the politicians are able to garner for themselves.

There are also far more sides to the issues than are usually presented in the press. There are Jews who are anti-Zionist, as an example. There are many Arabs, perhaps even a majority, who are against the radicalism of Hamas and Hezbollah but cannot speak for fear of reprisals. Ordinary Arabs are the people most victimized by Arab terrorists. King Abdullah II of Jordan, as an example, is extremely popular among his people because of his opposition to radical Islam and his pursuit of peace with Israel.

As mentioned in one of the previous notes, I failed to adequately exploit the development of the relationship between Walter and Lori. On rewrite, I'll focus more on my two stars.

Another thing I failed to exploit was the track-down section during the climactic sequence. I should have Walter close in on one more wrong place as the clock is ticking down. He might find it with just minutes left.

Also, I'll have to make changes in the backstory. Nora and Walter are divorced. At the beginning of the story, I show that he's still mad about her and she takes advantage of this to milk him for money, but they are divorced. Otherwise, some of the audience could be turned off by his attraction to Lori.

I've spent a few days now on my boat thinking about the climax since stepping it out in the step sheet. I now realize I should have Harry being slowly choked to death in the slaughterhouse as he's forced to watch Mary's beheading. As he is near death, it would give this scene even more urgency. I could have him rescued by Walter—by a master shot with his old Colt, cutting the rawhide that's choking him. Then I'll let Harry be the one who chops Josh's head off. He can bask in media glory and take all the credit. He's destined to have his own "reality" TV show. Walter and Lori don't mind; they don't care who gets the credit.

13

■ All About a Satisfying Resolution

Movement V. *Resolution. Tells what happens to the major characters as a result of the hero's victory or defeat.*

Remember, as you read this, I need not have rising conflict in the resolution as in the rest of the story. Also, I have written this assuming the change in the climax where Harry, not Mary, chops Josh's head off.

1. Directly following the climax, the media descend on the slaughterhouse. Walter, who never shows the least perturbation, is severely perturbed at Lori and lets her know, even though she is being tended to by medics. How dare she put herself in harm's way? She wants to know how dare he send her on a fool's errand? She already realized she'd fallen for the fossil; now she realizes he's fallen for her, too. She shocks him by kissing him passionately, not only in front of the folks, but on national TV, too. Meanwhile, Harry is basking in media glory, and Mary is being brave and stoic and charming for the cameras.

   Mary, of course, will be writing a book about this. Her advance will be huge.

2. That evening, the treaty is signed. The participants of the conference may not love one another, but they all love peace. Walter looks on. Mary is there, hugging everyone. Achmed and Daphne have a civil discussion that gets just a little heated. Harry is there, telling his story for the thousandth time, now with lots of embellishments—all about how he saved Mary and meted out justice to Josh Pape, making this wonderful peace agreement possible. Word comes that there's a protest going on at City Hall. The reporters all pack up and leave.

3. We're at Walter's stately home in the mountains. Walter and Lori are sitting on the veranda in the afternoon heat, sipping wine coolers and watching the horses graze in the meadow. Mary is there, writing her book. Daisy is being the perfect southern hostess. Nora comes by and wants money, and Walter tells her no. Nora turns on the charm, but it has no effect (*transformation in the hero*). After she leaves, Walter asks Lori if she could get used to living in the nineteenth century. She says she might like to try it out for a few decades and see.

   About the rumors of him being a bootlegger, he says . . .

   She says they'll have to have a long discussion about that.

■ **End of the *Peace Day* Step Sheet**

◼ End Note

In closing, I want to give you some advice. I know, I know, "Preach not" is one of the cardinal rules of writing how-to books like this one. But a lot of the writers I've worked with have found this advice helpful. So here it is.

When you start constructing your thriller, it will help a great deal if you have the right attitude. I wrote a little about attitude earlier, about how lots of things we think of as craft are really a matter of attitude. Let's put it this way: To write a damn good thriller, you need a killer attitude. I suggest you make a pledge to yourself to do the following:

- Commit yourself to creating strong conflicts in every line of every scene.

- Decide you will have fresh, snappy dialogue and not a single line of conversation.

- Decide to write quickly when drafting. Fast is golden.

- Give yourself production quotas of at least a thousand words every day, even if you have a tough day job like kissing up to bad bosses. Three or four thousand would be better.

- If your significant other complains your thriller writing is taking up too much of your time, get a new significant other.

- Commit yourself to this: You will not have any major characters that are bland and colorless. They will all be dramatic types, theatrical, driven, larger than life, clever.

- Create a step sheet for the whole novel or screenplay. You might start your first draft if you know your opening and have an idea for the climax.

- Trick the expectations of the reader and create nice surprises from time to time.

- Have your characters in terrible trouble right from the beginning, and never let them get free of terrible trouble until the climax.

- Have powerful story questions operating at all times.

- End each scene or section of dramatic narrative with a bridge, a story question to carry the reader to the next one.

- Always keep brainstorming and think about what's happening off scene. Make charts for the major characters that tell you what they're doing when they're not on scene.

- Try to be fresh. Don't use the same old clichés. Be sure your prose is colorful and sensuous.

- Keep the clock ticking and the excitement mounting right to the climactic moment.

Remember that you are creating dreams that others will dream. As you hone your craft as a storyteller, you will be able to create powerful stories that touch people's hearts and change people's minds. Before the Nazis incinerated the Jews, the Gypsies, and the Communists, there were fiction writers demonizing these groups. Fiction writers created the Native Americans as heartless, heathen savages before the cavalry rode out to annihilate them.

Fiction writing is a great responsibility, and you should use your powers for good and not for evil. Resist the temptation to create thrillers full of mindless violence. Such thrillers are nothing more than bloody pornography, and it should be beneath you to create such dreck, no matter how many BMWs it will buy you.

Don't create cardboard stereotypes without humanity, caricatures for your readers to hate. There is enough hate in the world. Percy Shelley, the English Romantic poet, rightly proclaimed that creative writers are the unacknowledged legislators of the world. We create the cultural mores that people live by, and this is an awesome responsibility. Fiction writers define what is villainy and what is heroic for all the peoples of the earth, in every generation, for all time. We inspire people to rise above their own small, scared selves and give them a burning desire to imitate the greatness in the characters we create. There is no greater calling than ours.

Write with love, my friend.

JAMES N. FREY
jamesnfrey.com
jnfrey@jamesnfrey.com

■ Appendix

■ Films Cited

(Asterisk* indicates the film is highly recommended)

3:10 TO YUMA* (1957); written by Halsted Welles from a short story by Elmore Leonard; starring Glenn Ford and Van Heflin; directed by Delmer Daves.

3:10 TO YUMA* (2007); written by Halsted Welles and Michael Brandt from a short story by Elmore Leonard; starring Russell Crowe and Christian Bale; directed by James Mangold.

ABSOLUTE POWER* (1997); written by William Goldman from the novel by David Baldacci; starring Clint Eastwood and Gene Hackman; directed by Clint Eastwood.

THE ADVENTURES OF ROBIN HOOD* (1938); written by Norman Reilly Raine and Seton I. Miller; starring Errol Flynn and Olivia de Havilland; directed by Michael Curtiz and William Keighley.

AIRPLANE! (1980); written by Jim Abrahams and David Zucker; starring Lloyd Bridges, Kareem Abdul-Jabbar, and Peter Graves; directed by Jim Abrahams and David Zucker.

ALIEN* (1979); written by Dan O'Bannon and Ronald Shusett; starring Sigourney Weaver and Tom Skerritt; directed by Ridley Scott.

ALIENS* (1986); written by Dan O'Bannon and Ronald Shusett; starring Sigourney Weaver and Carrie Henn; directed by James Cameron.

THE ANDROMEDA STRAIN (1971); written by Nelson Gidding from the novel by Michael Crichton; starring Arthur Hill and David Wayne; directed by Robert Wise.

THE ANDROMEDA STRAIN (2008); written by Robert Schenkkan from the novel by Michael Crichton; starring Benjamin Bratt, Eric McCormack, and Christa Miller; directed by Mikael Salomon.

AUSTIN POWERS: INTERNATIONAL MAN OF MYSTERY* (1997); written by Mike Myers; starring Mike Myers and Elizabeth Hurley; directed by Jay Roach.

THE BAD SEED (1956); written by John Lee Mahin from the play by Maxwell Anderson, based on a novel by William March; starring Nancy Kelly and Patty McCormack; directed by Mervyn LeRoy.

THE BAD SEED (1985); written by George Eckstein from the play by Maxwell Anderson; starring Blair Brown, Lynn Redgrave, and David Carradine; directed by Paul Wendkos.

BEOWULF (2007); written by Neil Gaiman and Roger Avary from the ancient legend; starring Ray Winstone, Anthony Hopkins, and Angelina Jolie; directed by Robert Zemeckis.

BLACK SUNDAY* (1977); written by Ernest Lehman from a novel by Thomas Harris; starring Robert Shaw, Bruce Dern, and Marthe Keller; directed by John Frankenheimer.

BLINDNESS (2008); written by Don McKellar from the novel by José Saramago; starring Julianne Moore and Mark Ruffalo; directed by Fernando Meirelles.

BLOOD DIAMOND (2006); written by Charles Leavitt; starring Leonardo DiCaprio and Djimon Hounsou; directed by Edward Zwick.

BODY HEAT (1981); written by Lawrence Kasdan; starring William Hurt and Kathleen Turner; directed by Lawrence Kasdan.

BODY SNATCHERS (1993); written by Stuart Gordon and Dennis Paoli from the novel by Jack Finney; starring Gabrielle Anwar, Terry Kinney, and Meg Tilly; directed by Abel Ferrara.

THE BONE COLLECTOR* (1999); written by Jeremy Iacone from the novel by Jeffery Deaver; starring Denzel Washington and Angelina Jolie; directed by Phillip Noyce.

BONNIE AND CLYDE* (1967); written by David Newman and Robert Benton; starring Warren Beatty and Faye Dunaway; directed by Arthur Penn.

DAS BOOT* (1981); written by Lothar G. Buchheim and Wolfgang Petersen; starring Jürgen Prochnow and Herbert Grönemeyer; directed by Wolfgang Petersen.

THE BOURNE IDENTITY* (TV 1988); written by Carol Sobieski from the novel by Robert Ludlum; starring Richard Chamberlain and Jaclyn Smith; directed by Roger Young.

THE BOURNE IDENTITY* (2002); written by Tony Gilroy and W. Blake Herron from the novel by Robert Ludlum; starring Matt Damon; directed by Doug Liman.

THE BOURNE SUPREMACY* (2004); written by Tony Gilroy from the novel by Robert Ludlum; starring Matt Damon and Franka Potente; directed by Paul Greengrass.

THE BOURNE ULTIMATUM* (2007); written by Tony Gilroy, Scott Z. Burns, and George Nolfi from the novel by Robert Ludlum; starring Matt Damon and Julia Stiles; directed by Paul Greengrass.

THE BOYS FROM BRAZIL* (1978); written by Heywood Gould from the novel by Ira Levin; starring Gregory Peck, Laurence Olivier, and James Mason; directed by Franklin J. Schaffner.

BUNNY LAKE IS MISSING* (1965); written by John Mortimer from the novel by Evelyn Piper; starring Laurence Olivier and Carol Lynley; directed by Otto Preminger.

BUTCH CASSIDY AND THE SUNDANCE KID* (1969); written by William Goldman; starring Paul Newman, Robert Redford, and Katharine Ross; directed by George Roy Hill.

CAPE FEAR* (1962); written by James R. Webb from the novel *The Executioners* by John D. MacDonald; starring Gregory Peck, Robert Mitchum, and Polly Bergen; directed by J. Lee Thompson.

CAPE FEAR* (1991); written by James R. Webb from the novel *The Executioners* by John D. MacDonald; starring Robert De Niro, Nick Nolte, and Jessica Lange; directed by Martin Scorsese.

CASABLANCA* (1942); written by Julius J. Epstein, Philip G. Epstein, and Howard Koch from the play *Everybody Comes to Rick's* by Murray Burnett and Joan Alison; starring Humphrey Bogart and Ingrid Bergman; directed by Michael Curtiz.

CASINO ROYALE (2006); written by Neal Purvis and Robert Wade based on characters created by Ian Fleming; starring Daniel Craig and Eva Green; directed by Martin Campbell.

CHARADE* (1963); written by Peter Stone; staring Cary Grant and Audrey Hepburn; directed by Stanley Donen.

CHARLEY VARRICK* (1973); written by Howard Rodman from the novel *The Looters* by John Reese; starring Walter Matthau and Joe Don Baker; directed by Don Siegel.

LA CHÈVRE* (1981); written by Francis Veber; starring Richard Pierre and Gérard Depardieu; directed by Francis Veber.

A CHRISTMAS CAROL (1910*); written by J. Searle Dawley from the novel by Charles Dickens; starring Marc McDermott and Charles S. Ogle; directed by J. Searle Dawley.

A CHRISTMAS CAROL (1951*); written by Noel Langley; starring Alastair Sim and John Charlesworth; directed by Brian Desmond Hurst.

CITIZEN KANE* (1941); written by Herman J. Mankiewicz; starring Joseph Cotten and Dorothy Comingore; directed by Orson Welles.

COMA (1978); written by Robin Cook and Michael Crichton; starring Geneviève Bujold and Michael Douglas; directed by Michael Crichton.

CONSPIRACY THEORY (1997); written by Brian Helgeland; starring Mel Gibson and Julia Roberts; directed by Richard Donner.

THE CONSTANT GARDENER (2005); written by Jeffrey Caine from the novel by John le Carré; starring Ralph Fiennes and Rachel Weisz; directed by Fernando Meirelles.

THE COUNT OF MONTE CRISTO* (2002); written by Jay Wolpert from the novel by Alexandre Dumas, père; starring James Caviezel and Richard Harris; directed by Kevin Reynolds.

DANTE'S PEAK (1997); written by Leslie Bohem; starring Pierce Brosnan and Linda Hamilton; directed by Roger Donaldson.

DAVE* (1993); written by Gary Ross; starring Kevin Kline and Sigourney Weaver; directed by Ivan Reitman.

THE DA VINCI CODE (2006); written by Akiva Goldsman from the novel by Dan Brown; starring Tom Hanks and Audrey Tautou; directed by Ron Howard.

THE DAY OF THE JACKAL* (1973); written by Kenneth Ross from a novel by Frederick Forsyth; starring Edward Fox and Terence Alexander; directed by Fred Zinnemann.

DEAD CALM* (1989); written by Terry Hayes from the novel by Charles Williams; starring Nicole Kidman, Sam Neill, and Billy Zane; directed by Phillip Noyce.

THE DESPERATE HOURS* (1955); written by Joseph Hayes from his novel (1954) and his play (1955); starring Humphrey Bogart and Fredric March; directed by William Wyler.

THE DESPERATE HOURS (1990); written by Lawrence Konner and Mark Rosenthal; starring Mickey Rourke; directed by Michael Cimino.

DIE HARD* (1988); written by Jeb Stuart and Steven E. de Souza from the novel *Nothing Lasts Forever* by Roderick Thorp; starring Bruce Willis and Bonnie Bedelia; directed by John McTiernan.

DIE HARD 2* (1990); written by Steven E. de Souza and Doug Richardson from the novel *58 Minutes* by Walter Wager; starring Bruce Willis and Bonnie Bedelia; directed by Renny Harlin.

DIE HARD: WITH A VENGEANCE* (1995); written by Jonathan Hensleigh and Roderick Thorp; starring Bruce Willis and Jeremy Irons; directed by John McTiernan.

DIRTY HARRY* (1971); written by Harry Julian Fink and Rita M. Fink; starring Clint Eastwood and Harry Guardino; directed by Don Siegel.

DOG DAY AFTERNOON* (1975); written by Frank Pierson; starring Al Pacino and John Cazale; directed by Sidney Lumet.

DOLORES CLAIBORNE* (1995); written by Tony Gilroy from the novel by Stephen King; starring Kathy Bates and Jennifer Jason Leigh; directed by Taylor Hackford.

DOUBLE INDEMNITY* (1944); written by Billy Wilder and Raymond Chandler from the novel by James M. Cain; starring Fred MacMurray and Barbara Stanwyck; directed by Billy Wilder.

DR. JEKYLL AND MR. HYDE (1931); written by Samuel Hoffenstein from the novel by Robert Louis Stevenson; starring Fredric March and Miriam Hopkins; directed by Rouben Mamoulian.

DR. NO (1962); written by Richard Maibaum and Johanna Harwood from the novel by Ian Fleming; starring Sean Connery and Ursula Andress; directed by Terence Young.

DR. STRANGELOVE* (1964); written by Stanley Kubrick from the novel *Red Alert* by Peter George; starring Peter Sellers, Peter Sellers, Peter Sellers, George C. Scott, and Sterling Hayden; directed by Stanley Kubrick.

AN ENEMY OF THE PEOPLE* (1978); written by Alexander Jacobs and adapted by Arthur Miller from the play by Henrik Ibsen; starring Steve McQueen, Bibi Andersson, and Charles Durning; directed by George Schaefer.

THE EXORCIST* (1973); written by William Peter Blatty from his novel; starring Ellen Burstyn, Max von Sydow, and Lee J. Cobb; directed by William Friedkin.

DAS EXPERIMENT (2001); written by Mario Giordano; starring Moritz Bleibtreu and Christian Berkel; directed by Oliver Hirschbiegel.

EYE OF THE NEEDLE* (1981); written by Stanley Mann from the novel by Ken Follett; starring Donald Sutherland and Kate Nelligan; directed by Richard Marquand.

FAHRENHEIT 451* (1966); written by François Truffaut from the novel by Ray Bradbury; starring Oskar Werner and Julie Christie; directed by François Truffaut.

FARGO* (1996); written by Joel Coen and Ethan Coen; starring Frances McDormand and William H. Macy; directed by Joel Coen.

FATAL ATTRACTION* (1987); written by James Dearden; starring Michael Douglas and Glenn Close; directed by Adrian Lyne.

FORBIDDEN PLANET (1956); written by Cyril Hume; starring Walter Pidgeon, Anne Francis, and Leslie Nielsen; directed by Fred M. Wilcox.

FOR WHOM THE BELL TOLLS* (1943); written by Dudley Nichols from the novel by Ernest Hemingway; starring Gary Cooper, Ingrid Bergman, and Akim Tamiroff; directed by Sam Wood.

FRANKENSTEIN* (1994); written by Steph Lady from the novel by Mary Shelley; starring Robert De Niro and Kenneth Branagh; directed by Kenneth Branagh.

FRANTIC* (1988); written by Roman Polanski and Gérard Brach; starring Harrison Ford and Betty Buckley; directed by Roman Polanski.

FROM RUSSIA WITH LOVE* (1963); written by Johanna Harwood and Richard Maibaum from the novel by Ian Fleming; starring Sean Connery and Daniela Bianchi; directed by Terence Young.

FUTUREWORLD (1976); written by George Schenck and Mayo Simon; starring Peter Fonda and Blythe Danner; directed by Richard T. Heffron.

GASLIGHT* (1944); written by John Van Druten, Walter Reisch, and John L. Balderston from the play *Angel Street* by Patrick Hamilton; starring Charles Boyer and Ingrid Bergman; directed by George Cukor.

GET SHORTY* (1995); written by Scott Frank from the novel by Elmore Leonard; starring John Travolta and Gene Hackman; directed by Barry Sonnenfeld.

THE GODFATHER* (1972); written by Mario Puzo and Francis Ford Coppola from the novel by Mario Puzo; starring Marlon Brando, Al Pacino, and James Caan; directed by Francis Ford Coppola.

GOLDFINGER* (1964); written by Richard Maibaum and Paul Dehn from the novel by Ian Fleming; starring Sean Connery, Honor Blackman, and Gert Fröbe; directed by Guy Hamilton.

GONE WITH THE WIND* (1939); written by Sidney Howard from the novel by Margaret Mitchell; starring Clark Gable, Vivien Leigh, and Butterfly McQueen; directed by Victor Fleming.

GRAN TORINO* (2008); written by Nick Schenk and Dave Johannson; starring Clint Eastwood, Christopher Carley, and Bee Vang; directed by Clint Eastwood.

THE GREEN MILE* (1999); written by Frank Darabont from the novel by Stephen King; starring Tom Hanks and David Morse; directed by Frank Darabont.

THE HAND THAT ROCKS THE CRADLE* (1992); written by Amanda Silver; starring Annabella Sciorra and Rebecca De Mornay; directed by Curtis Hanson.

THE HAUNTING* (1963); written by Nelson Gidding from the novel *The Haunting of Hill House* by Shirley Jackson; starring Julie Harris and Claire Bloom; directed by Robert Wise.

THE HAUNTING (1999*); written by David Self from the novel *The Haunting of Hill House* by Shirley Jackson; starring Liam Neeson, Catherine Zeta-Jones, and Owen Wilson; directed by Jan de Bont.

HIDE AND SEEK (2005); written by Ari Schlossberg; starring Robert De Niro and Dakota Fanning; directed by John Polson.

HIGH NOON* (1952); written by Carl Foreman and John W. Cunningham from the short story "The Tin Star" by John W. Cunningham; starring Gary Cooper and Grace Kelly; directed by Fred Zinnemann.

HOMBRE* (1967); written by Irving Ravetch and Harriet Frank Jr. from the novel by Elmore Leonard; starring Paul Newman and Richard Boone; directed by Martin Ritt.

THE HUNCHBACK OF NOTRE DAME* (1939); written by Sonya Levien from the novel by Victor Hugo; starring Charles Laughton and Maureen O'Hara; directed by William Dieterle.

INDIANA JONES AND THE KINGDOM OF THE CRYSTAL SKULL (2008); written by David Koepp and George Lucas; starring Harrison Ford and Cate Blanchett; directed by Steven Spielberg.

INDIANA JONES AND THE LAST CRUSADE* (1989); written by George Lucas and Philip Kaufman; starring Harrison Ford and Sean Connery; directed by Steven Spielberg.

INDIANA JONES AND THE TEMPLE OF DOOM* (1984); written by George Lucas and Willard Huyck; starring Harrison Ford; directed by Steven Spielberg.

INFERNO* (1953); written by Francis M. Cockrell; starring Robert Ryan; directed by Roy Ward Baker.

THE INVASION (2007); written by Oliver Hirschbiegel from the novel *The Body Snatchers* by Jack Finney; starring Nicole Kidman and David Craig; directed by Oliver Hirschbiegel.

INVASION OF THE BODY SNATCHERS* (1956); written by Daniel Mainwaring from the novel by Jack Finney; starring Kevin McCarthy and Dana Wynter; directed by Don Siegel.

INVASION OF THE BODY SNATCHERS* (1978); written by W. D. Richter from the novel by Jack Finney; starring Donald Sutherland, Jeff Goldblum, and Brooke Adams; directed by Philip Kaufman.

THE IPCRESS FILE* (1965); written by Len Deighton and W. H. Canaway from the novel by Len Deighton; starring Michael Caine, Nigel Green, and Guy Doleman; directed by Sidney J. Furie.

IRON MASK (1929); written by Douglas Fairbanks from the novel *The Man in the Iron Mask* by Alexandre Dumas, père; starring Douglas Fairbanks; directed by Allan Dwan.

IT'S A MAD MAD MAD MAD WORLD* (1963); written by William Rose and Tania Rose; starring Spencer Tracy and Milton Berle; directed by Stanley Kramer.

IVANHOE (1952); written by Noel Langley from the novel by Sir Walter Scott; starring Robert Taylor and Elizabeth Taylor; directed by Richard Thorpe.

THE JACKAL (1997); written by Kenneth Ross and Chuck Pfarrer; starring Bruce Willis and Richard Gere; directed by Michael Caton-Jones.

JACOB'S LADDER (1990); written by Bruce Joel Rubin; starring Tim Robbins and Danny Aiello; directed by Adrian Lyne.

JAWS* (1975); written by Peter Benchley based on his novel; starring Roy Scheider, Robert Shaw, and Richard Dreyfuss; directed by Steven Spielberg.

JEWEL OF THE NILE* (1985); written by Mark Rosenthal and Lawrence Konner; starring Michael Douglas and Kathleen Turner; directed by Lewis Teague.

KAGEMUSHA* (1980); written by Masato Ide and Akira Kurosawa; starring Tatsuya Nakadai and Tsutomu Yamazaki; directed by Akira Kurosawa.

THE LAST OF THE MOHICANS (1992); written by John L. Balderston from the novel by James Fenimore Cooper; starring Daniel Day-Lewis and Madeleine Stowe; directed by Michael Mann.

LETHAL WEAPON* (1987); written by Shane Black; starring Mel Gibson and Danny Glover; directed by Richard Donner.

LETHAL WEAPON 2* (1989); written by Shane Black; starring Mel Gibson and Danny Glover; directed by Richard Donner.

LETHAL WEAPON 3 (1992); written by Shane Black and Jeffrey Boam; starring Mel Gibson and Danny Glover; directed by Richard Donner.

LETHAL WEAPON 4 (1998); written by Shane Black and Jonathan Lemkin; starring Mel Gibson and Danny Glover; directed by Richard Donner.

LIVE FREE OR DIE HARD* (2007); written by Mark Bomback; starring Bruce Willis and Timothy Olyphant; directed by Len Wiseman.

THE LORD OF THE FLIES (1990); written by Sara Schiff from the novel by William Golding; starring Balthazar Getty and Chris Furrh; directed by Harry Hook.

MACBETH* (1948); written by Orson Welles from the play by William Shakespeare; starring Orson Welles and Jeanette Nolan; directed by Orson Welles.

THE MANCHURIAN CANDIDATE* (1962); written by George Axelrod from the novel by Richard Condon; starring Frank Sinatra, Laurence Harvey, and Janet Leigh; directed by John Frankenheimer.

THE MAN IN THE IRON MASK* (1977); written by William Bast from the novel by Alexandre Dumas, père; starring Richard Chamberlain and Patrick McGoohan; directed by Mike Newell.

THE MAN IN THE IRON MASK* (1998); written by Randall Wallace from the novel by Alexandre Dumas, père; starring Leonardo DiCaprio; directed by Randall Wallace.

THE MAN WHO KNEW TOO MUCH (1956); written by John Michael Hayes and Charles Bennett; starring James Stewart and Doris Day; directed by Alfred Hitchcock.

THE MAN WITH ONE BLACK SHOE (*Le grand blond avec une chaussure noire*)* (1972); written by Yves Robert and Francis Veber; starring Pierre Richard; directed by Yves Robert.

THE MAN WITH ONE RED SHOE (1985); written by Francis Veber and Yves Robert; starring Tom Hanks and Dabney Coleman; directed by Stan Dragoti.

THE MAN WITH THE GOLDEN GUN (1974); written by Richard Maibaum and Tom Mankiewicz from the novel by Ian Fleming; starring Roger Moore and Christopher Lee; directed by Guy Hamilton.

M*A*S*H* (1970); written by Ring Lardner Jr. from the novel by Richard Hooker; starring Donald Sutherland and Elliott Gould; directed by Robert Altman.

THE MATRIX (1999); written by Andy Wachowski and Larry Wachowski; starring Keanu Reeves and Laurence Fishburne; directed by Andy Wachowski.

MIDNIGHT RUN* (1988); written by George Gallo; starring Robert De Niro and Charles Grodin; directed by Martin Brest.

MISERY* (1990); written by William Goldman from the novel by Stephen King; starring Kathy Bates and James Caan; directed by Rob Reiner.

MISS CONGENIALITY* (2000); written by Marc Lawrence, Caryn Lucas, and Katie Ford; starring Sandra Bullock, Michael Caine, and Benjamin Bratt; directed by Donald Petrie.

MOBY DICK* (1956); written by Ray Bradbury from the novel by Herman Melville; starring Gregory Peck and Richard Basehart; directed by John Huston.

MOLL FLANDERS (1996); written by Pen Densham from the novel by Daniel Defoe; starring Robin Wright Penn and Morgan Freeman; directed by Pen Densham.

MURDERS IN THE RUE MORGUE (1932); written by Robert Florey from the short story by Edgar Allan Poe; starring Sidney Fox, Leon Ames, and Bela Lugosi; directed by Robert Florey.

THE NAKED PREY (1966); written by Clint Johnston and Don Peters; starring Cornel Wilde and Ken Gampu; directed by Cornel Wilde.

NINETEEN EIGHTY-FOUR* (1984); written by Michael Radford from the novel by George Orwell; starring John Hurt and Richard Burton; directed by Michael Radford.

THE NINTH GATE (1999); written by John Brownjohn and Enrique Urbizu from the novel *El club Dumas* by Arturo Pérez-Reverte; starring Johnny Depp and Frank Langella; directed by Roman Polanski.

NORTH BY NORTHWEST* (1959); written by Ernest Lehman; starring Cary Grant and Eva Marie Saint; directed by Alfred Hitchcock.

OCTOPUSSY (1983); written by George MacDonald Fraser and Richard Maibaum based on characters created by Ian Fleming; starring Roger Moore, Louis Jourdan, and Maud Adams; directed by John Glen.

THE OLD MAN AND THE SEA (1958); written by Peter Viertel from the novel by Ernest Hemingway; starring Spencer Tracy; directed by John Sturges.

THE PETRIFIED FOREST* (1936); written by Charles Kenyon and Delmer Daves from the play by Robert E. Sherwood; starring Humphrey Bogart, Leslie Howard, and Bette Davis; directed by Archie Mayo.

THE PIT AND THE PENDULUM (1961); written by Richard Matheson based on the short story by Edgar Allan Poe; starring Vincent Price and Barbara Steele; directed by Roger Corman.

PLAY MISTY FOR ME* (1971); written by Jo Heims and Dean Riesner; starring Clint Eastwood and Jessica Walter; directed by Clint Eastwood.

THE POSTMAN ALWAYS RINGS TWICE* (1946); written by Harry Ruskin and Niven Busch from the novel by James M. Cain; starring John Garfield and Lana Turner; directed by Tay Garnett.

THE POSTMAN ALWAYS RINGS TWICE* (1981); written by David Mamet from the novel by James M. Cain; starring Jack Nicholson and Jessica Lange; directed by Bob Rafelson.

PREMATURE BURIAL (1962); written by Charles Beaumont from a short story by Edgar Allan Poe; starring Ray Milland and Hazel Court; directed by Roger Corman.

PRIDE AND PREJUDICE (1940*); written by Aldous Huxley from the novel by Jane Austen; starring Laurence Olivier, Greer Garson, and Edna May Oliver; directed by Robert Z. Leonard.

PRIDE AND PREJUDICE (1945*); written by Andrew Davies from the novel by Jane Austen; starring Jennifer Ehle and Colin Firth; directed by Simon Langton.

PRIDE AND PREJUDICE (2005*); written by Deborah Moggach; starring Keira Knightly and Matthew MacFadyen; directed by Joe Wright.

THE PRINCE AND THE PAUPER* (1937); written by Laird Doyle from the novel by Mark Twain; starring Errol Flynn and Claude Rains; directed by William Keighley.

THE PRISONER OF ZENDA* (1937); written by John L. Balderston from the novel by Anthony Hope; starring Ronald Colman and Madeleine Carroll; directed by John Cromwell.

PSYCHO* (1960); written by Joseph Stefano from the novel by Robert Bloch; starring Janet Leigh and Anthony Perkins; directed by Alfred Hitchcock.

THE PUBLIC ENEMY* (1931); written by Kubec Glasmon and John Bright; starring James Cagney and Jean Harlow; directed by William Wellman.

PURE LUCK (1991); written by Herschel Weingrod; starring Danny Glover and Martin Short; directed by Nadia Tass.

QUANTUM OF SOLACE (2008); written by Paul Haggis and Neal Purvis based on characters created by Ian Fleming; starring Daniel Craig and Olga Kurylenko; directed by Marc Foster.

RAIDERS OF THE LOST ARK* (1981); written by George Lucas and Philip Kaufman; starring Harrison Ford and Karen Allen; directed by Steven Spielberg.

RAWHIDE* (1951); written by Dudley Nichols; starring Rita Hayworth and Tyrone Power; directed by Henry Hathaway.

REAR WINDOW (1954); written by John Michael Hayes from the short story "It Had to Be Murder" by Cornell Woolrich; starring James Stewart and Grace Kelly; directed by Alfred Hitchcock.

ROMANCING THE STONE* (1984); written by Diane Thomas; starring Michael Douglas, Kathleen Turner, and Danny DeVito; directed by Robert Zemeckis.

RONIN (1998); written by J. D. Zeik and David Mamet; starring Robert De Niro and Jean Reno; directed by John Frankenheimer.

SAMSON AND DELILAH* (1949); written by Jesse Lasky Jr. and Fredric M. Frank from the Book of Judges; starring Victor Mature and Hedy Lamarr; directed by Cecil B. DeMille.

SAN FRANCISCO* (1936); written by Anita Loos and Robert E. Hopkins; starring Clark Gable, Spencer Tracy, and Jeanette MacDonald; directed by W. S. Van Dyke.

SCARFACE* (1932); written by Armitage Trail and Ben Hecht; starring Paul Muni and Ann Dvorak; directed by Howard Hawks and Richard Rosson.

THE SCARLET PIMPERNEL* (1934); written by Lajos Biró and S. N. Behrman from the novel *The League of the Scarlet Pimpernel* by Baroness Orczy; starring Leslie Howard, Merle Oberon, and Raymond Massey; directed by Harold Young.

SERGEANT YORK* (1941); written by Abem Finkel and Harry Chandlee; starring Gary Cooper and Walter Brennan; directed by Howard Hawks.

SERPICO* (1973); written by Peter Maas, Waldo Salt, and Norman Wexler; starring Al Pacino; directed by Sidney Lumet.

SEVEN DAYS IN MAY* (1964); written by Rod Serling from the novel by Fletcher Knebel and Charles W. Bailey II; starring Burt Lancaster and Kirk Douglas; directed by John Frankenheimer.

THE SHAWSHANK REDEMPTION* (1994); written by Frank Darabont from the short story "Rita Hayworth and the Shawshank Redemption" by Stephen King; starring Tim Robbins and Morgan Freeman; directed by Frank Darabont.

SHE (1965); written by David T. Chantler from the novel by H. Rider Haggard; starring Ursula Andress, Peter Cushing, and Christopher Lee; directed by Robert Day.

THE SHINING* (1980); written by Stanley Kubrick and Diane Johnson from the novel by Stephen King; starring Jack Nicholson, Shelley Duvall, and Scatman Crothers; directed by Stanley Kubrick.

THE SHOOTIST* (1976); written by Miles Hood Swarthout and Scott Hale from the novel by Glendon Swarthout; starring John Wayne and Lauren Bacall; directed by Don Siegel.

THE SILENCE OF THE LAMBS* (1991); written by Ted Tally form the novel by Thomas Harris; starring Jodie Foster and Anthony Hopkins; directed by Jonathan Demme.

SINGLE WHITE FEMALE* (1992); written by Don Roos from the novel *SWF Seeks Same* by John Lutz; starring Bridget Fonda and Jennifer Jason Leigh; directed by Barbet Schroeder.

THE SIXTH SENSE* (1999); written by M. Night Shyamalan; starring Bruce Willis and Haley Joel Osment; directed by M. Night Shyamalan.

SLEEPING WITH THE ENEMY (1991); written by Ronald Bass from the novel by Nancy Price; starring Julia Roberts; directed by Joseph Ruben.

THE SNOW WALKER* (2003); written by Charles Martin Smith from a short story by Farley Mowat; starring Annabella Piugattuk and Barry Pepper; directed by Charles Martin Smith.

SPARTACUS* (1960); written by Dalton Trumbo from the novel by Howard Fast; starring Kirk Douglas and Laurence Olivier; directed by Stanley Kubrick.

SPELLBOUND (1945); written by Ben Hecht from the novel *The House of Dr. Edwardes* by Francis Beeding; starring Ingrid Bergman and Gregory Peck; directed by Alfred Hitchcock.

THE SPY WHO CAME IN FROM THE COLD* (1965); written by Paul Dehn from the novel by John le Carré; starring Richard Burton and Claire Bloom; directed by Martin Ritt.

STAKEOUT (1987); written by Jim Kouf; starring Richard Dreyfuss and Emilio Estevez; directed by John Badham.

STRANGERS ON A TRAIN* (1951); written by Raymond Chandler and Czenzi Ormonde from a novel by Patricia Highsmith; starring Farley Granger, Ruth Roman, and Robert Walker; directed by Alfred Hitchcock.

SUSPICION (1941); written by Samson Raphaelson, Joan Harrison, and Alma Reville from the novel *Before the Fact* by Anthony Berkeley Cox (writing as Francis Iles); starring Cary Grant and Joan Fontaine; directed by Alfred Hitchcock.

THUNDERBALL (1965); written by Kevin McClory and Jack Whittingham based on the characters created by Ian Fleming; starring Sean Connery and Claudine Auger; directed by Terence Young.

TITANIC (1997); written by James Cameron; starring Leonardo Di Caprio and Kate Winslet; directed by James Cameron.

THE TOWERING INFERNO* (1974); written by Thomas N. Scortia from the novel *The Glass Inferno* (1974) by Thomas N. Scortia and Frank M. Robinson; starring Steve McQueen and Paul Newman; directed by John Guillermin and Irwin Allen.

TREASURE ISLAND (1934); written by John Lee Mahn from the novel by Robert Louis Stevenson; starring Wallace Beery, Jackie Cooper, and Lionel Barrymore; directed by Victor Fleming.

TREASURE ISLAND (1950*); written by Lawrence Edward Watkin from the novel by Robert Louis Stevenson; starring Bobby Driscoll, Robert Newton, and Basil Sydney; directed by Byron Haskin.

TREASURE ISLAND (1972); written by Wolf Mankiewitz from the novel by Robert Louis Stevenson; starring Orson Welles, Walter Slezak, and Kim Burfield; directed by John Hough.

TROY (2004); written by David Benioff from an epic poem by Homer; starring Brad Pitt and Julian Glover; directed by Wolfgang Petersen.

WAIT UNTIL DARK* (1967); written by Robert Carrington from the 1966 play by Frederick Knott; starring Audrey Hepburn and Efrem Zimbalist Jr.; directed by Terence Young.

WAR AND PEACE* (1956); written by Bridget Boland, Robert Westerby, King Vidor, Mario Camerini, Ennio de Concini, Ivo Perilli, Gian Gaspare Napolitano, and Mario Soldati from the novel by Leo Tolstoy; starring Audrey Hepburn, Mel Ferrer, and Henry Fonda; directed by King Vidor.

WAR AND PEACE* (1967); written by Sergei Bondarchuck and Vasili Solovyov from the novel by Leo Tolstoy; starring Lyudmila Savelyeva, Vyacheslav Tikhonov, and Sergei Bondarchuk; directed by Sergei Bondarchuk.

THE WIZARD OF OZ* (1939); written by Noel Langley and Florence Ryerson from the novel *The Wonderful Wizard of Oz* by L. Frank Baum; starring Judy Garland and Frank Morgan; directed by Victor Fleming.

■ Written Works Cited

Anonymous. *Samson and Delilah*. In the Book of Judges, the Bible, King James version, 1611. Peabody, MA: Hendrickson Publishers, 2006.

Anonymous, oral tradition. *Beowulf* circa 800 A.D. New York: Signet Classic, 2008.

Anonymous, oral tradition. "A Gest of Robyn Hode." In *Robin Hood and Other Outlaw Tales*. Kalamazoo, MI: Medieval Institute Publications, 1997.

Austen, Jane. *Pride and Prejudice*. London: White's Books Ltd., 2009.

Baldacci, David. *Absolute Power*. New York: Warner Books, 1996.

Baum, L. Frank. *The Wonderful Wizard of Oz*. Chicago and New York: George M. Hill, 1900.

Beeding, Francis. *The House of Dr. Edwardes*. London: Hodder & Stoughton, 1927.

Benchley, Peter. *Jaws*. New York: Doubleday & Co., Inc., 1974.

Black, Cara. *Murder in the Rue de Paradis*. New York: Soho Press, 2008.

Blatty, William Peter. *The Exorcist*. New York: Harper & Row, 1971.

Bloch, Robert. *Psycho*. New York: Simon & Schuster, 1959.

Bradbury, Ray. *Fahrenheit 451*. New York: Ballantine Books, 1953.

Brown, Dan. *The Da Vinci Code*. New York: Bantam Press, 2005.

Browne, Ian, Dr. *The Da Vinci Mole: A Philosophical Parody*. Cyberspace: Ben-Bella Books, 2006.

Bryant, Peter. *Red Alert*. New York: Ace Books, 1958.

Cain, James M. *The Postman Always Rings Twice*. New York: Alfred Knopf, 1934.
———. *Double Indemnity*. New York: Avon Books, 1945.

Campbell, Joseph. *The Hero with a Thousand Faces*. Princeton, NJ: Princeton University Press, 1948.

Condon, Richard. *The Manchurian Candidate*. New York: McGraw-Hill, 1959.

Cook, Robin. *Coma*. New York: Little, Brown, 1977.

Cooper, James Fenimore. *The Last of the Mohicans*. Philadelphia: H. C. Carey & I. Lea, 1826.

Crichton, Michael. *The Andromeda Strain*. New York: Alfred A. Knopf, 1969.

Cunningham, John W. "The Tin Star." Originally published in *Collier's* magazine, December 6, 1947.

Deaver, Jeffery. *The Bone Collector*. New York: Viking Press, 1997.

Defoe, Daniel. *Moll Flanders*. New York: W. W. Norton & Co., 2003.

Deighton, Len. *The Ipcress File*. New York: Simon & Schuster, 1963.

Dostoevsky, Fyodor. *The Double*. Originally published 1846. In *The Double and the Gambler*. New York: Vintage, 2007.

Doyle, Sir Arthur Conan. "A Scandal in Bohemia." Available online at http:// www.eastoftheweb.com/short-stories/UBooks/ScanBohe.shtml.

Dumas, Alexandre, père. *The Man in the Iron Mask*. Originally published in French, 1848. New York: Signet Classics, 2006.

——. *The Count of Monte Cristo*. Originally published in French, 1845. New York: Penguin Classics, 2007.

Egri, Lajos. *The Art of Dramatic Writing*. New York: Simon & Schuster, 1946.

Ellis, David. *Line of Vision*. New York: Putnam Adult, 2001.

Finney, Jack. *The Body Snatchers (Invasion of the Body Snatchers)*. New York: Dell Books, 1955.

Fleming, Ian. *Dr. No*. London: Jonathan Cape, Ltd., 1958.

——. *Goldfinger*. London: Jonathan Cape, Ltd., 1959.

——. *The Man with the Golden Gun*. London: Jonathan Cape, Ltd., 1965.

Follett, Ken. *Eye of the Needle*. New York: Arbor House, 1978.

Forsyth, Frederick. *The Day of the Jackal*. New York: Viking Press, 1971.

Frey, James N. *How to Write a Damn Good Novel*. New York: St. Martin's Press, 1987.

——. *How to Write a Damn Good Novel II: Advanced Techniques for Dramatic Storytelling*. New York: St. Martin's Press, 1994.

——. *The Key: A Fiction Writer's Guide to Writing Damn Good Fiction Using the Power of Myth*. New York: St. Martin's Press, 2002.

——. *How to Write a Damn Good Mystery*. New York: St. Martin's Press, 2004.

Gardner, John. *On Moral Fiction*. New York: Basic Books, 1979.

Golding, William. *Lord of the Flies*. London: Faber & Faber Ltd., 1954.

Haggard, H. Rider. *The Annotated She: A Critical Edition with Notes by Norman Etherington*. Bloomington: Indiana University Press, 1991.

Hamilton, Patrick. *Angel Street: A Victorian Thriller in Three Acts*. New York: Samuel French, Inc., 1966.

Harris, Thomas. *Black Sunday*. New York: G. P. Putnam's Sons, 1975.

——. *The Silence of the Lambs*. New York: St. Martin's Press, 1988.

Hayes, Joseph. *The Desperate Hours: A Novel of Suspense*. New York: Random House, 1954.

——. *The Desperate Hours: A Play by Joseph Hayes*. New York: Random House, 1955.

Hemingway, Ernest. *For Whom the Bell Tolls*. New York: Charles Scribner's Sons, 1940.

——. *The Old Man and the Sea*. New York: Charles Scribner's Sons, 1951.

Hiaasen, Carl. *Skinny Dip*. New York: Alfred A. Knopf, 2004.

Highsmith, Patricia. *Strangers on a Train*. New York: Harper & Brothers, 1950.

Homer. *The Iliad*. An epic poem from the Greek oral tradition, probably created around the eighth or ninth century B.C. In *The Iliad and Odyssey*. New York: Penguin Classics, 1999.

———. *The Odyssey*. An epic poem from the Greek oral tradition, probably created around the eighth or ninth century B.C. In *The Iliad and Odyssey*. New York: Penguin Classics, 1999.

Hooker, Richard. *M*A*S*H*. New York: William Morrow, 1968.

Hope, Anthony. *The Prisoner of Zenda*. New York: Henry Holt, 1894.

Hugo, Victor. *The Hunchback of Notre Dame*. Philadelphia: Carey, Lea & Blachard, 1834.

Ibsen, Henrik. *An Enemy of the People*. Copenhagen: F. Hegel & Son, 1882.

Iles, Francis (Anthony Berkeley Cox). *Before the Fact*. London: Macmillan, 1931; reprint 1999.

Jackson, Shirley. *The Haunting of Hill House*. New York: Viking Press, 1959.

Katzenbach, John. *The Wrong Man*. New York: Ballantine Books, 2006.

King, Stephen. *Misery*. New York: Viking Press, 1971.

———. *Dolores Claiborne*. New York: Viking Press, 1993.

———. *The Green Mile*. New York: Plume, Inc., 1997.

———. "Rita Hayworth and the Shawshank Redemption." In *Different Season*. New York: Viking Press, 1982.

———. *The Shining*. Garden City, NY: Doubleday, Inc., 1977.

———. *Danse Macabre*. New York: Everest House, 1981.

Knebel, Fletcher, and Charles W. Bailey II. *Seven Days in May*. New York: Harper & Row, 1962.

Knott, Frederick. *Wait Until Dark*. New York: Dramatists Play Services, 1967.

Koontz, Dean. *How to Write Best-Selling Fiction*. Cincinnati: Writer's Digest Books, 1981.

le Carré, John. *The Spy Who Came in from the Cold*. London: Victor Gollancz, Ltd., 1963.

———. *The Constant Gardener*. London: Hodder & Stoughton, 2001.

Leonard, Elmore. "3:10 to Yuma." Originally published in 1952. In *Three-Ten to Yuma and Other Stories*. New York: HarperTorch, 2006.

———. *Hombre*. New York: Ballantine Books, 1961.

———. *Get Shorty*. New York: Delacorte Press, 1990.

Levin, Ira. *The Boys from Brazil*. New York: Random House, 1976.

London, Jack. "To Build a Fire." Originally published in 1908. In *To Build a Fire and Other Stories by Jack London*. Toronto: Bantam Books, 1986.

Ludlum, Robert. *The Bourne Identity*. New York: Robert Marek, 1980.

Lutz, John. *SWF Seeks Same*. New York: St. Martin's Press, 1990.

Maas, Peter. *Serpico*. New York: Viking Press, 1973.

MacDonald, John D. *The Executioners*. New York: Simon & Schuster, 1958.

March, William. *The Bad Seed*. New York: Rinehart & Co., 1954.

Melville, Herman. *Moby-Dick*. New York: Harper & Brothers, 1851.

Mitchell, Margaret. *Gone With the Wind*. New York: Macmillan Company, 1936.

Mowat, Farley. "Walk Well, My Brother." In *The Snow Walker*. Mechanicsburg, PA: Stackpole Books, 2004.

Orczy, Baroness Emmuska. *The League of the Scarlet Pimpernel*. London: Cassell & Co., 1919.

Orwell, George. *Nineteen Eighty-Four*. London: Secker & Warburg, 1949.

Pérez-Reverte, Arturo. *The Club Dumas*. English edition. New York: Harcourt & Brace, 1997.

Piper, Evelyn. *Bunny Lake Is Missing*. Harper & Brothers, 1957.

Poe, Edgar Allan. *Complete Stories and Poems*. New York: Doubleday, 1984.

Price, Nancy. *Sleeping with the Enemy*. New York: Simon & Schuster, 1987.

Puzo, Mario. *The Godfather*. New York: G. P. Putnam's Sons, 1969.

Reese, John. *The Looters* (aka *Charley Varrick*). New York: Pyramid Books, 1973.

Roberts, Adam (Don Brine). *The Da Vinci Cod: A Fishy Parody*. New York: Harper Paperbacks, 2005.

Scortia, Thomas N., and Frank M. Robinson. *The Glass Inferno*. New York: Pocket Books, 1974.

Shakespeare, William. *Macbeth*. Originally published in 1606. In *William Shakespeare: Complete Works*. New York: Modern Library, 2007.

———. *The Tempest*. Originally published in 1610. In *William Shakespeare: Complete Works*. New York: Modern Library, 2007.

Shelley, Mary. *Frankenstein*. New York: W. W. Norton & Co., 1995.

Sherwood, Robert E. *The Petrified Forest: A Play in Three Acts*. New York: Dramatists Play Service, 1998.

Stevenson, Robert Louis. *Treasure Island*. London: Cassell & Co., 1883.

———. *The Strange Case of Dr. Jekyll and Mr. Hyde*. London: Longmans, Green & Co., 1886.

Stowe, Harriet Beecher. *Uncle Tom's Cabin*. Boston: John P. Jewett & Co., 1852.

Swartout, Glendon. *The Shootist*. Garden City, NY: Doubleday, Inc., 1975.

Thorp, Roderick. *Nothing Lasts Forever*. New York: W. W. Norton & Co., Inc., 1979.

Tolstoy, Leo. *War and Peace*. 6 vols. New York: William S. Gottsberger, 1886.

Twain, Mark. *The Prince and the Pauper*. Boston: James R. Osgood & Co., 1882.

Wager, Walter. *58 Minutes*. New York: Macmillan Inc., 1987.

Williams, Charles. *Dead Calm*. New York: Viking Press, 1963.

Woolrich, Cornell. "It Had to Be Murder." In *The Cornell Woolrich Omnibus: Rear Window and Other Stories*. New York: Penguin, 1998.

◼ Index